Network Strategies for Regional Growth

Network Strategies for Regional Growth

Edited by

Martin Johanson

and

Helène Lundberg

palgrave
macmillan

First published 2011 by
PALGRAVE MACMILLAN

Palgrave Macmillan in the UK is an imprint of Macmillan Publishers Limited, registered in England, company number 785998, of Houndmills, Basingstoke, Hampshire RG21 6XS.

Palgrave Macmillan in the US is a division of St Martin's Press LLC, 175 Fifth Avenue, New York, NY 10010.

Palgrave Macmillan is the global academic imprint of the above companies and has companies and representatives throughout the world.

Palgrave® and Macmillan® are registered trademarks in the United States, the United Kingdom, Europe and other countries.

ISBN: 978–0–230–27330–6 hardback

This book is printed on paper suitable for recycling and made from fully managed and sustained forest sources. Logging, pulping and manufacturing processes are expected to conform to the environmental regulations of the country of origin.

A catalogue record for this book is available from the British Library.

Library of Congress Cataloging-in-Publication Data

Network strategies for regional growth / edited by Martin Johanson, Heléne Lundberg.
p. cm.
ISBN 978–0–230–27330–6
1. Regional planning. 2. Regional economics. 3. Business networks. I. Johanson, Martin. II. Lundberg, Heléne, 1960– III. Title.

HT391.N4425 2011
307.1′2—dc22 2010034137

10 9 8 7 6 5 4 3 2 1
20 19 18 17 16 15 14 13 12 11

Printed and bound in Great Britain by
CPI Antony Rowe, Chippenham and Eastbourne

Contents

Illustrations

Figures

Tables

Preface

The year 2001 saw the initiation of the Strategic Networks project at Mid Sweden University in Sundsvall, Sweden. Its aims were to study inter-firm networks founded in specific regions for regional development purposes, and to interact with practitioners and businesspeople to provide feedback to participants in such initiatives. We have previously reported findings from the project in a book called *Regionala strategiska nätverket i praktiken* (Regional strategic networks in practice) in 2009.[1] Over the years, we have extended the research team by establishing contact with other researchers, in Sweden and abroad, who were studying the same phenomena. We decided to publish some of our findings jointly, resulting in the present book. In the process we have enjoyed financial support from several organisations, and are grateful for the generous assistance of EU Mål 2 Regionala fonden, Framtidens bio-raffinaderi, Landstinget och Länsstyrelsen i Västernorrland, Tillväxtverket, and Centre for Research on Innovation and Industrial Dynamics at Uppsala University (CIND).

Sundsvall and Uppsala, Sweden, 15 October 2010
Martin Johanson
Heléne Lundberg

[1] L. Hallén, M. Johanson and T. Roxenhall, eds, *Regionala strategiska nätverk i praktiken* (Lund, Sweden: Studentlitteratur, 2009).

Contributors

Edith Andresen is a doctoral student and teacher at Mid-Sweden University. Her research interests concern regional business development through cooperation between private companies, the public sector, and academic institutions. Her research interests are in business-to-business relationships, entrepreneurship and engineered network initiatives.

Alsones Balestrin is a professor and researcher at the School of Management, UNISINOS (University of Sinos Valley, Brazil). He was awarded his Ph.D. in Business Administration by the Federal University of Rio Grande do Sul. He has also received a doctorate in Information Science and Communication from the University of Poitiers, France. He has written books and articles in the social sciences field, concerning organizational management, cooperation networks, and open innovation.

Björn Berggren is an assistant professor at the Centre for Banking and Finance, the Royal Institute of Technology, Stockholm, Sweden. His research interests include the development of financial systems and studying the relationship between small and medium-sized enterprises and financial actors.

Anette Bergman is a doctoral student at Mid-Sweden University. Her research is mainly focused on managerial communication in regional strategic networks, especially email communication and its impact on relationship development.

Petter Boye is a senior lecturer in Business Administration at Linnaeus University, Sweden. He specializes in strategy and business development. Since the early 1990s he has, as researcher and consultant, worked with strategic development processes of regional and transnational industrial platforms. This work ranges from internationalization of small and medium-sized enterprises to regional policy issues.

Staffan Brege is a professor of industrial marketing and Head of the Division of Industrial Marketing at Linköping University, Sweden. His research is mainly focused upon issues within the areas of business-to-business marketing and business development, including topics such as relationship marketing, value-added strategies, industrial services, outsourcing, and functional sales.

Sylvie Chetty is a professor of marketing at Massey University, New Zealand, and a research associate at Uppsala University, Sweden. Her research interests are in the internationalization process of small and medium-sized enterprises , business networks, industry clusters, and learning. She is a member of the editorial boards of several academic journals in marketing.

Christer Ekelund is an associate professor at the Centre for Business Studies, Kristianstad University College, Sweden. His previous research has been on relationships in business networks and the significance of these networks for firm performance. Present research concerns knowledge transfer from academy to firm/organization.

Karolina Elmhester is an assistant professor in Industrial Marketing at Linköping University, Sweden. Her research interest is business development in small and medium-sized enterprises, especially cooperation in strategic networks. She has previously worked as a researcher at CTF (Service Research Center), Karlstad University.

Simone Guercini is a full professor in business economics at the University of Florence, Italy. He received his Ph.D. from the Sant'Anna School of Advanced Study. His research interests include buyer–seller relationships, internationalization, entrepreneurship, and intercultural marketing.

Lars Hallén is Professor of Business Administration at Mid-Sweden University, where he holds the chair of marketing and is the head of the Centre for Research on Economic Relations (CER). His publications include journal articles and books dealing with markets-as-networks, business-to-business relationships, transition economies, tourism, and regional development.

Hans Jansson is Professor of International Marketing and Director of the Baltic Business Research Center at Linnaeus School of Business and Economics, Linnaeus University, Sweden. He has published a large number of books and articles on internationalization, international strategic marketing, and organization of large and small firms relating to emerging markets.

Martin Johanson is a professor in business administration at the Department of Business Studies at Uppsala University, Sweden. Prior to his academic career he worked for many years as a diplomat and business consultant. He is now a member of the consultancy company, IM-Gruppen. His primary research interests concern transformation of turbulent economies, firm entry into emerging markets, and regional growth strategies.

Nicolaus Lundahl is a Ph.D. student at the Centre for Banking and Finance, the Royal Institute of Technology, Stockholm, Sweden. His research interests include studying the relationship between small and medium-sized enterprises and their financiers and advisers.

Heléne Lundberg is a senior lecturer at Mid-Sweden University. She received her Ph.D. from the University of Uppsala. Her main research interests include markets-as-networks, business-to-business relationships, engineered network initiatives, entrepreneurship, and regional development.

Snejina Michailova is a professor of international business at the University of Auckland Business School, New Zealand. Her academic work is in the areas of international management and knowledge management. Snejina is currently Associate Editor of *Critical Perspectives on International Business* and a member of the editorial boards of several academic journals.

Kai Mietzner studied business administration and economics at Leibniz University of Hanover, Germany. In 2007 he joined Siemens Healthcare in Düsseldorf. In his thesis he studied the assessment of regional agglomeration systems, focusing on the significance and impact of a firm's cluster membership for its strategic management.

Peter E. Parker is an associate professor at the Department of Urban Studies, Malmö University, Sweden. His previous research has been on social networks in business and the significance of these networks for firm development. Present research interests concern challenges of organizing cross-sectional urban development initiatives.

Håkan Pihl, Ph.D., is a senior lecturer at Kristianstad University College, Sweden, and Dean of the Department of Business Administration at Lund University, Sweden. He has published books and articles in areas such as environmental economics and international business. His research interests are connected to applications and developments of new institutional economic theory.

Andrea Runfola is an assistant professor in business economics at the University of Perugia, Italy. He received his Ph.D. from the University of Urbino. His research interests include business marketing, supply-chain management and international and cross-cultural retailing.

Holger Schiele is Professor of Technology Management – Innovation of Operations at the University of Twente, The Netherlands. He earned his Ph.D. and his habilitation (*venia legendi*) from Leibniz University of Hanover. For the past 15 years he has been researching innovative clusters. Other research topics focus on innovation generation in buyer–supplier relations and methods enabling academic–practitioner collaborative research.

Lars Silver is an associate professor at the Centre for Banking and Finance, the Royal Institute of Technology, Stockholm, Sweden. His research interests include studying the relationship between small and medium-sized enterprises and financial actors, the development of the financial system and the evolution of savings banks.

Claus Steinle has been a full professor for organizational behaviour and management at the Leibniz University of Hanover since 1986. He works on general management topics, planning, controlling, organizational behaviour, leadership, and change management. His current research focuses on clusters, start-ups, and internationalization of SMEs.

Jorge Renato Verschoore holds a doctorate in business administration from UFRGS (Federal University of Rio Grande do Sul, Brazil) and is a senior lecturer and researcher at UNISINOS (University of Sinos Valley, Brazil) as well as a policy consultant for the state government. His main interests are network governance, small-firm internationalization, and collaborative innovation.

1
Network Strategies for Regional Growth

Heléne Lundberg and Martin Johanson

The past twenty years have seen a shift in the economic policies pursued in many countries. Networks and networking have become buzz words in business, academe, and regional and national governments as the traditional macro-perspective on economic conditions has increasingly been superseded by a greater interest in the micro-economic business environment (Wilson 1995). The focus is no longer on specific companies or on the market in general; instead, specific relationships and networks between companies in a region are the object of policy-makers' priorities. Vast public resources are now being poured into projects and programmes that aim to support the development of relationships between various companies in a specific region in order to achieve growth (see Figure 1.1). Governments worldwide are addressing regional and local development issues using a more decentralized approach, paying increased attention to resources and knowledge available at the local level and accessible through networking. As a result, regional plans and strategies often incorporate the aim of developing and maintaining relationships between companies in a region in order to achieve growth.

This tendency apparently started in the 1980s in small countries such as Denmark and New Zealand, which are highly dependent on foreign trade and on strong small and medium-sized enterprises (SMEs). However, accompanied by achievements in the research community, which introduced concepts such as relationships, partnerships, alliances, clusters, and networks, all emphasizing the strengths arising from cooperation and interaction between companies, this development also took off in the USA and in the European Union. In Europe, regional development is viewed as a key to achieving national growth, and the structural funds have distributed vast resources to support various regional network strategies. Although this tendency has become prevalent, the logic just presented is relatively under-researched and merits greater research attention. This book therefore aims to improve our understanding of these types of regional development networks, exploring why they exist, how they function, and what they achieve.

Figure 1.1 The logical chain: economic policy–networks–growth

Background

Increased interest in regional development among policy-makers was spurred by an upsurge in interest in regional issues on the part of researchers, which was manifested in greater attention to the cluster concept and the somewhat overlapping concept of industrial districts. That some industries tend to co-locate in agglomerations has been well known and documented since the works of Marshall (1891). However, interest in this observation was revived and strengthened late in the 20th century, as Porter (1990, 1998a, 1998b, 2000) and Piore and Sable (1984) brought the issue of regional advantages back into focus with their research into the value and importance of regional clusters and successful flexible production in industrial districts. In particular, the social dimension, emphasizing local networks of social relationships and interactions giving rise to both the voluntary and involuntary transfer of information and experience, has become a salient and often-cited characteristic of modern agglomeration theory (Saxenian 1994; Maskell 2001).

However, the cluster concept not only serves an analytical purpose but has also become 'a key political tool' (Martin and Sunley 2003: 6), providing important inspiration for regional development measures worldwide. Academic interest in clusters, however, has still not resulted in any fully elaborated models or hypotheses able to give guidance on how to undertake cluster development or cluster support measures. Such research is hampered by the fact that most of the successful clusters currently under study were not planned from the beginning, and, in addition, the conditions under which they currently exist are unlikely to be identical to those that originally set the cluster formation process in motion (Bresnahan *et al.* 2001). The cluster phenomenon thus remains elusive: each cluster is unique, with its own long path-dependent history. It follows that regional development measures come in various shapes and sizes. However, there is usually a common theme of local interaction and mutual learning as the intended path towards regional development. In a survey of 238 cluster development initiatives around the world, fostering networks among people and companies was found to be the most frequent objective (Sölvell *et al.* 2003: 9).

Cluster theories discuss a number of potential advantages accruing to companies as a result of co-location in a particular region. Some of these advantages are available to all companies, often due to pure agglomeration effects, such as economies of scale regarding transportation, education, and a common labour pool. Other externalities are more specific and of interest or accessible only to particular kinds of companies; for example, competitors may cooperate in certain business areas or intensify their competition through ongoing comparisons and rivalry. The extent and importance of cluster advantages, however, has been questioned. Enright (1996) argues that here has been too much focus on the internal operation of clusters, to the neglect of external factors important for the success or failure of clusters, a point also made by Lazerson and Lorenzoni (1999). Appold (2005: 19) concludes that 'while there is an impressive and growing literature documenting the co-location of critical economic activities, evidence for local connections is limited'. He suggests that co-location results partly from mimetic behaviour, as location decisions are made under conditions of uncertainty with symbolic connotations of identity and legitimacy.

However, despite unsolved theoretical issues and the lack of specific guidelines for cluster support and development, governments and international institutions still formulate policies and support programmes to promote regional development. Although they should perhaps refrain from such action, doing so would still influence business conditions, as it would prolong present conditions for better or worse. The alternative to passivity is to undertake some sort of action, usually under the influence of a particular theoretical understanding of economic life. The cluster concept is attractive to regional development practitioners as it concerns the critical issues of knowledge development, innovation, and competitiveness, which are fundamental to economic development. It is thus not particularly surprising that the increased research interest in clusters should be reflected in the inclusion of the concept in international, national, and regional economic development plans (Sölvell *et al.* 2003). What is surprising is the limited number of studies and evaluations of regional development programmes informed by cluster theory, especially considering the vast resources dedicated to such programmes (Sölvell *et al.* 2003).

Engineered network contexts

Interaction and communication between individuals in a community is often described as a key factor determining regional success, as in Saxenian's (1994) study of the networks in Silicon Valley, California. However, although cluster theory pays close attention to social interaction as a vehicle for knowledge transfer, knowledge development, and business exchange, in real life social interaction cannot be taken for granted, even within agglomerations. It is not uncommon, even in the presence of physical industrial agglomeration, for there to be only minor interaction among the companies in an area. 'In Massachusetts, for example, more than four hundred companies...were involved in some way in medical devices.... Executives in the cluster had never come together before despite the fact that firms shared many common constraints, problems, and opportunities' (Porter 1998b: 204).

There is therefore an underlying assumption on the part of researchers and policy-makers that increased mutual knowledge and interaction among individuals and companies in a region will benefit the business community and thereby the region. Attempts to stimulate interaction have accordingly become prevalent in development ventures, supplemented by other common measures, such as providing business consultation and training (Sölvell *et al.* 2003).

As the cases presented in this book indicate, regional development programmes worldwide increasingly focus on the networking characteristics of successful clusters. Networking programmes use an engineered process, whereby a triggering entity actively strives to create some sort of cooperation among a group of actors (Doz *et al.* 2000). The opposite of an engineered process is an emergent one, in which no intervention by a triggering entity is required. Emergent processes develop spontaneously, often when environmental changes in the market present a threat or an opportunity for a number of companies with perceived interdependence. Over time, however, emergent forms will become intentionally or rationally structured as a result of institutionalizing pressures (Powell *et al.* 1996).

Emergent processes are characterized by member self-selection, but Doz *et al.* (2000) argue that the presence of a triggering entity gathering a group of companies is essential to the emergence of networks when interdependencies or other grounds for increased interaction and cooperation are difficult for the actors themselves to recognize. Government agencies, consultants, specific companies, or entrepreneurial individuals may then assume this triggering role and set out to create a shared, unifying perception of the need for increased collaboration among a group of selected members. An appointed hub will be needed to organize and coordinate the interaction between them. Such gatherings of companies in a particular region, usually chosen on the basis of a number of cluster criteria, thus form an engineered network context that is created to stimulate communication, interaction, and learning among member companies, thereby acting as a vehicle to foster regional development.

However, due to the broad and varied definitions of cluster – for example, 'a geographically proximate group of interconnected companies and associated institutions in a particular field, linked by commonalities and complementarities' (Porter 2000: 15) – what is labelled a 'cluster' may vary greatly in theory and practice. 'What are claimed to be clusters often turn out, on closer empirical inspection, to be small and only loosely connected collections of similar or related firms' (Martin and Sunley 2003: 21). The local conditions called 'clusters' by local politicians and civil servants, forming the basis of engineered regional strategic networks, display great variation. This variation, of course, gravely hampers the development of best practice for the triggering entity. It does not, however, diminish the need to study these arrangements in order to improve their processes and outcomes.

Strategic networks in relation to clusters and industrial districts

Companies are thus often gathered in engineered regional strategic networks, an arrangement displaying similarities to the strategic networks defined by Jarillo (1988: 32) as 'long-term, purposeful arrangements among distinct but related for profit organizations that allow those companies in them to gain or sustain competitive advantage vis-à-vis their competitors outside the network'. Being planned and formalized, strategic networks have appealed to politicians and public administrations as a means to achieve regional development in a purposeful and manageable way.

Strategic networks are in some respects similar to clusters/industrial districts but display several key differences. First, strategic networks may span vast geographical distances, and social interaction is mainly discussed with regard to the relationships among the companies included in the network. As member companies may be located in different countries, the spatial dimension in such cases is likely to present obstacles to communication and cooperation in terms of cultural differences and lack of trust (Ford 2002; Boschma 2005). Cluster researchers, on the other hand, emphasize the importance of local 'in the air' transfer of knowledge between individuals and companies through social interaction in various local arenas, outside as well as during working hours (Maskell 2001; Dahl and Pedersen 2004). Being co-located in the area implies access to information and knowledge, while embeddedness confers contextual meaning on the information obtained, facilitating its use. In this tradition, the social network is a crucial concept and a key success factor.

Second, network boundaries may affect the activities undertaken, as in strategic networks the hub is restricted to dealing with a specified set of actors. However, these actors still have ties to other companies that, although they are not participating in the strategic network, will influence it via the restraints inherent in the relationships (Blois 1998). There are boundaries to clusters as well, but these are more 'in the eye of the beholder', as clusters can be studied at varying levels of aggregation to expose different issues (Porter 2000).

Third, the word 'strategic' indicates that strategic networks are planned and rationalized *ex ante*. Companies scan the market for suitable partners, in search of complementary skills and resources needed to handle a particular threat or to take advantage of a particular opportunity. Clusters, on the other hand, are self-organizing entities that evolve over long periods.

Fourth, in strategic networks, working arrangements are specified in written contracts and fulfilled in a formal organization based on control. Clusters, on the other hand, are said to involve the interplay between production and daily life activities, resulting in a governance mechanism characterized by mutual trust and underpinned by an underlying threat of community social sanctions (for instance, Becattini 1991). There is therefore less need for formal agreements.

Fifth, in strategic networks, goals are specified for a predetermined time horizon, although the underlying purpose is long-term in nature, while cooperation in clusters is described as being of a long-term, evolving character.

In summary, strategic networks are more manageable than clusters, as they encompass only a limited number of companies. Furthermore, they have specific boundaries and a formal organization. The activities and processes in strategic networks, however, may be hampered by a lack of trust and personal relationships – characteristics said to be crucial to successful clusters – and by the relationships member companies have with external actors. The hubs of strategic networks thus face a major challenge in promoting interaction and cooperation among member companies. Furthermore, when strategic networks are created for regional development purposes, new dimensions are added and the picture becomes even more complex.

Regional strategic networks

There are two key differences between the strategic networks discussed by Jarillo (1988) and the *regional* strategic networks discussed here. First, the strategic networks of Jarillo are formed by companies themselves on the basis of some kind of business opportunity, whereas in regional strategic networks formed for a regional development purpose, the sample of companies is taken from companies located in a particular region. Second, this sample of companies, often supplemented by university representatives and/or government agencies, is often made by consultants or civil servants as part of a regional development strategy formulated by a regional government. It thus follows that while the strategic networks discussed by Jarillo (1988: 32) are governed and coordinated by a 'hub' having 'special relationships with the other members of the network' on a business-exchange basis, regional strategic networks have a much looser business-exchange basis on which to build and therefore need extra resources to finance the hub function. Some sort of hub/coordinator is accordingly usually appointed and paid by state sources. However, the hub/coordinator's role is very complex, since there are few business relationships on which to build from the beginning – that being the reason for the undertaking. The hub must therefore motivate the chosen companies to participate in the network by means of promotional and coordinating activities that they will find useful and valuable. These activities will lead to the development of social and business relationships that foster the interaction among regional companies that is claimed to characterize economically successful regions. The hub thus plays a key role in the network, and Porter (1998b: 265) argues that 'instigating communications is the essence of successful cluster initiatives'.

Regional strategic network initiatives are often supported by international, national, or regional funding and organized according to a political logic as projects with a predetermined life span and a focus on distinct targets, measurable objectives, short-term assessments, and evaluations of specific activities. In the political agenda, however, network initiatives are expected to become gradually transformed into processes operating according to a business logic with characteristics such as interaction, emergent goals, long-term processes, and relational performance with unclear dimensions. When network initiatives mature, they are expected to become transformed into structures sharing some of the typical characteristics ascribed to clusters or industrial districts, that is, socially embedded business relationships, trusting personal relationships between business actors, and knowledge spillovers (Capello and Faggian 2005).

Hallén and Johanson (2009) contrast emergent with engineered cooperation, and interregional with regional cooperation (Table 1.1). Business networks, clusters/industrial districts, and industrial networks all represent emergent forms of cooperation, while strategic networks and regional strategic networks represent engineered attempts to build inter-firm cooperation and learning. Though each of these four types of cooperation has specific characteristics, the types are not mutually exclusive. Business networks, per definition, are all-embracing, as they are based on all the direct and indirect relationships between the actors in the market (Johanson and Mattsson 1994). Business networks thus subsume and include the companies that are part of more specific forms of cooperation. Furthermore, regional strategic networks constitute a subset of strategic networks, distinguished by differences in formation and processes.

Table 1.1 Four types of cooperation among companies

	Emergent	**Engineered**
Interregional cooperation	Business networks	Strategic networks
Regional cooperation	Clusters and industrial districts	Regional strategic networks

Regional strategic networks aim to enhance knowledge capital and social capital in a particular region to enable its resident businesses to compete more comprehensively and successfully. The central vision is that such networks should 'unlock important synergies, encourage innovativeness, raise efficiency, and thus strengthen the competitive advantages of the regional economy.... As a byproduct, local network building may also enhance political competencies and social commitments' (Staber 1996: 4).

Their geographical delimitations give regional strategic networks a resemblance to industrial districts but constitute a major difference from strategic networks, as defined in business theory by Jarillo (1988) and others, as such networks may cover vast areas.

Regional strategic networks tend to be less formal and use weaker membership contracts than do business-exchange or R&D-oriented strategic networks. Furthermore, regional strategic networks often include a rather large number of companies gathered under vaguely formulated goals. Under such circumstances, formulating a common purpose is problematic as members differ, for example, in maturity, cost structures, and business strategy (Staber 1996).

The above comparison of industrial districts, strategic networks, and regional strategic networks in terms of geographical proximity, boundaries, organization, governance mechanism, and time horizon is summarized in Table 1.2, adapted from Lundberg (2008).

In summary, we find that regional strategic networks constitute a very complex phenomenon involving simultaneous ongoing process at three

Table 1.2 Comparison of clusters/industrial districts, strategic networks, and regional strategic networks

Characteristics	**Clusters/industrial districts**	**Strategic networks**	**Publicly financed regional strategic networks**
Origin	Emergent	Engineered by leading (hub) company	Engineered
Motive	Business exchange	Business exchange or R&D cooperation	Regional development through increased regional business exchange
Geographical proximity	Close to varied	Varied	Close
Organization	Self-organization, based on shared culture and social relationships	Hub company	Hub appointed but with a mission to foster sustainable self-organization

levels: the region, the participating organizations, and the individuals representing their organizations in the regional strategic network. At each level, various tangible and intangible effects may develop. However, several challenges face initiators, coordinators, and participants if the visions and goals of these networks are to be realized. These networking initiatives are undertaken in various settings and under varying circumstances, so it is important to improve our understanding of the effects of such variation on processes and outcomes. More research is also needed into how outcomes can be registered, measured, and valued to enable the improvement of processes and outcomes in terms of efficiency and goal fulfilment at all three levels. In addition, further knowledge of outcomes would provide valuable information on the purposes for which regional networking initiatives may be used.

> We have surprisingly little systematic knowledge of these [cluster] initiatives, their structure, and their outcomes. As more and more resources are devoted to efforts to foster cluster development, the need to understand best practices has become urgent. Cluster initiative practitioners have to find the approach that both builds on the international experience and reflects their unique local environment.
>
> (Sölvell *et al.* 2003: 5)

Some characteristics of regional strategic networks

We feel it is impossible simply to cherry-pick the advantages presented in the literature on clusters, business networks, and strategic networks and expect them to emerge automatically from regional strategic networks, which superficially share some characteristics with these other types of industrial agglomeration. Based on Sölvell *et al.*'s (2003) observations and the above analysis, one can identify three main areas in which these specific characteristics are evident: network arrangement and structure, actor roles and functions, and network processes.

Network arrangement and structure

A network has a structure, a set of relationships between companies, but this does not mean that all networks share the same qualities. The number of companies and the number of relationships vary, as does the strength of these relationships. The number of companies joining a regional strategic network determines how many relationships could potentially be developed among the network participants, and since relationships are the cornerstones of a network, the number of companies is crucial. In other words, the more companies in a network, the more relationships can be developed. However, as time and resources are limited, in business in general and in engineered networks in particular, the greater the number of relationships that are to be developed in a network, the weaker these relationships are likely to be. This may not be a disadvantage, however, depending on what the network aims to achieve. Weak relationships are beneficial for information access (Granovetter 1973) and also favour the seeking and obtaining of resources (Lin 2001). Such relationship benefits arise not only from direct relationships between network participants but also from relationships with more distant actors, as relationships can provide access to other networks and span structural holes (Burt 2004). If such relationships with other networks can be mobilized, they will be strategic assets for the network and counteract the threat of lock-in effects (Grabher 2004) that might otherwise impinge on networks oriented towards a particular region.

Relationships with other companies may provide information and knowledge, but this may not be enough to make weak, newly developed relationships function as a cooperation platform in the way intended by financers and policy-makers. It has been indicated that weak relationships are less suited for transferring complex knowledge, which tends to require a trusting, frequently renewed, and strong relationship between the two parties (Hansen 1999). A smaller network may therefore be better suited to facilitating the development of a few strong and deep relationships, which may be more effective for participants if the aim is to cooperate closely in production, R&D, marketing, or other business areas. Nevertheless, a lot of companies and a lot of relationships mean that companies can distribute the costs of network activities among more participants, thereby achieving increased economies of scale. In other words, if the aims of the network are costly to achieve, it would be advantageous to have more companies in the network.

The arrangements of companies and relationships in networks vary, possibly significantly influencing both network operations and results. It is

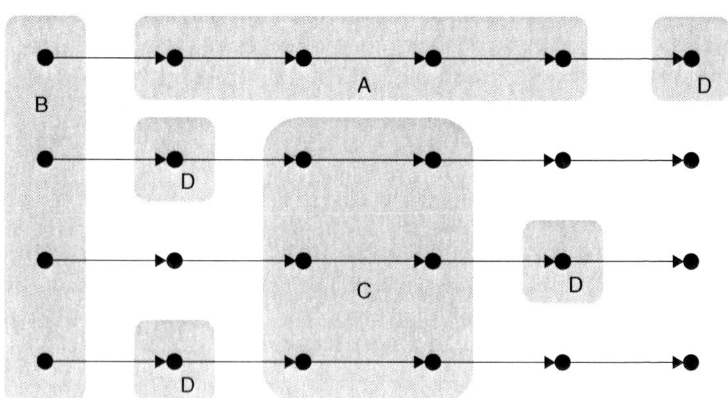

Figure 1.2 Four network types

possible to identify four types of networks. In Figure 1.2, which attempts to illustrate a number of value chains, the arrows symbolize buyer–seller relationships between companies.

1. Networks consisting of buyer–seller relationships (see A in Figure 1.2)

These networks consist of existing or future relationships, in which companies currently or in the future will buy or sell from each other. This means not only that they share interfaces but also that they have a common goal, namely to do business. On this basis the network activities can be designed and performed, which also implies that it will be relatively easy to specify and plan what the network should do and achieve before it commences operations. The critical question in this case is whether these relationships already exist – that is, are the participating companies currently buying and selling? – or whether this a goal for the future. The shared logic and goal can constitute a platform for developing new or improving existing relationship-related activities, such as transportation and logistics, production processes, and product development. However, this process is likely to take more time in a network founded to develop buyer–seller relationships than in pre-existing networks. In existing relationships, companies are likely to have developed a shared language and knowledge base, and mutual experience and trust prevail. For networks of existing buyer–seller relationships, it can therefore be questioned why anyone should financially support already-viable companies and relationships.

2. Networks consisting of relationships between competitor companies (see B in Figure 1.2)

In this type of network, companies share a language and a knowledge base; they also all possess almost the same resources, since they produce similar goods or services. However, the network companies do not have a shared goal. They act according to the same business logic but do not do business with each other, only with other companies; instead, they compete to do business better than the other companies in the network. This gives rise to two prevalent situations in a network of competitors, situations with quite different consequences. The first situation implies that the companies follow the competition logic and maintain distance from the other companies in the network. However, maintaining distance from other companies runs counter to the whole idea of developing new relationships and creating a network, posing a significant obstacle to the network in its ambition to produce positive outcomes for the member companies. In the second situation, in contrast, the companies act according to the cooperation logic. They cooperate, sharing information and knowledge, but this leads to complicated new situations and questions: What are these networks planned to achieve? What are the side effects when competing companies begin to cooperate? Are these networks compatible with existing legislation? Should governments and public organizations stimulate and support the development of cooperative relationships among competitors?

3. Networks consisting of companies in an industry (see C in Figure 1.2)

This type of network is a mixture of the previous two types and resembles what we tend to denote as a cluster. Companies in these networks have largely the same background, being part of the same industry and possessing similar resources and competencies. These companies easily understand each other's problems and opportunities. This also means that they share a single view of business. Here we find companies that are both business partners and competitors. Since they are located in the same region, they also share the same labour market, which means that, over the years, workers tend to shift among the companies in the networks. These networks are characterized not only by predictability but also by some suspicion. The shared location implies shared social networks and social control but can engender fear that another firm, in particular a competitor, may take undue advantage of transferred information or other resources. The critical issue is finding the right balance in the network in terms of numbers and competencies and developing a trusting and open interaction climate in which the companies share experiences and knowledge for the common good.

4. Network consisting of dispersed companies (see D in Figure 1.2)

These networks are fairly common and are often put together for political reasons, such as to reduce unemployment, increase equality, or strengthen the link between universities and business. In this network type, we find companies from different industries that neither buy from or sell to each other nor compete with each other. In business terms, they are very distant from each other. This means that they lack a common denominator and have a limited absorptive capacity (Cohen and Levinthal 1990) for information transfer and knowledge development.

Consequently, these networks tend to have vague goals, remote from the participating companies' daily operations, making it difficult for the coordinating hub to offer the participants anything other than general network activities. Instead, the regional development goal, or maybe a more general social context, must provide the glue that holds the network together. The social context can be a substitute for the lack of experience gained from doing business together. Nevertheless, despite such social platforms, these networks have difficulties finding shared goals for the involved companies, goals from which all companies can benefit. This means that such networks must spend considerable time defining what activities should be performed. All these factors imply long-term preparation and a long start-up period. Overall, these networks risk being vague, insipid, and characterized by low participant commitment, which, in turn, reduces the chance of achieving positive outcomes.

Roles and functions in network

Market logic is simple: companies do business with each other to make a profit. Almost all corporate actors follow this logic. However, regional strategic networks are, if not dominated by, at least well populated by actors acting according to a different logic. A characteristic actor in a regional strategic network is the hub organization, which is a company, organization, group of people, or sometimes just a single person. The hub fulfils a critical function in these networks, as it coordinates all the network's activities. From this it follows that one of the hub's main tasks is to keep all the other actors well informed about what is going on in the network. Its competence, enthusiasm, and commitment are especially important in the first phase of a network's existence. Usually its importance tends to fade if the other network actors develop relationships that exclude the need for a third party. The hub organization's existence is closely related to the financial support the network enjoys. Some network activities arranged by the hub are financed by the companies and organizations involved in the network. However, a network may also obtain significant financial resources from external sources, which are themselves stakeholders with their own agendas and intentions for the network. These stakeholders cannot be neglected by the hub, which must make arrangements and advocate goals that will satisfy them as well.

Moreover, the network needs an administration of its own, a role which is, in most cases, played by the hub, though the administrative and hub functions can be split. In any case, it is not the companies in the networks that are in charge of the administration. Finally, the people or organizations commissioned to evaluate the network and its activities play a specific role. The network needs external resources to get started, and the sources of these resources, for example government or regional administration, require that the network's use of their subsidies be evaluated. This is traditionally done after a period of financial support has ended, but, more recently, more networks are being evaluated midway through the process. Nevertheless, these evaluators seldom have any direct knowledge of the network: they are engaged just to conduct the evaluation and report their observations and conclusions, after which they are expected to leave the network. Thus, in regional strategic networks, four important functions – hub, financial support, administration, and evaluation – are not handled by the participating companies, as they are in other kinds of business networks, but by other actors who exert their own influence on network activities and outcomes.

Processes and phases in the network

Regional strategic networks are not established to exist indefinitely. They are usually initiated by organizations outside the network, such as consultants, public organizations, or governments, to exist for a specific period. With their help, networks gain financial support to achieve specific goals in advance. Among other things, this means that network operations are performed outside the ongoing operations of participating companies. The companies' ongoing operations and the regional strategic network's operations can to some extent be regarded as competing for the same resources in terms of time, people, and money.

The processes in the networks pass through various phases. A critical question is whether the network companies have any previous experience of working together. If there is positive prior experience of interaction between the companies in the network, the network will likely pass through some kind of honeymoon phase, when everyone expects good things to happen. On the other hand, in a network in which the participating companies have little experience of interacting with each other, the first phase will be critical, as it is when everyone involved must identify common goals and problems. However, it is most important that the network clearly, and preferably quickly, demonstrates that it can achieve goals and solve problems. If it cannot demonstrate this ability, the companies' commitment to the network will fade.

Another typical aspect of regional strategic network processes is that they emerge from plans devised by people often not directly involved in the network. Financial support is given on the basis of these plans, and the aim, of course, is that the plans should be fulfilled. However, when companies begin to interact, unanticipated matters arise, matters sometimes incompatible with the plans. This especially concerns networks in which companies are unknown to each other at the outset.

As already touched on, regional strategic networks do not survive solely on their own merits. In addition to their goals and plans, these networks mainly survive due to the outside financial support they enjoy. The sights are often set very high when a network is launched, in order to recruit participants and financers. Although there are often hopes that the network will transform itself into a self-sufficient and enduring organization, the reality is often that when financial support ends and the results turn out to be not very impressive, all but vestigial interaction dies. These network initiatives have thus been questioned and warrant further study.

An introduction to the themes and chapters of this book

This book takes a management perspective on the operations and processes in these networks and addresses the need for additional knowledge of regional strategic networks. In subsequent chapters, various case settings, processes, and outcomes are described and analysed. These chapters provide a deeper understanding of several key topics regarding regional development initiatives in the form of regional networking. This understanding can

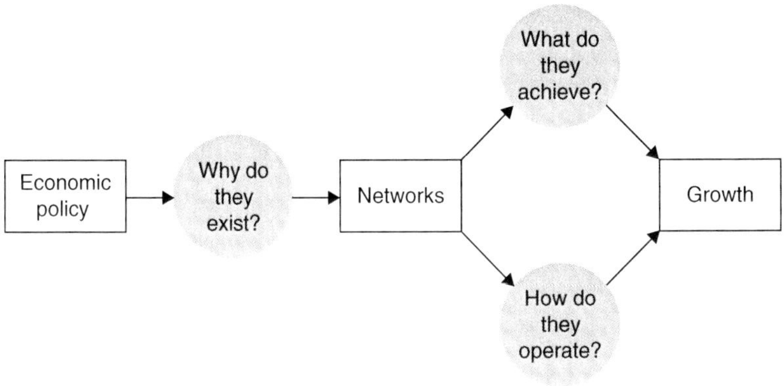

Figure 1.3 Main chapter themes

be divided into three areas, corresponding to the discussion in first section of this chapter (see Figure 1.3). The relationships between the three areas are dealt with in this book.

How economic policy influences the existence and function of these networks is an important area that can be scrutinized by answering the key question: Why do these networks exist? The second relationship, between networks and growth, can be divided into two areas, giving rise to two further questions: How do they operate? What do they achieve?

Why do these networks exist?

This question concerns the institutions and policy bodies that initiate networks. To begin with, in Chapter 2, Peter Parker and Christer Ekelund challenge the present role of regional governments and their espoused ways of managing publicly funded regional network development initiatives. They argue that there is a fundamental mismatch between the espoused aims of promoting knowledge development and the bureaucratic control usually employed to ensure the proper use of funding in these initiatives. Referring to the literature on complex project management and its application to a case analysis, they argue for a need to redefine and clarify roles in regional development initiatives and for a shift in control mechanisms from sponsoring activities towards buying results. They argue that these changes would increase the ability of regional governments to achieve results in regional development initiatives and increase their ability to communicate these results.

In Chapter 3, Håkan Pihl uses a new theory on institutional change in analysing the establishment of the hub organizations responsible for coordinating publicly supported regional strategic networks. The theory, developed by North (2005), extends new institutional economics and introduces human belief systems, learning, and institutional entrepreneurs to explain institutional change. Pihl uses the 'Northian' theory in analysing a case, 'the Rich Wetlands of Kristianstad'. Changes in the institutional structure were initiated by institutional entrepreneurs, and the case describes how a few individuals gradually established a small hub organization in the municipality of Kristianstad, Sweden, for the purpose of conserving and sustainably developing the surrounding wetlands. The activities of the organization include changing attitudes, building relationships, and initiating projects in collaboration with various stakeholders. The institutional framework provided incentives for entrepreneurs to develop new knowledge, which led to a path-dependent development.

How do these networks operate?

The driving factors of the networks, including communication, cooperation, interaction, learning, shared values, and trust, are studied and discussed in Chapters 4–6. In Chapter 4, Claus Steinle, Holger Schiele, and Kai Mietzner address the issue of the actual interaction between the actors in a regional–sectoral agglomeration. Recognizing that the mere existence of a structure consisting of a number of related companies and institutions does not automatically lead to all the benefits associated with clusters, this chapter follows a path suggested by the milieu approach focusing on the local interaction. However, while most research into milieus relies on qualitative case studies, here a survey-based approach to regional assessment is suggested and applied in analysing a medical technology cluster. The results underscore that a cluster analysis is not complete without a dedicated investigation of the interaction taking place. Such an analysis can help position a cluster in an assumed cluster life cycle; it also provides information that may guide a support initiative aiming to foster increased interaction among cluster companies, thereby increasing their ability to benefit from being in a cluster location.

The ability of network initiatives to achieve their aims has been questioned (Lindström 2005). In Chapter 5, Jorge Renato Verschoore and Alsonses Balestrin cast additional light on this question by measuring outcomes generated by small-firm networks in southern Brazil. They use a conjoint analysis of a sample of 443 owners out of a population of 3,087 companies associated with the 120 networks of the Cooperation Networks Program, supported by the government of Rio Grande do Sul state. The results indicate that promoting cooperation through small-firm networks can be a functional way to promote local economic development. The study confirmed the relevance of five outcomes produced by the networks, in the following order of importance:

1. collective solutions;
2. scale and market power;
3. learning and innovation;

4. social relationships;
5. cost and risk reduction.

On the basis of the results, the authors presented an analysis of the outcomes of small-firm networks, taking account of their age and size.

In Chapter 6, Edith Andresen, Anette Bergman, and Lars Hallén address the development of email communication in a regional strategic network in which the use of email was part of a deliberate communication strategy that was supposed to contribute to both efficient communication and improved computer skills in member firms. The total dataset of emails sent and received by the hub manager was sampled for three periods of one month each. The email communication pattern is analysed in terms of communicating partners, communication direction and frequency, and information content. Within the brief time frame of three years, the communication pattern did not change much. It was difficult to implement the new communication strategy, which is discussed against the background of communication preferences, the atmosphere in the relationships between the firms and the hub, the geographic location of the members, and the tasks to be performed. The findings illustrate problems associated with temporary organizations when long-term conditions, such as preferences and atmosphere, have an impact on desired development effects.

What do these networks achieve?

Networks can also be approached from another angle: the results they produce or are intended to produce. In an increasingly globalized world, increased exports and internationalization are common goals. Supporting small businesses and regional entrepreneurship by attracting capital and building business-angel networks is another popular goal. Networks engineered to help companies develop marketing activities and distribution systems or to improve supply-chain management and foster the emergence of supplier networks are deemed critical for company well-being. These goals set the stage for the question 'What do these networks achieve?', which the book addresses in Chapters 7–11.

In Chapter 7, Snejina Michailova and Sylvie Chetty examine the potential benefits for SMEs of a cluster location by addressing the increasing importance of knowledge in corporate internationalization processes. They focus on the links between cluster membership, knowledge processes, and SME internationalization. They distinguish between *access* to knowledge, found to be more frequently associated with component knowledge, and knowledge *acquisition*, found to be typically associated with architectural knowledge. They find that cluster membership is beneficial to both information access and acquisition, and thus to SME internationalization, and that governments can help by stimulating cluster interaction.

Chapter 8, by Karolina Elmhester and Staffan Brege, examines the potential benefits of interaction in a regional context, even among competitors. They present a Swedish case of regional cooperation among potential competitors which jointly developed their competencies to live up to the demands of their shared dominant customer, IKEA. Under the guidance of a network hub, they managed to radically shorten the time from order to delivery and to share knowledge, despite their competitive situation. Network membership provided knowledge and motivation that helped these companies undertake important improvement actions in their companies. The identified success factors were as follows.

1. The network was strategically important to the suppliers and driven by high involvement.
2. The network was supplier driven, with support from its biggest customer.
3. The network was administered by a competent coordinator and a stable administrative organization.
4. The participants were competent.
5. Project management was professional and possessed clear objectives.
6. The projects were flexible.
7. There were strong personal bonds among participating CEOs.

In Chapter 9, Simone Guercini and Andrea Runfola address networking benefits from the perspective of the Italian fashion industry. In this context, new forms of marketing cooperation emerge in local networks of fashion companies, including the integration of cooperative retail strategies (for example, store openings) and branding (for example, brand management). These new forms seem to be characterized by the more complex integration of marketing processes. The development of these new forms was initiated by leading entrepreneurs who activated cooperation among companies that also gained public/institutional support. Empirically, the chapter presents three cases of marketing cooperation innovation in local networks of fashion companies that are investigated in depth. The cases illustrate how consortia of companies with a large number of associated actors have been formed in cooperation. These units have been able to specialize in marketing tasks, thereby reaping economies of scale and scope.

Engineered networks are further discussed in Chapter 10 by Lars Silver, Nicolaus Lundahl, and Björn Berggren. This chapter focuses especially on the evolution and development of business-angel networks, a kind of network that is increasing in number, totalling approximately 300 in Europe in 2007. The studied network divides into two groupings because of divergent views on how best to perform the role of business angels. This chapter illustrates how engineered networks must be context-dependent and adapted to the situation at hand. The authors emphasize the importance of policy-makers' ability to accurately portray the decisions an investment business-angel network must make in order to succeed.

Chapter 11 deals with how the internationalization of SMEs can be improved through export cooperation. The authors Hans Jansson and Petter Boye describe and explain how SMEs can increase their internationalization by establishing joint export networks using local resources and competencies to exploit international markets. To specify the relationship between internationalization at the firm and network levels, a joint export network model is developed. It consists of a joint export network organization structure, based on a shared knowledge base, resource base, and institutional structure. This joint export network is anchored in an industrial region. The network builds competitiveness through being involved in a gradually evolving internationalization process. The chapter mainly presents the theoretical framework developed to describe how SMEs increase their internationalization through joint network organizations. The methodology used is explained and the framework is illustrated by two empirical examples.

Finally, in Chapter 12, Heléne Lundberg summarizes and discusses the findings of the previous chapters, focusing particularly on major challenges in publicly backed network initiatives, the complexity of evaluating network initiatives, and the advantages identified in regional network initiatives. Furthermore, some concluding managerial implications for initiators and facilitators are presented, and three major topics for further research are suggested.

References

S. J. Appold, 'Location Patterns of US Industrial Research: Mimetic Isomorphism and the Emergence of Geographic Charisma', *Regional Studies,* 39 (2005): 17–39.

G. Becattini, 'Italian Industrial Districts: Problems and Perspectives', *International Journal of Management and Organization,* 21 (1991): 83–90.

K. Blois, 'Don't All Firms Have Relationships?', *Journal of Business and Industrial Marketing,* 13 (1998): 256–70.

R. A. Boschma, 'Proximity and Innovation: A Critical Assessment', *Regional Studies,* 39 (2005): 61–74.

T. Bresnahan, A. Gambardella, and A. Saxenian, '"Old Economy" Inputs for "New Economy" Outcomes: Cluster Formation in the New Silicon Valleys', *Industrial and Corporate Change,* 10 (2001): 835–60.

R. S. Burt, 'Structural Holes and Good Ideas', *American Journal of Sociology,* 110 (2004): 349–99.

R. Capello and A. Faggian, 'Collective Learning and Relational Capital in Local Innovation Processes', *Regional Studies,* 39 (2005): 75–87.

W. M. Cohen and D. A. Levinthal, 'Absorptive Capacity: A New Perspective on Learning and Innovation', *Administrative Science Quarterly,* 35 (1990): 128–52.

M. S. Dahl and C. O. R. Pedersen, 'Knowledge Flows through Informal Contacts in Industrial Clusters: Myth or Reality?', *Research Policy,* 33 (2004): 1673–86.

Y. L. Doz, P. M. Olk, and P. S. Ring, 'Formation Processes of R&D Consortia: Which Path to Take? Where Does It Lead?', *Strategic Management Journal,* 21 (2000): 239–66.

M. Enright, 'Regional Clusters and Economic Development: A Research Agenda', in U. Staber, N. Schaefer, and B. Sharma (eds), Business *Networks: Prospects for Regional Development* (Berlin: Walter de Gruyter, 1996).

D. Ford, 'The Development of Buyer–Seller Relationships in Industrial Markets', in D. Ford (ed.), *Understanding Business Marketing and Purchasing* (London: Thomson Learning, 2002).

G. Grabher, 'The Weakness of Strong Ties: The Lock-in of Regional Development in the Ruhr Area', in G. Grabler and W. W. Powell (eds), *Networks* (Cheltenham: Elgar Edward, 2004).

M. Granovetter, 'The Strength of Weak Ties', *American Journal of Sociology,* 78 (1973): 1360–80.

L. Hallén and M. Johanson, 'Vad är regionala strategiska nätverk?', in L. Hallén, M. Johanson, and T. Roxenhall (eds), *Regionala strategiska nätverk i praktiken* (Lund: Studentlitteratur, 2009).

M. T. Hansen, 'The Search-Transfer Problem: The Role of Weak Ties in Sharing Knowledge across Organization Subunits', *Administrative Science Quarterly,* 44 (1999): 82–111.

J. C. Jarillo, 'On Strategic Networks', *Strategic Management Journal,* 9 (1988): 31–41.

J. Johanson and L.-G. Mattsson, 'The Market-As-Network Tradition in Sweden', in G. Laurent, G. L. Lilien, and B. Pras (eds), *Research Traditions in Marketing* (Boston, MA: Kluwer Academic Publishers, 1994).

M. H. Lazerson and G. Lorenzoni, 'The Firms That Feed Industrial Districts: A Return to the Italian Source', *Industrial and Corporate Change,* 8 (1999): 235–65.

N. Lin, 'Building a Network Theory of Social Capital', in N. Lin, K. Cook and R. S. Burt (eds), *Social Capital* (New York: Aldine de Gruyter, 2001).

B. Lindström, *Regionalpolitiken som tillväxtpolitik: Retorik och substans i den regionala utvecklingspolitiken* (Östersund: Institutet för tillväxtpolitiska studier, 2005).

H. Lundberg, *Geographical Proximity Effects and Regional Strategic Networks* (Uppsala: Department of Business Administration, Uppsala University, 2008).

A. Marshall, *Principles of Economics* (London: Macmillan, 1891).

R. Martin and P. Sunley, 'Deconstructing Clusters: Chaotic Concept or Policy Panacea', *Journal of Economic Geography,* 3 (2003): 5–35.

P. Maskell, 'Towards a Knowledge-based Theory of the Geographical Cluster', *Industrial and Corporate Change,* 10 (2001): 921–43.

D. C. North, *Understanding the Process of Economic Change* (Princeton, NJ: Princeton University Press, 2005).

M. Piore and C. Sabel, *The Second Industrial Divide: Possibilities for Prosperity* (New York: Basic Books, 1984).

M. Porter, *The Competitive Advantage of Nations* (London: Macmillan, 1990).

M. Porter, 'Clusters and the New Economics of Competition', *Harvard Business Review,* 98 (1998a): 77–90.

M. Porter, *On Competition* (Boston, MA: Harvard Business School, 1998b).

M. Porter, 'Location, Competition, and Economic Development: Local Clusters in a Global Economy', *Economic Development Quarterly,* 14 (2000): 15–34.

W. W. Powell, K. W. Koput, and S.-D. Laurel, 'Interorganizational Collaboration and the Locus of Innovation: Networks of Learning in Biotechnology', *Administrative Science Quarterly,* 41 (1996): 116–45.

A. Saxenian, *Regional Advantage: Culture and Competition in Silicon Valley and Route 128* (Cambridge, MA: Harvard University Press, 1994).
U. Staber, 'Networks and Regional Development: Perspectives and Unresolved Issues', in U. Staber, N. Schaefer, and B. Sharma (eds), *Business Networks: Prospects for Regional Development* (Berlin: Walter de Gruyter, 1996).
Ö. Sölvell, G. Lindqvist, and C. Ketels, *The Cluster Initiative Greenbook* (Stockholm: VINNOVA, 2003).
P. A. Wilson, 'Embracing Locality in Local Economic Development', *Urban Studies,* 32 (1995): 645–59.

2
A New Role for Government in Regional Development

Peter E. Parker and Christer Ekelund

Introduction

Significant funds are channelled into regional development initiatives every year. The Swedish Agency for Economic and Regional Growth, NUTEK, estimates that in the first years of the new millennium, approximately SEK 10 billion (more than €1 billion) were annually channelled into regional development projects in Sweden. Structural funds, national and regional governmental agencies, and private enterprises each contribute roughly a third of the total investment (NUTEK 2004). Though there is clearly enormous interest in promoting regional development, well-known and serious managerial challenges remain to be addressed in publicly funded regional development efforts (Gullander *et al.* 2004); this chapter concerns these challenges. Particular attention is paid to initiatives seeking to promote beneficial business networks and partnerships as a means of facilitating knowledge transfer and development at the regional level.

The chapter begins by briefly reviewing the rationales for regional development initiatives to promote knowledge transfer and development. This review provides an important backdrop to discussions of how knowledge transfer and development can be facilitated. We then seek to identify some key managerial challenges in publicly funded regional development initiatives, particularly those using a network approach. Analysis of these managerial challenges indicates that the problems facing network-development initiatives are known in the literature on the management of complex projects, and that this literature can be drawn on in addressing these challenges.

Arguments for government involvement in regional development

Before discussing the managerial challenges facing regional development initiatives, we must briefly address why regional development initiatives are needed at all. A grasp of the underlying rationale of publicly funded regional development initiatives will provide a better sense of the challenges involved.

Policies to promote regional business development all seem to be rooted in two broad assumptions. First, in important respects, knowledge is considered a public good. Therefore, markets are understood to provide insufficient mechanisms for generating and transferring knowledge. Second, knowledge development, in particular, enlarging the knowledge component of products and processes, is central to corporate competitiveness and therefore economic development (Metcalfe 1997; Hallin and Österhol 2004).

The belief that markets provide insufficient mechanisms for knowledge transfer and development is based on two assumptions. First, firms have difficulties estimating returns on investments in new knowledge, and this creates a certain amount of conservatism. Second, firms have difficulties capturing the returns on knowledge they develop, as certain kinds of knowledge may be circulated at little cost and one person's use of the knowledge does not preclude another's. The possibility of the 'free' circulation of knowledge is significant in many respects. While such freely circulating knowledge may be of enormous help to people facing similar challenges, it is problematic for individual firms seeking to capture returns on knowledge investments. Difficulties estimating and capturing returns lead firms to invest less in knowledge development than may be beneficial from a societal perspective (Metcalfe 1997).

Arguments as to the insufficiency of market mechanisms for creating and transferring knowledge acquire increased significance in light of the widely held belief that innovation, that is, the commercialization of knowledge development, is key to firm and regional competitiveness. For example, Porter's (1990) influential work argues that regional development depends on forms of rivalry, the network connections of firms, proximity to demanding customers, and employee skill – all key ingredients of dynamic development (Porter 1990). Dynamic regions are thus characterized by the presence of firms that maintain high-quality communication with front-line suppliers and demanding customers and by their ability to draw on available knowledge to create improved products and processes (Saxenian 2000).

Given these starting points, it is natural that governments should take a keen interest in promoting effective knowledge transfer and development mechanisms in business. In principle, governments should be able to do something to alleviate underinvestment in the development and dissemination of knowledge that could be put to business use.

One approach to stimulating knowledge development in business is to promote the development of business networks. The underlying premise is that personal networks linking organizations with complementary knowledge may provide an important non-market means of developing and transferring knowledge between organizations. These networks are not incompatible with markets but are fuelled by slightly different incentives, such as reputation building and individual need to acquire the information necessary to navigate a complex and shifting environment (Parker 2004). The knowledge developed and transferred in these networks is highly context-specific and provides a sound basis for commercial application.

By promoting the development of business networks, regional governments seek to augment regional knowledge transfer and development. By promoting better connectivity between firms, research facilities, and other agencies, regions hope to facilitate innovation and long-term competitiveness. Such networks, linking people from various firms and organizations, can be conceived of as regional resources: a regionally based system for knowledge transfer and development.

Management challenges

While publicly funded initiatives to stimulate business networks could play an important role in economic development, realizing this potential is not a trivial task. In this section, we seek to outline four interrelated managerial challenges confronting publicly funded network initiatives. The list of challenges is not exhaustive. Our intent is merely to capture key issues that are widely noted in evaluations and documentation and that affect the legitimacy of these initiatives in the eyes of funding agencies and businesses. This list of problems then forms the basis for further analysis and discussion of possible ways forward.

Not crowding out private initiative

A first challenge lies in avoiding the risk that publicly funded initiatives may crowd out private financing – the risk that public financing simply replaces private financing of projects that would have taken place anyway. Such crowding out of private financing is a concern because such an addition of public resources achieves no additional development effects but may introduce new administrative problems for both firms and governmental agencies. Empirical evidence on crowding out is ambiguous (David *et al.* 2000), though the concern is real. Clearly, regional development initiatives must seek to create regional resources over and above those normally created by private actors. This consideration has an important impact on the kinds of initiatives supported and on the fund control mechanisms used. Initiatives are devised to minimize the risk that funding may be seen as an industry subsidy.

Creating business involvement

In a sense, the challenge of creating business involvement is the inverse of crowding out private initiative and may even stem from learning that first lesson too well. Many regional development initiatives suffer from too little, rather than too much, business interest. It has often proven difficult for publicly funded initiatives to foster sufficient business involvement in creating regional resources. Reports from various initiatives have repeatedly warned of failures to foster such involvement, both in Sweden (Berggren *et al.* 1998; ITPS 2004b) and in the case of European Community (EC) structural funds generally (NUTEK 2005). In a summary report, NUTEK notes the general lack of business involvement in EC-funded regional development initiatives, despite a widespread conviction that business participation is an essential means of keeping the initiatives relevant (NUTEK 2005).

The second problem to be addressed in managing regional development issues is therefore the fostering of adequate business involvement. Regional development ultimately takes place through businesses, as returns are realized and employment is created in them. Coordination with existing business should obviously be a pivotal element of most regional development initiatives.

Bureaucracy

Part of the problem in fostering business involvement seems to be related to the large-scale bureaucratic procedures used in many regional development initiatives. These procedures are developed to ensure accountability in public funding use; as such, they are commendable. However, bureaucratic control is singularly ill adapted to creating the innovative exchanges and increased connectivity the initiatives seek to promote. The problem is not specific to publicly funded initiatives but has more to do with the nature of knowledge development, which does not lend itself to long-term planning. Traditional top-down planning and control mechanisms are simply ineffective at promoting knowledge creation and innovation (Kreiner 1995; ITPS 2004a).

The bureaucracy involved in managing regional development initiatives is, in our experience, often perceived as both burdensome and relatively unrelated to actual practice by the businesses involved. However, it is not a point we find explicitly mentioned in evaluations, perhaps because it reflects poorly on the funding agency imposing these controls. While monitoring and controlling of the use of public funding is important, it is easy to understand how control mechanisms established centrally in broad funding schemes can become increasingly detached from business reality over time. Nor is it difficult to imagine how the imposition of seemingly irrelevant bureaucratic procedures burdens project participants and further undermines trust in governmental agencies.

In interviews with firms taking part in network-development initiatives, we learn that funding is rarely perceived as a *reward* for ends achieved. Instead, funding is perceived as a kind of handout only loosely coupled to firm activities. Thus, the *form* in which support is given for such regional development initiatives makes them seem antithetical to business practice: businesses are reimbursed for demonstrating certain project outputs rather than business outcomes. Accordingly, 'taking the path of government aid' tends to be seen to indicate that a business cannot manage on its own. This is precisely opposite to what is intended in most initiatives: that programme participation should be seen as advancing business practice in a region to greater heights. In certain initiatives, the logic of producing and documenting project outputs counteracts any attempts to direct the initiative towards more business-relevant activities. In such cases, public funding becomes a hindrance rather than a boon to development.

Government funding of development initiatives clearly allows for valuable activities that would not otherwise take place. Nonetheless, it is also clear that these initiatives introduce a foreign bureaucratic logic according to which firms are reimbursed for activities rather than rewarded for results. Relatively involved bureaucratic procedures do allow for a degree of control over resources but may well be counterproductive in terms of achieving business-relevant results.

Demonstrating results

A final management challenge in regional development initiatives is their relative inability to produce demonstrable positive effects. This may be partly due to inherent difficulties in measuring diffuse developmental outcomes (Rosenfeld 1996; Keast *et al.* 2004). How, for example, does one measure the results of increased insight and knowledge in a region? However, a lack of measurable outcomes would also seem to reflect management problems. For example, an extensive independent review of the impact of structural funds in Sweden, 1995–2000, finds no quantifiable effect whatsoever of funding on target variables, such as per-capita income, employment rate, or proportion of the population of working age. Moreover, the report finds no support linking EC funding to any of the 15 intermediary variables capturing various aspects of business dynamism, skills, and labour-market development, or the attractiveness of a region as a place of work or recreation. The Swedish Institute for Growth Policy Studies (ITPS) has concluded that this should be interpreted as a serious warning signal with respect to programme implementation, and the agency also states there is a need to develop effective evaluation mechanisms (ITPS 2004a). Difficulties both achieving and measuring results may contribute to the lack of visible impact of EC structural funds in Sweden. In any case, an inability to demonstrate positive outcomes diminishes the political legitimacy of regional development initiatives and exacerbates the difficulty of fostering business involvement (Human and Provan 2000).

An illustration of managerial challenges: the systems-network initiative

A development initiative that the authors were able to monitor closely illustrates how the managerial challenges described above come together.

The initiative concerned developing the capacity of small suppliers to jointly take on larger and more complex orders (systems). This initiative was rooted in widespread concern that small regional suppliers were fragmented and unable to exploit market opportunities that required taking more responsibility for integrating the components of larger systems. An important customer for many of the firms had also clearly signalled that it wished for fewer interfaces with suppliers.

The idea underlying the systems-network initiative was that public funding could be used to develop the ability of firms to coordinate, produce, and deliver complex systems that used the various competencies of the network firms. The project envisioned that the firms would develop their collective competence in several ways. First, the project required that the firms acquire a certain amount of technical knowledge of how the components of larger systems are integrated. Second, the project called for the development of inter-firm coordination mechanisms, so that orders could be successfully coordinated. Finally, the initiative required that the firms be able to market themselves as potential suppliers of larger systems. Funding for the systems-network project was obtained from EC structural-adjustment funds and coordinated by the participating firms under the aegis of regional government.

Though strong customers may sometimes take the initiative to coordinate and develop their suppliers, the firms in this case lacked a proactive customer. The targeted firms had to be the driving force in developing the capacity to sell to large customers. The suppliers seemed unable to implement such an initiative by themselves but required the aid of an independent third party. In this sense, there was a case for this being an area in which market failure could be remedied by public funding.

The initiative took its starting point in groups of eight firms in related fields of mechanical engineering, metals, and plastics. The former purchasing head of a large customer firm was hired as project consultant. The project was to start with educational programmes in the participating firms, to establish a basis for cooperation and transfer relevant knowledge from a purchaser's perspective. The consultant was then to organize a set of intensive one-day workshops involving various potential customers. These workshops would help the firms collectively identify and discuss improvements that customers might want in their production processes. When an interesting area of potential improvement was identified, the firms would combine their understandings of the problem and use their collective know-how to create an offer. If the offer was met with interest, further development would follow, and it was hoped that new orders and more productive relationships with the customer would result.

Significant competence was involved in the development initiative, as well as sufficient funding and a focus that seemed relevant to both the firms and the region. Nonetheless, the project quickly faltered.

A preliminary indication of problems was that the participating firms tended to choose educational packages unrelated to the overarching aim of designing and delivering whole systems. Interviews with participants revealed that they doubted the ability of the project to bring about the necessary inter-firm coordination, so each firm tended to respond by maximizing its own benefit from the programme regardless of the other firms' interests. The funding of the initiative provided no direct incentives for the consultant to bring the firms into line. In fact, funding was assured via a complex alliance of funding sources, and it turned out to be nearly impossible to change project direction. Regional government could have chosen to abort the programme completely at this point but instead tried to salvage some value by letting it run its course. There was a risk that no regional resources would be created in this case.

The four managerial problems outlined above come together in this case to create an intricate problem complex. The initiative was founded on a perceived need for knowledge development among the suppliers, so they could take advantage of more advanced demand. A case was made that the needed form of coordination was not forthcoming, so there was a role for regional government to play in boosting the suppliers' competitiveness by helping them help each other. To maintain control over public resources, the project had to fulfil the detailed requirements of various funding agencies. The project was thus plagued by multiple and burdensome bureaucratic control procedures and, precisely because of this, had no real overall means of governance. The regional government had no way to induce firms to exploit opportunities identified at the beginning of the project. Since the project lacked convincing leadership, the participating firms naturally sought to extract the maximum benefit for themselves, regardless of whether this was a regional interest. Businesses became less involved as the credibility of the project decreased. In essence, businesses were opting out of involvement in a common project. This project might still yield interesting results, quite apart from those originally intended, but it would be difficult if not impossible to capture these potential results and link them directly to the systems-network project.

Understanding the complexity of network development

In the previous sections, we have sought to demonstrate that network-development initiatives could have an important role to play in regional development but that important managerial challenges must be considered. In the following, we seek to demonstrate that these managerial challenges can be met.

The first part of this argument entails analysing the underlying complexity of network development. Complexity arises in network development because there is uncertainty as to what is to be achieved, that is, how firms can best help each other and how to bring this about. Such complexity can, within limits, be managed. Indeed, there is a growing body of literature and considerable experience regarding the handling of complex projects, which do require a different kind of management thinking.

A useful understanding of the problems confronting network-development initiatives can be achieved if we analyse the challenges involved in terms of two underlying dimensions commonly distinguished in the relevant literature (Kreiner 1995; Williams 1999; Lindkvist *et al.* 2001; Schwaber 2004).

First, there is a dimension along which we assess project complexity in terms of how difficult it is to set specifications. In some projects, desired outcomes are relatively easy to specify by the primary stakeholders. In other cases, specifications are very difficult to set, perhaps due to a considerable knowledge gap between stakeholders or to the shift of requirements over time (Koppenjan and Klijn 2004; Klijn 2007).

Second, there is a project-complexity dimension that concerns the degree to which project components are systemically interrelated. In simple cases, we can break down a project into its components and implement these more or less separately in a planned manner. In other cases, project components are significantly interrelated and planning becomes more difficult, since minor changes in one component may significantly affect many others. In this kind of project, detailed sequential planning is difficult or impossible because minor changes are inevitable.

When a project scores reasonably high on both these dimensions, it is considered complex. In such projects it is difficult to specify both what should be achieved and how. We argue that network-development initiatives generally are complex projects and need to be managed as such.

To highlight the complexity of network-development projects, it may be useful to continue citing the systems network outlined above. In this development initiative, there was a knowledge gap between the regional government and the participating firms. This gap derived from the fact that the publicly funded agencies and participating firms were part of different fields of activity with different rules and priorities. The government employees may be assumed to have limited knowledge of the particular realities facing firms, and vice versa. Difficulties communicating across this gap were exacerbated by the complicated relationship between the aims and means of these two main stakeholders. Firms may be assumed to take part in regional development efforts for reasons of self-interest, so to them the primary question is whether an initiative benefits the firm. For a regional development agency, however, business interest is a means to achieve aims that are perhaps more difficult to convey, such as regional knowledge transfer and development. The difficulty of specifying aims for a network-development initiative may be exacerbated by the necessity of using multiple funding sources, each with its own purposes, and demands.

It is safe to say that network-development initiatives often score high on the first dimension, that is, difficulty setting adequate specifications.

Network-development initiatives are also complex with respect to the second dimension: there can be considerable uncertainty as to how to achieve project aims due to the complex interrelationships between project components. In the case of the systems network discussed earlier, inter-firm coordination and firm ability to meet the needs of particular large customers depended in complex ways on all other participating firms. There was no simple way to plan how this network should develop, as changes in one firm would likely necessitate changes throughout the project. Network development as a whole therefore depends on a complex interplay of autonomous actors whose priorities may change over time. Trust between actors and internal communications are therefore critical and unpredictable factors in successful network development (Vangen and Huxham 2003; Neergaard and Ulhöi 2006). In the case of the system network, and others like it, we find complexity in a process or technological sense, as various project components are systemically interrelated in a manner that defies simple planning.

If it is correct that regional development projects are complex in these ways, then it is easy to understand how imposing a heavy bureaucratic burden, based on a simple planning logic, will cause serious problems. In complex projects, traditional planning and control methods premised on the predictability of means and results quickly lose their relevance. Defining requirements for the outcome is almost impossibly time consuming, due to knowledge gaps between parties. Even if it is possible to establish a reasonable set of requirements, these will necessarily be subject to change as the project develops and new areas are explored. Detailed, long-term planning is therefore useless and may even hinder development (Blomberg 2003). Unfortunately, and counterproductively, repeated project failures tend to strengthen calls for more and better planning and control, rather than lead to a questioning of methods (Tjäder and Söderlund 2001).

Many problems confronting network-development initiatives can be understood to stem from the collision between bureaucratic control and complex reality. Bureaucratic logic is pervasive in the funding and execution of regional development initiatives. For example, competence-raising programmes may be initiated in hopes that greater competence will generate higher incomes or more productive work. However, the question of *how* the education provided is actually applied ultimately falls outside the programme's scope. In other words, control is exercised to ensure that funds are used according to plan, not that they are used to achieve desired ends. Similarly, business-development agencies may be initiated and run without any built-in feedback regarding actual business improvements. The logic is one of controlling *funding outputs* while ignoring actual outcomes. This logic enables us to spend billions of euro on laudable projects that achieve no demonstrable effect.

Managing complex projects

The past decade has seen the proliferation of theories concerning the management of complex projects. The following sections briefly review the fundamental principles of this approach; we subsequently argue that network-development initiatives can be managed using similar principles.

This field of complex project management was given important impetus from experience in software development. Markets and technology have been developing rapidly in this field, creating uncertainty in terms of both what developers can deliver and the best ways of solving problems. Software products are highly systematic, that is, there is considerable interrelatedness between components, creating complexity with respect to how ends are to be achieved. In this situation, extensive or long-term planning can be counterproductive. In response, there has been a massive shift in this field away from plan-based bureaucratic control towards more agile forms of management. Iterative or agile project management is held to be an alternative that allows better exploration and learning while meeting customer or management control needs (Chin 2004; Highsmith 2004; Schwaber 2004).

The basic principles of agile approaches to complex project management are straightforward. Because such projects are complex with respect to specification setting, simple, regular, and meaningful communication is needed with important stakeholders, particularly the main customer/buyer. Because such projects are complex in the sense that they are difficult to plan, frequent and meaningful communication is needed between project participants. Achieving these ends arguably requires two important shifts: first, clarification and simplification of the roles involved in the project and, second, a shift towards iterative methods in which communication is based on the results achieved in the previous interval rather than on complex, predetermined planning about what to achieve in the long term. These principles are applied similarly but on different time scales to augment external and internal communication in complex projects. A more detailed description of how this works is provided below.

Creating simple, regular, and meaningful communication with external stakeholders

Most complex projects have multiple important stakeholders, yet it may be difficult to induce their representatives to reach joint decisions or even to be present at the same time. Since stakeholders have different perspectives on and competence in setting specifications, both formulating adequate aims and reviewing progress become challenging in complex projects. In traditional project management, responsibility for understanding and weighing the interests of multiple stakeholders falls on the project manager. For complex projects, however, it has been suggested (Schwaber 2004) that a role representing all external stakeholders be created. This effectively shifts the responsibility for communicating with diverse stakeholders from the project manager to this new role, which we may call 'owner/buyer'. The owner/buyer is also responsible for negotiating directly with those driving the development, namely, the project participants. Clearly, this new owner/buyer role is central and difficult; to make the role feasible, simplifying structures are imposed.

First, direct communication between the owner/buyer and project participants occurs in structured forms at regular intervals, to review results from the previous interval and set priorities for the next. Interval duration is predetermined and should be reasonable in terms of risk to the owner/buyer, but should be sufficient to allow project participants to achieve substantial results. Between these meetings, there should be no communication between owner/buyer and participants. This allows participants to work wholeheartedly and to focus on achieving the results to which they committed at the start of the interval.

Second, project priorities are defined in terms of the *functionality* that the owner/buyer wants and the project participants commit to achieving. Likewise, results demonstrated in each interval should be tangible, testable, and functional for the owner/buyer. In essence, the owner/buyer and project participants negotiate and review thin and manageable 'slices' of finished product at regular intervals. This helps keep communication meaningful, despite knowledge gaps between parties.

Fostering frequent and meaningful communication among project participants

According to the same school of thought (Schwaber 2004), three important principles help foster meaningful communication among project participants.

First, limit the number of participants, preferably to no more than six to eight people. This allows flexible and tight communication in meetings. Second, help institute regular short meetings where results and immediate future work are discussed. Work taken on by various participants should be of a nature that allows frequent reporting of meaningful results. In this case, 'meaningful' refers to something relatable to the entire project effort, a tangible result comprehensible by other project participants so that they can agree on its value. Third and finally, the participants as a group must manage themselves: they must be entirely responsible for the work the group commits to delivering and for finding appropriate means to deliver it.

The methodology as a whole

The project methodology described here is designed to make the best possible use of the disparate knowledge of the various project stakeholders. It attempts to do so by creating the best possible communication given a high level of uncertainty regarding requirements and process. The key mechanism is to communicate tangible results pertaining to delivered functionality rather than about ideas *about* possible results. The process includes mechanisms that allow the project to evolve without loss of control as new areas are explored. In fact, the sense of control is usually enhanced by periodic delivery and demonstration of functionality and the higher-quality communication this facilitates.

In the following section, we will attempt to demonstrate that a more agile approach to regional development is possible and would be advantageous. We argue that this approach would alleviate the managerial problems from which network-development initiatives suffer.

A new role for government: managing network-development initiatives as complex projects

A critical step towards creating better management practices in network-development initiatives is to initiate the role of owner/buyer with a real mandate to negotiate regarding the development of initiatives. Initiating the owner/buyer role would be pivotal in creating better communication concerning project aims. This would also be the critical step in moving from a system of bureaucratic control to one of controlling outcomes, and thus improving accountability (Agranoff and McGuire 2001; Kenis and Provan 2006).

As a means of further explaining what this role entails and how the approach could be put into practice, it would be useful to revisit the earlier example of the systems-network initiative. As described earlier, a regional government representative had initiated a project with a consultant involving eight supplier firms. The initiative aimed to enable a set of suppliers to coordinate, produce, and deliver systems improvement to larger customers. Could such a project be run in accordance with the principles outlined above? Although the answer is necessarily speculative, we see no reason why it could not.

We can imagine that the owner/buyer, a regional representative, lacks the competence to plan how the desired development is to take place among the group of suppliers. This is not only because the owner/buyer does not know the specific circumstances of these suppliers but also because setting adequate project specifications is probably not viable. We expect there to be significant learning in the process and that the project must be adaptable to changing circumstances.

The first step in the initiative is to set the stage for negotiation. The owner/buyer and the supplier-firm representatives set aside a limited time in which to negotiate the results to be delivered over the course of the project and in the next interval of, say, two months. The exact duration of these intervals is unimportant. What is important is that the time allotted to both negotiation and delivery be determined before negotiating the content and that everyone be clear that these time limits are fixed.

Successful negotiation might produce a list of requirements consisting of a set of competencies for the firms to develop and demonstrate during the project. Clearly, these competencies must be aligned with the interests of the businesses involved, as they have to see their business potential. The achieved competencies must also, in the owner/buyer's view, provide a foundation for future business and regional development. In this example, the project goal was that participating firms should develop into proficient systems suppliers. This goal could be broken down into three basic intervals, each of which could be broken down into a set of requirements. By way of example, the following intervals could be imagined:

1. *Competence in integrating technical solutions* for a potential customer is acquired in the firm network: the suppliers will analyse a particular system of a larger customer firm and cooperate to find an alternate technical solution for this system that improves substantially on its current configuration. This will be reviewed at the end of the first interval by an external consultant and by the customer firm.
2. *Partnering competence* is developed in the firm network: solution production and delivery require cooperative arrangements between the firms. In this case, the firms devise arrangements for delivering a complex product like the one developed in the first interval. This interval requires the development of cooperation forms and the establishment of legal arrangements to enable satisfactory production and delivery. Each firm should agree to the arrangements to demonstrate functionality.
3. *Market/sales competence* for systems is developed in the network: the suppliers must be able to sell improvements to large customers in an advantageous manner. This calls for a marketing organization and the creation of credibility in terms of supplying and maintaining the delivered systems. Functionality is demonstrated by successfully meeting prospective customer firms and conducting technical analysis, as in interval 1, and making an offer for the construction and delivery of a new system in accordance with agreements developed in interval 2.

Initially, only the requirements of the first interval (of two months) are defined in detail; these requirements are prioritized by the owner/buyer. The group of firms negotiates what can reasonably be achieved in the first interval, given the resources available. The suppliers must then commit to delivering the agreed-on functionality at the end of the interval, after which both the results and process are reviewed and priorities and commitments for the next interval are reviewed. Of course, either individual firms or owners/buyers may wish to discontinue the project. This is relatively unproblematic in that the delivered functionality is a sufficient and demonstrable result.

As for the group of suppliers, they organize themselves. Work in each interval is conducted entirely on the terms of the participating firms. They own the problem and have the best knowledge of how to advance the situation.

In doing this, the firms also develop their ability to solve joint problems and build trust. Naturally, the firms will account for their use of the public resources made available to them, but this is of secondary interest. What is of most significance is what they achieve and can demonstrate at the end of each interval. Thus, the project imposes a minimum amount of bureaucracy and encourages the firms to find cost-effective means of achieving the results. After all, an important part of the project result is that the firms find efficient means of coordination.

In sum, the approach described here relies on initiating the role of owner/buyer. This is a person, probably from regional government, mandated to negotiate directly with participating firms and to 'buy' regional development. The approach also stipulates using relatively brief intervals, to keep risk at a reasonable level and to promote communication based on what has been developed and can be demonstrated, that is, small 'slices' of regional development. At the end of each interval, renegotiation occurs, allowing either the process to advance or the parties to leave with what they have achieved so far.

Advantages of an agile approach

An agile approach to managing network-development initiatives provides a means to address several serious managerial challenges.

A first, important advantage of the approach is that it invites business and key regional development actors to explore the best means of creating regional resources and to do so on their own terms. The methodology focuses on buying results that the businesses have negotiated and committed to; as such, it is compatible with business logic. Furthermore, the iterative development cycles proposed in the methodology are conducive to generating trust and solving problems in small cohesive groups of firms (Vangen and Huxham 2003; Provan and Kenis 2007). This helps to alleviate key problems in fostering business involvement.

A second important advantage of the methodology is increased transparency and accountability. The use of short development intervals ending in demonstrations of the achieved results provides a solid basis for assessing development initiatives, even ongoing ones. The methodology thus provides much greater transparency, both internally and externally. Since the owner/buyer is also clearly identified as responsible for representing external stakeholders, this increased transparency also allows for increased public accountability.

Third, the proposed approach is light on bureaucracy. Instead of ensuring control over public funding by ascertaining that funds are being used for designated activities, in this methodology accountability is achieved by transparency of results and the clear responsibility of the owner/buyer. This is a critical point in creating flexibility, so network-development initiatives can take fullest advantage of available opportunities. In an agile approach, we are less interested in how funds are used but more interested in the results achieved in each interval using these funds. There is little need for the elaborate paperwork that plagues current EC-funded projects in Sweden.

Finally, the agile approach provides a basis for learning. Its open iterative methodology lends itself well to periodic control and reflection. Process evaluation can be undertaken to facilitate both improving business interaction and negotiations between businesses and owners/buyers. Learning is expected to give rise to significant advantages for subsequent intervals of the same project and for subsequent projects. One aspect of this learning seems particularly relevant, namely, that owner/buyers will develop their understanding of how to define and negotiate the development of regional as opposed to private resources. This provides a basis for addressing concerns of whether public financing is actually creating public goods or simply crowding out private investment.

In sum, an agile approach to managing network-development initiatives puts development, not bureaucratic procedure, at the centre. It helps involve key actors, demonstrates relevant results, and promotes accountability for these results. The approach is also conducive to learning so that management can be improved over time. Adopting such an approach would mark an important step forward in addressing the serious managerial challenges that characterize complex projects such as network-development initiatives.

Limitations

We have suggested transposing a model for managing complex projects, one rooted in software development, to the regional development context. This may seem a daring leap. Our arguments hinge on whether we have correctly identified common underlying problems and opportunities. The starting point is that business-network development is indeed characterized by complexity stemming from knowledge gaps, systemic interconnectedness, and shifting resource bases. A critical claim made in the argument is that it is possible to demonstrate meaningful regional development in incremental steps, similar to how software is delivered in blocks of functionality. Although it would be possible to use an agile approach even when the above criteria are not met, the advantages decrease with decreasing complexity. The disadvantages may be more obvious in simple projects. For example, an agile approach makes it more difficult to conduct centralized, long-term planning and budgeting.

A further limitation of the approach lies in the government effort required to establish the new role we propose. There must also be a sufficient number of initiatives under way to make this role meaningful and accepted.

Summary

This chapter takes as its starting point the assumption that markets provide insufficient mechanisms for knowledge transfer and development. This is an important basis for regional development initiatives, particularly in conjunction with the assumption that regional development relies for its success on the ability of firms to access and develop knowledge for process and product development. This implies an important role for governments in creating beneficial knowledge transfer and development mechanisms. Promoting appropriate business-network development still seems to be one of the most viable means of doing this. However, the role of regional government in promoting development will remain only a potential one if managerial problems hinder the practical realization of this. The chapter has sought to clarify the nature of the managerial challenges encountered in promoting business-network development and to propose a way forward.

We discuss four major managerial challenges encountered in publicly supported network-development initiatives. This list is not exhaustive but does reflect important recurring criticisms. We particularly noted the following: the difficulty of assessing whether public funding is crowding out private investment, the lack of business involvement in publicly supported network-development initiatives, the problems created by involved bureaucratic procedures, and, finally, the inability of regional development initiatives to produce demonstrably positive effects.

We have argued that these managerial problems stem from, or are greatly exacerbated by, a mismatch between the inherent complexity of network development and the control mechanisms imposed to ensure the legitimate use of public funds.

We also argued that there are alternative ways to govern network-development initiatives, alternatives based on practices developed for managing complex projects. We have sought to demonstrate that the underlying complexity is similar and that similar control mechanisms are viable. We therefore posit that it is possible and, moreover, advantageous to implement a more agile approach in promoting business-network development. Such an approach creates better grounds for securing the commitment of key stakeholders, provides transparency and clear accountability, and uses a less-burdensome control system. Finally, the transparency created in the approach facilitates learning and better evaluation of the initiatives.

A more agile approach to business-network development is premised on the empowerment of regional governments to buy and review regional resource development. It would require mandating regional government representatives to fulfil the new and visible role of the owner/buyer of regional development. While it may be difficult to create such a role, it would be an important step towards conferring greater legitimacy on publicly funded business-development initiatives.

References

R. Agranoff and M. McGuire, 'Big Questions in Public Network Management Research', *Journal of Public Administration Research and Theory,* 11 (3) (2001): 295–326.

C. Berggren, G. Brulin, and L. Gustavsson, *Från Italien till Gnosjö: Om det sociala kapitalets betydelse för livskraftiga industriella regioner* (Stockholm: Rådet för arbetslivsforskning, 1998).
J. Blomberg, *Projektorganisationen: Kritiska analyser av projektprat och praktik* (Malmö: Liber Ekonomi, 2003).
G. Chin, *Agile Project Management: How to Succeed in the Face of Changing Project Requirements* (New York: AMACOM, 2004).
P. A. David, B. H. Hall, and A. A. Toole, 'Is Public R&D a Complement or Substitute for Private R&D? A Review of the Econometric Evidence', *Research Policy,* 29 (4) (2000): 497–529.
S. Gullander, A. Öhrwall Rönnbäck, and NUTEK, *Produktutveckling för företag i samverkan: Studie av små och medelstora svenska verkstadsföretag* (Stockholm: Verket för näringslivsutveckling – NUTEK, 2004).
G. Hallin and A. Östhol, *På den tillväxtpolitiska agendan* (Östersund: Institutet för tillväxtpolitiska studier, 2004).
S. E. Human and K. G. Provan, 'Legitimacy Building in the Evolution of Small-Firm Multilateral Networks: A Comparative Study of Success and Demise', *Administrative Science Quarterly,* 45 (2) (2000): 327–65.
J. A. Highsmith, *Agile Project Management: Creating Innovative Products* (Boston, MA: Addison-Wesley, 2004).
ITPS (Institutet för tillväxtpolitiska studier), *The EC Regional Structural Funds Impact in Sweden 1995–2000* (Östersund: Institutet för tillväxtpolitiska studier, 2004a).
ITPS (Institutet för tillväxtpolitiska studier), *Effektutvärdering av de geografiska målprogrammen inom EG:s* (Östersund: Institutet för tillväxtpolitiska studier, 2004b).
R. Keast, M. P. Mandell, K. Brown, and G. Woolcock. 'Network Structures: Working Differently and Changing Expectations', *Public Administration Review,* 64 (3) (2004): 363–71.
P. Kenis and K. G. Provan. 'The Control of Public Networks', *International Public Management Journal,* 9 (3) (2006): 227–47.
E. H. Klijn, 'Managing Complexity: Achieving the Impossible', *Critical Policy Analysis,* 1 (3) (2007): 252–77.
J. F. M. Koppenjan and E. H. Klijn, *Managing Uncertainties in Networks: A Network Approach to Problem Solving and Decision Making* (London: Routledge, 2004).
K. Kreiner, 'In Search of Relevance: Project Management in Drifting Environments', *Scandinavian Journal of Management,* 11 (4) (1995): 335–46.
L. Lindkvist, J. Söderlund, and F. Tell, 'Styrning av produktutvecklingsprojekt: Om fontäner och deadlines in projekt', in C. Berggren and L. Lindkvist (eds), *Organisation för målorientering och lärande* (Lund: Studentlitteratur, 2001).
J. S. Metcalfe, 'Science Policy and Technology Policy in a Competitive Economy', *International Journal of Social Economics,* 24 (75) (1997): 723–40.
H. Neergaard and J. P. Ulhöi, 'Government Agency and Trust in the Formation and Transformation of Interorganizational Entrepreneurial Networks', *Entrepreneurship: Theory and Practice,* 30 (4) (2006): 519–39.
NUTEK, *Tillsammans utvecklar vi Sverige* (Stockholm: Verket för näringslivsutveckling – NUTEK, 2004).
NUTEK, *Organisera för näringslivets medverkan* (Stockholm: Verket för näringslivsutveckling – NUTEK, 2005).
P. Parker, *How Personal Networks Shape Business: An Anthropological Study of Social Embeddedness, Knowledge Development and Growth of Firms* (Lund: Department of Sociology, Lund University, 2004).

M. Porter, *The Competitive Advantage of Nations* (New York: Free Press, 1990).
K. G. Provan and P. Kenis, 'Modes of Network Governance: Structure, Management, and Effectiveness', *Journal of Public Administration Research and Theory,* 18 (2007): 229–52.
S. A. Rosenfeld, 'Does Cooperation Enhance Competitiveness? Assessing the Impacts of Inter-firm Collaboration', *Research Policy,* 25 (2) (1996): 247–63.
A. Saxenian, *Regional Advantage: Culture and Competition in Silicon Valley and Route 128* (Cambridge, MA: Harvard University Press, 2000).
K. Schwaber, *Agile Project Management with Scrum* (Redmond, WA: Microsoft Press, 2004).
J. Tjäder and J. Söderlund, 'Ledning av IT-projekt 75–98', in C. Berggren and L. Lindkvist (eds), *Projekt: Organisation För Målorientering Och Lärande* (Lund: Studentlitteratur, 2001).
S. Vangen and C. Huxham, 'Nurturing Collaborative Relations: Building Trust in Interorganizational Collaboration', *The Journal of Applied Behavioral Science,* 39 (1) (2003): 5–31.
T. Williams, 'The Need for New Paradigms for Complex Projects', *International Journal of Project Management,* 17 (5) (1999): 269–73.

3

Strategic Networks as Institutional Change: The Rich Wetlands of Kristianstad

Håkan Pihl

Introduction

Research on strategic networks has provided new opportunities to analyse areas such as industry structure, market power, and firm positioning in an industry (Gulati *et al.* 2000). Analysing strategic networks has provided new insight into issues such as governance, contracting, and coordination and into firm value and knowledge creation (Gulati *et al.* 2000; Kogut 2000; Möller and Svahn 2006). An area of special interest concerns how public organizations (governmental agencies at various levels) can initiate and support strategic networks, thereby promoting publicly desired developments.

In analysing strategic networks, one focuses on existing hub organizations and relationships and discusses how strategic networks are coordinated and how network relationships influence firm performance. The characteristics and dynamic aspects of various types of networks are also considered. How hub organizations and their networks are established, however, is seldom theoretically analysed.

Strategic networks have been successfully analysed using transaction cost theory, as first noted by Jarillo (1988). Transaction cost theory is part of the 'new institutional economics' tradition, which analyses the economic function and impact of various societal institutions, that is, modes of coordination (Ménard 2000; Williamson 2000). In a recent monograph, *Understanding the Process of Economic Change* (2005), Douglass North suggests a new theoretical approach in this tradition, useful for understanding how institutions are created. This chapter will investigate whether this new 'Northian' contribution to institutional economics can be used as a theoretical basis for analysing how hub organizations are established.

The following analysis is based on a case describing how a small publicly initiated organization was developed in the municipality of Kristianstad, Sweden. The organization was initially named the 'Ecomuseum for the Rich

Wetlands of Kristianstad', later renamed the 'Man and Biosphere Office'. The organization has built extensive relationships with various stakeholders and acts in various projects to foster the sustainable use of wetlands surrounding the city of Kristianstad. After a description of the theoretical approach suggested by North (2005) the case is presented. Then the theoretical framework is used to analyse the case, after which the possible development of the theory is discussed.

A Northian view of institutional change

North describes institutions as 'the rules of the game' – the various formal and informal regulations humans impose on their interactions (North 1984, 1990, 1992). Given this, how can the process of institutional change be understood? North (2005) starts by assuming that humans strive to reduce uncertainty and increase predictability. Another assumption is that the world is 'non-ergonic': there is no underlying stable structure to keep variation within certain limits, and the world changes in novel and unforeseeable ways. Development is based on the knowledge currently possessed by the actors. It is impossible to know today the new knowledge that will underlie the development tomorrow, so it is impossible to know the future. This fact, and the limited cognitive capacity of the human mind, creates a non-ergonic process of development in which humans cannot fully grasp the complexities faced and in which feedback is incomplete.

The new institutional economics tradition distinguishes *institutions* from economic activities/outcomes and analyses how the former affects the latter. North also distinguishes individual *belief systems* from institutions and activities/outcomes. Belief systems are the internal representations or mental constructs that humans develop to cope with their situations. They are models of the realities and dominant beliefs that individuals have internalized. Analytically, these belief systems come between institutions and activities/outcomes and interact with both sides. Belief systems determine how institutions are interpreted and, therefore, how institutions affect individual behaviours and outcomes. Belief systems are partly based on cultural heritage (informal institutions) and partly on individual experiences.

If belief systems are introduced, economic theory must also embrace cognitive science and learning theory. Learning is the construction of systems for classifying and interpreting the external environment, a process shaped by the environment we experience. However, learning is an imperfect process, involving misinterpretations and mistakes and leading to the development of a variety of models. Belief systems affect institutional structure and how it changes. Prior beliefs and institutions provide the basis for the development of new ones, creating path dependencies. Thus, the stock of knowledge is an underlying determinant of institutional change and the development of new knowledge constitutes a major influence on the evolution of institutions.

Changes in institutional structure are initiated by *institutional entrepreneurs*. These are organizations (or individuals in them) that intentionally try to change institutions to gain advantages, based on the belief systems they have developed. Hence, institutional structure reflects the bargaining power of institutional entrepreneurs. Over time, institutional entrepreneurs will have incentives to invest in new knowledge and skills, which will influence future actions and institutional change.

North concludes that this is the beginning of a new research agenda and a more dynamic economic theory. There is much more to learn, for example, about the evolution of informal constraints and about the relationship between changes in belief systems, informal institutions, and formal institutions. The following five propositions summarize the posited theory (North 2005: 59):

1. The continuous interaction between institutions and organizations in the economic setting of scarcity, and, hence, the competition, is the key to institutional change.
2. Competition forces organizations to continually invest in skills and knowledge to survive. The kinds of skills and knowledge individuals and their organizations acquire will shape evolving perceptions about opportunities and, hence, choices that will incrementally alter institutions.
3. The institutional framework provides the incentives that dictate the kinds of skills and knowledge perceived to have the maximum pay-off.
4. Perceptions are derived from the mental constructs of the players.
5. The economics of scope, complementarities, and network externalities of an institutional matrix make institutional change overwhelmingly incremental and path dependent.

The hub organization of 'The Rich Wetlands of Kristianstad'

The hub-organization dealing with 'The Rich Wetlands of Kristianstad' is today called the Man and Biosphere Office and is located in the municipality of Kristianstad, Sweden. The office has five employees and a budget of approximately €200,000 a year (2006). The office acts as a centre for administering various joint projects with external participants. In 2006, the office was involved in approximately 200 projects involving some 200 people (Hahn *et al.* 2006).

The establishment process of the office has been studied by a group of researchers (comprising Per Olsson, Thomas Hahn, Carl Folke, and Kristin Johansson) at the Centre for Transdisciplinary Environmental Research at Stockholm University. Their research analyses the process in a specific theoretical context, stressing concepts such as social–ecological systems, resilience, adaptive co-management, and ecosystem management. This chapter applies the empirical descriptions these researchers formulated, based on interviews and other information, as well as documents produced at the Man and Biosphere Office, such as the form for nominating an area to become a biosphere reserve (Magnusson *et al.* 2005), and other material published on its website (www.vattenriket.kristianstad.se). Finally, an interview was conducted on 28 March 2006 with Karin Magntorn and Sven-Erik Magnusson, two central actors in the process working at the Man and Biosphere Office in Kristianstad municipality.

Various uses of the wetlands

The wetlands surrounding the Helge river were traditionally used for harvesting hay and grazing. In the early 1600s, the town of Kristianstad was built in the area for defence reasons. In the 1800s and 1900s, the need for defence diminished, and new technologies facilitated transforming the wetlands into permanent agricultural land. The river was also increasingly used for waste disposal. In the early 1900s, untreated industrial and household sewage drastically reduced the water quality. Public opinion held that the wetlands were of low value and ought to be transformed into permanent farming land; seasonal flooding of the river should be eliminated, and the river should serve merely as a reservoir and a distribution channel for waste (Magnusson 2004). Some protests were heard from conservation groups, for example, when the garbage dump was established near the city in the 1960s. In the 1970s, the state declared some parts of the wetlands to possess international nature-conservation significance. In 1975, the Convention on Wetlands – known as the Ramsar Convention – declared that the wetlands were of international significance, but little happened. In the 1980s, observations indicated that the wetlands' biodiversity and bird populations had declined. There were also signs of lake degradation and the decreased use of the floodplain meadows for haymaking and grazing. The floodplain areas were inadequately managed, the meadows were overgrown, the river was polluted, and leachate from the garbage dump was entering the aquifer and river (Magnusson 2004).

Today, the wetlands represent a resource that poses managerial and coordination challenges of many kinds. Due to traditional cultivation methods, rich biodiversity still prevails, and large bird populations live in the area. However, modern large-scale agricultural methods are increasingly being introduced, for example, for growing vegetables. The area is also used for recreation, and several golf courses are situated there. The city also needs new land for expansion, and there is demand for residential development near the water. At the same time, the area is situated on one of Europe's largest aquifers, and the rich supply of fresh water is regarded as a valuable asset. In addition, the river that runs through the area experiences periodic seasonal flooding, necessitating the maintenance of sufficient buffer zones. How can these competing interests be reconciled? The case illustrates a response to these many challenges.

Inventories and an outdoor museum

Olsson *et al.* (2004) identify one individual, Sven-Erik Magnusson, as especially important for the establishment of the Man and Biosphere Office. In 1977, Magnusson was working as a curator at the Museum of Kristianstad. At the time, the museum was hosting a national touring exhibit on Swedish wetlands, but that did not cover the local wetlands. As Magnusson gathered material about local conditions, he learned that the wetlands had shrunk over the past three centuries, so he presented the social processes underlying this change. A year later, Magnusson was involved in another exhibition, celebrating the 200th anniversary of the death of Carl von Linné. The exhibition described the history of the local landscape and showed that many of the key biodiversity values of the wetlands were the results of traditional agricultural practices. At this time, Magnusson founded an 'outdoor museum'. The idea was to provide on-site information (such as panel displays and exhibition buildings) at selected places in the landscape, to help visitors interpret and understand the values associated with it. Magnusson also developed close ties with local media, which provided positive publicity.

In 1986, the municipality initiated a cultural-heritage programme. The County Museum and Magnusson were responsible for inventories of meadows and pastures. Using existing maps and inventories, Magnusson was able to identify several habitats with unique flora, but not what sustained them. Therefore, in 1989, he initiated a special inventory of the cultivation status of the floodplain meadows. A leading member of the local birdwatching society, Hans Cronert, later closely connected with the Man and Biosphere Office, became involved in designing the inventory. The local birdwatching society had produced continuous bird inventories since the 1950s and had recorded declining waterfowl populations, a development possibly related to the decreasing use of floodplain meadows for grazing and haymaking.

Magnusson finished mapping the land-use practices in 1989. The national inventories at the time were based on very general information, excluding the local context necessary for producing a detailed policy plan for defining and prioritizing areas for improved land-use practices and for estimating the funding needed to maintain and develop these practices.

In those years, Magnusson learnt that the various actors involved in activities relevant to the area were seldom aware of each other and shared no overview of its problems. To address this lack of an overarching framework, Magnusson worked to gather these activities under a single concept, 'The Rich Wetlands of Kristianstad' (Swedish: *Kristianstads Vattenrike*).

Proposal to establish an ecomuseum office

A subsequent idea was to create an ecomuseum, inspired by other European ecomuseums, such as the French Musée Camarguais. By early 1988, the proposed 'Ecomuseum of the Rich Wetlands of Kristianstad' (Ekomuseum Kristianstads Vattenrike) represented both the outdoor museum concept and an organization working to protect and develop the wetland areas. At this time, Magnusson presented a proposal to the municipality, the county administrative board, and other potential collaborators. The proposal was presented in one-to-one encounters, focusing on special aspects of the wetlands that might interest the person or group in question. The aim was to establish trusting relationships with key individuals in the organizations approached, who included a Lund University researcher, a World Wildlife Federation (WWF) official, the rector of and a senior lecturer at Kristianstad University College, a hotel director and former president of the local tourism board, and a director of the National Museum of Natural History. The wetlands were depicted as a resource to serve many ends: environmental protection, nature conservation, tourism, educational, and cultural history, all of which could be furthered by the development of an outdoor museum.

Several parties had interests impinging on the wetlands: the municipality wanted to market the city and to strengthen its image and identity, the county administrative board was interested in the nature-conservation and regional-development aspects of the wetlands, while the WWF wanted to support biodiversity in the floodplain meadows. Magnusson observed that:

> 'The key was to avoid a one-size-fits-all proposal that would be so neutral that nobody would be interested in it. Instead, it had to approach each person and identify what their specific needs and interests might be and emphasize the parts of the project proposals they could identify with'.
>
> (Olsson *et al.* 2004: 13)

By late 1988 and early 1989, the proposal had gained wide support, including from the municipality, county administrative board, WWF Sweden, the Swedish Museum of Natural History, the Swedish Research Council, the local birdwatching society, and the farmers' association. A 1988 meeting between Magnusson and a senior municipal politician was crucial to the process. The politician later explained in an interview that Sven-Erik Magnusson (SEM):

> presented the area in a different way than anyone had done before and I became aware of the values. Many considered the wetlands as a problem.…SEM presented a nature conservancy plan that didn't close the area but, opened it up and made it accessible to the public.…I was impressed by the way SEM marketed the idea and the broad support he had. He managed to engage and involve several important groups in the project, even farmers.
>
> (Olsson *et al.* 2004: 11)

The senior politician convinced the chair of the municipal executive board to support the idea; according to Magnusson, these two politicians were central to realizing the project – they were the ones who made things happen in the municipality at the time.

Certain circumstances at that time worked in favour of this process. The city had earlier lost its role as a centre for legislative functions in southern Sweden, and now its historical role as a military centre was severely threatened. One of two military campuses in the city had been closed down, and the other would probably soon follow. This created local anxiety, prompting discussion of the need for a new civic identity. The change in perceptions of the wetlands also coincided with a national and international trend to increased environmental awareness. In the 1988 Swedish elections, environmental issues were the focus of political discussion, and the new Green Party attracted many voters. This was partly an international trend, as green parties had emerged in many nations and the UN had initiated the concept of 'sustainable development'.

From ecomuseum to man and biosphere office

In February 1989, a press release describing the ecomuseum was used to promote the idea to the public and to build broad support. A month later, the municipality assumed responsibility for the project and opened an office for the ecomuseum. That office would later become the hub of a strategic network comprising various actors connected with the wetlands. A few people were employed in the office to develop the project, and Magnusson was appointed project leader. This way, the municipality declared its desire to increase its efforts to maintain and restore the wetlands and to protect the area's natural and cultural values.

The new office was organized as a unit reporting directly to the municipal board. The aim of the office was to facilitate and coordinate local collaboration processes, involving participants in, for example, international associations, national, regional, and local authorities, as well as researchers, non-profit associations, and landowners. The unit was also involved in developing policy, designing projects, resolving conflicts, and administering conservation and restoration efforts. It developed goals for 'The Rich Wetlands of Kristianstad', as well as management plans, agreements, follow-up reports, and updates for specific areas (Olsson *et al.* 2004). The intention was to co-manage the wetland ecosystems, together with other stakeholders, but without having property rights and without having special regulations to enforce its policies. The office was described as a bridging organization, creating opportunities for new interactions between actors at various organization levels and serving as an arena for trust-building, sense-making, learning, collaboration, and conflict resolution. Financial support for projects would come from various sponsors in the network, providing diverse funding opportunities (Olsson *et al.* 2006).

Early this century, local, regional, and national authorities began preparing to apply to UNESCO to declare 'The Rich Wetlands of Kristianstad' the first Swedish Man and Biosphere Reserve. This status was granted in 2005, indicating that the area is considered an international model for sustainable development. Swedish authorities at local, regional, and national levels have committed themselves to allowing the area to fulfil the multiple functions of biodiversity conservation, sustainable development, and logistical support (Swedish EPA 2006).

Magnusson had considered applying for Man and Biosphere Reserve status in the 1980s, but did not expect to get support for the idea. By the early 2000s, however, the time was right (Olsson *et al.* 2006): the political environment had changed, and there was increased emphasis on sustainable development. By 2002, sustainable development had become central to national development strategy, and eight core areas were focused on, including regional development and cohesion and community development (Ministry of the Environment 2002).

Building relationships and initiating projects

Today, the Man and Biosphere Office works on protecting and developing the biosphere reserve. After initially focusing on the floodplain meadows, its work has expanded into new projects, such as reintroducing the white stork and European catfish. Its collaboration networks have expanded and now include international associations, national, regional, and local authorities, researchers, non-profit associations, and landowners. Examples of sustainable development projects include the introduction of ecotourism, new technology for haymaking in wetlands, and new irrigation technologies. The Man and Biosphere Office also supports farmers who market locally produced high-quality meat under a single brand, emphasizing the fact that cattle grazing on these unique pastures has helped conserve the black-tailed godwit.

The Man and Biosphere Office does not provide subsidies or other financial support but does offer guidance on applying for financial support from other sources. It provides other consultation as well, and suggests projects to members of the network. For example, the idea of ecological, locally produced meat was first presented by the Man and Biosphere Office to local farmers, who developed the idea, reformulated the concept, and realized the project.

The Man and Biosphere Office also acts as a facilitator, handling problems that involve various groups with diverse interests. It initiates meetings and, in collaboration with stakeholders, suggests solutions to these problems. This is illustrated by a new phenomenon in the area: large numbers of cranes invading the wetlands in the spring. The birds have become not only a tourist attraction but also a problem for the local farmers. To handle the situation, the Man and Biosphere Office initiated meetings with farmers, birdwatchers, and local authorities, resulting in a solution in which cranes are fed in certain fields and scared off from others. The Man and Biosphere Office provides information about where to find the cranes, to direct tourists to the places where they feed.

Trust is vital in making collaboration between different interests work. The following quotation from an interview with a local landowner illustrates the trusting relationships that have developed:

> Landowner A: Previously I was almost afraid of authorities, it felt so bureaucratic somehow. But now, thanks to this project, I have learned a lot and I have a completely different attitude. Now it's more like we're all in the same boat. We've had open communication where everybody's opinion has the same value.
>
> (Hahn *et al.* 2006: 586)

Changing perceptions of the wetlands

The outdoor museum, followed by the ecomuseum and today's Man and Biosphere Office, also served to change local perceptions in favour of conservation and sustainability. Information–dissemination activities and initiatives have been undertaken to make the wetlands more accessible to the public – information centres, paths, footbridges, and birdwatching towers let people experience the various features of the wetlands. The establishment of an outdoor school in the area represented another step in this direction.

The task is to make people see the value and potential of the wetlands, not forcing them to belong to a specific organization or to follow new laws and regulations, but encouraging them to see the value of the biosphere reserve. Changing attitudes and conceptualizations is difficult and takes a long time. Setting good examples and conveying positive values to people with diverse interests are good ways to change attitudes. Magnusson clarified this in the interview of 28 March 2006 (which included Karin Magntorn):

> The tools of the Man and Biosphere Office are not laws and regulations. We operate in a different, amoeba-like space where we try to find engagement, commitment, idealism, influence, feeling, and attitude. All these are things you cannot make laws about... When we tell people about the biosphere reserve, we don't start by explaining what a natural reserve is or the laws and regulations surrounding it. And we don't try to force people to learn all the facts about, for example, the various kinds of birds that exist here. We start with experiences, engagement, and that sort of thing, and then search for a specific angle of approach – it could be a hunter, an angler, or a figure from local folklore. Some are interested in sports and open-air activities, and others are interested in health issues and medical aspects. To find strands of personal experience that those individuals may not be aware are linked to landscape, nature, and sustainability. To find these strands of experience, pull them first into awareness, and then transform this awareness into a change or strengthening of attitude, which eventually leads to the possibility of changing things. That

is how we work. To get people, in matters small and large, to gradually undertake mental reconstruction in the interests of sustainability.

Staff at the Man and Biosphere Office are convinced that the public view of the wetlands has changed since 'The Rich Wetlands of Kristianstad' concept was introduced in the late 1980s. When efforts started, many of the public believed that the wetlands were useless swamps, of little value to anyone. Today that view has changed. Many people with diverse interests have internalized the 'Rich Wetlands' concept and have come to value the wetlands (Magnusson 2004).

The hub organization and institutional change

The case traces the establishment of a publicly supported hub organization at the centre of a strategic network. From a new institutional economics perspective, this hub represents a new institution, developed to coordinate natural resources when market exchanges and state-enforced, hierarchical regulations are insufficient. Market exchanges may be insufficient due to externalities, such as the need to protect biodiversity and to create buffer zones against flooding. State-enforced regulations may be insufficient because of the need for flexibility and new solutions when conditions change. The hub organization, the ecomuseum/Man and Biosphere Office, has developed trusting relationships with key stakeholders, thereby reducing transaction costs in flexible projects and collaborations – a characteristic of strategic networks identified early on by Jarillo (1988). Below, the establishment of this new strategic network hub is analysed in light of the institutional-change theory formulated by North. The analysis follows propositions 1–5 as outlined above, except for proposition 4 ('perceptions are derived from the mental constructs of the players'), which provides a basic assumption and is touched on relative to the other propositions.

Changes in scarcity and competition underlie institutional change

According to North's first proposition, the key to institutional change is ongoing interaction between institutions and organizations in an economic setting of scarcity and competition. The Kristianstad wetlands can be used in diverse ways by individuals and organizations with a range of competing interests. The wetlands have long been used for defence and for traditional cultivation. Dredging and embankments have transformed parts of the wetlands into permanent agricultural land or land for the city's expansion. These efforts could be pursued further, allowing the city to expand more, creating new agricultural land, or allowing for new recreation areas, such as golf courses. Another alternative would be to use the wetlands and the river for waste disposal. Cultivation could be abandoned and the area allowed to return to wilderness, which in some areas was about to happen in the 1970s and 1980s when the meadows became overgrown, biodiversity decreased, and bird populations declined. Conservation, including traditional cultivation, is one of several possible competing uses of the geographical area, a use that was increasingly threatened in the 1970s and 1980s. This situation of increased scarcity and competition prompted the institutional change, leading to the creation of a strategic network with the Man and Biosphere Office as its hub. This change occurred gradually, in line with North's proposition of ongoing interaction between institutions and organizations in a setting of economic scarcity; hence, competition was the key to institutional change.

New knowledge influences perceptions and choices

North's second proposition states that competition forces organizations to continually invest in skills and knowledge, which shapes evolving perceptions of opportunities and hence the choices that incrementally change institutions. The institutional entrepreneurs (Magnusson and his colleagues) incrementally acquired knowledge of the ecological and biological values of the wetlands and developed personal beliefs that the wetlands were valuable and warranted conservation. At the time, few local individuals shared this knowledge or these values. The institutional entrepreneurs invested in new knowledge and in methods to transfer knowledge and values to decision-makers and the public. The entrepreneurs acted with intentionality and started the process by convincing the local authorities to support information initiatives, for example, the early proposal for outdoor museums.

A further example is inventories mapping the cultivation status of the floodplain meadows, showing declining use of traditional grazing and hay-making methods and declining waterfowl populations. This knowledge was used when lobbying authorities to take conservation action, resulting in a proposal to the municipality to establish the hub organization (the ecomuseum, later the Man and Biosphere Office) and build relationships with stakeholders – farmers, businesspeople, and other groups and individuals. The development was non-ergonic: no one at the time could have foreseen the new knowledge and initiatives that would follow. This supports North's proposition that competition forces organizations to invest in skills and knowledge on an ongoing basis and that the kinds of skills and knowledge individuals and their organizations acquire shapes evolving perceptions of the opportunities and, hence, choices that incrementally alter institutions.

Institutional change gives incentives for knowledge development

According to North's third proposition, the kinds of skills and knowledge perceived to yield the maximum pay-off are dictated by the incentives provided by the institutional framework. In the late 1980s, environmental issues were ascendant in Sweden. This 'pro-environmental' change in the institutional framework coincided with another change at the local level, the search for a new identity for the city of Kristianstad. Hence, the proposal to the municipality to investigate wetlands use and invest in information-dissemination projects, such as outdoor museums, came at a time when environmental concern had increased and the search for a new identity and profile was peaking. 'The Rich Wetlands of Kristianstad' concept offered a way to make the city unique and attractive.

These changes in institutional framework at the international, national, and local levels increased the pay-off from acquiring knowledge. This is illustrated by the increased interest on the part of the county administrative board in nature conservation and regional development and by the positive attitudes towards the environment among local politicians and other participants.

Later on, the increased emphasis on sustainable development strengthened incentives for further investments and initiatives. In 2002, sustainable development became the focus of the Swedish government's national strategy, a shift in institutional framework that provided new incentives to apply for Man and Biosphere Reserve status. The formal and informal institutions changed over time, strengthening incentives to develop knowledge and values of conservation and sustainability. In the words of North, the institutional framework changed and provided new incentives, which dictated the kinds of skills and knowledge perceived to yield the maximum payoff.

Institutional change is incremental and path dependent

In his fifth proposition, North states that economics of scope, complementarities, and network externalities of an institutional matrix make institutional change overwhelmingly incremental and path-dependent. The institutional development studied in the case is the result of changes that developed stepwise over several years, one activity leading to another. This is illustrated by the national exhibition in the late 1970s, which was developed further in a subsequent exhibition. Building on the earlier study, the biodiversity created by traditional agricultural practices was now emphasized. This change gave rise to further investigations and the idea of an outdoor museum, which reflected an awareness of the importance of information and accessibility. The knowledge gained by developing these exhibitions was built path-dependently, one inventory building on another, pointing to a need for information and management. The wetlands were degrading, and there was a need for protective action. Therefore, the ecomuseum combined the functions of an outdoor museum with an organization that would work actively to manage various issues in the wetlands, initiating projects and building extensive networks that provided opportunities for interaction between actors. Some years later, the existence of the office was proved an important prerequisite for fulfilling the requirements to become a Man and Biosphere Reserve. The functions of the ecomuseum were interpreted in terms of the UNESCO (United Nations Educational, Scientific and Cultural Organization) requirements, including conservation, sustainable development, and, especially, logistics. Following North, this institutional change was path-dependent and incremental, one change being a prerequisite for another.

To sum up: the above analysis suggests possibilities, in the framework suggested by North, for analysing the establishment of publicly supported strategic networks. The approach identifies institutional entrepreneurs that act with intentionality and develop their knowledge and skills. They thereby gain enough bargaining power to influence local institutional development. The process displays a non-ergonic, path-dependent pattern. One can also assume that the belief systems of individual actors influenced, and were influenced by, institutional development and the institutional framework. The entrepreneurs invested in knowledge, which was important for further development, while changes in the institutional framework provided incentives for the development of new knowledge.

Further theoretical developments

North emphasizes that changes in the institutional framework alter the payoffs and provide incentives to institutional entrepreneurs. The entrepreneurs act with intentionality, which implies that they develop strategic actions to increase their bargaining power, but North does not discuss how these strategies are crafted. Future theoretical developments could analyse such strategies. The case indicates that concept innovations and multi-interest proposals are used by institutional entrepreneurs to increase their bargaining power. The case also indicates that the institutional framework can be analysed in greater detail, identifying institutional levels.

Concept innovation

North states that imperfect feedback, and the problem that humans use mental constructs to study what is outside them, makes it possible for a variety of belief systems to develop. This opens up the possibility that entrepreneurial efforts could influence mental constructs. The case indicates that the innovation of new concepts can be an important bearer of such new models and a way for entrepreneurs to increase their bargaining power. This is illustrated in the case by the introduction of 'The Rich Wetlands of Kristianstad' concept and by the innovation of concepts such as 'outdoor museum' and 'ecomuseum'.

The 'Rich Wetlands' concept was the bearer of an entirely new interpretation of local surroundings, emphasizing conservation and traditional land use. From being viewed as swamps and wastelands, the 'Rich Wetlands' were now seen as providing a unique habitat for rare birds and plants, a buffer zone during flooding, and good haymaking and ecological cattle grazing. These lands also offered public recreation possibilities, an interesting research arena, and a basis for new businesses such as ecotourism. The 'Rich Wetlands' gave the city a new, positive, and unique profile at a time when its identity was being challenged. The concept conveyed that the traditional land use was valuable and that new uses and values could be developed, with optimism and moral justification. The institutional entrepreneur had formulated and launched a new concept that was important for gaining support for the establishment of a hub organization financed by the municipality. The concept innovation helped in building a strategic network and trusting relationships among stakeholders; the shared new interpretation of the wetlands reduced transaction costs in cooperative projects.

Multi-interest proposals

The case also implies that a concept innovation that conveys different proposals to different stakeholders strengthens the competitiveness of institutional entrepreneurs. The more loaded with positive values and the more attractive to different stakeholders a concept is, the more support is gained and the stronger the bargaining power of the entrepreneur.

When the idea of a hub organization ('Ecomuseum') to support the 'Rich Wetlands' was launched, the institutional entrepreneurs approached key individuals representing local organizations and presented arguments adapted to their diverse interests: research opportunities were promoted to a researcher, conservation issues to a WWF official, educational opportunities to members of the local university college, commercial possibilities (tourism) to a hotel director and former tourism-board president, and a positive civic profile to local politicians. It was vital to create a new concept and to load it with a set of multi-interest proposals in an effort to build trusting relationships with individuals and organizations, supporting the idea of the 'Rich Wetlands' and a hub organization. A conclusion is that institutional entrepreneurs can increase their bargaining power by means of concept innovations which are multi-interest proposals loaded with complementary meanings that attract a range of stakeholders.

Identifying levels in the institutional framework

A final theoretical development task is to increase the detail of the institutional framework analysis and to identify how changes at one level (for a classification of institutional levels, see Williamson 2000) influence changes at others. The introduction of the 'sustainable development' concept first occurred at the international level (namely, the United Nations [UN]). This ushered in changes at the national level, embodied in Swedish government strategy, which led to important changes in the local institutional framework. These local changes increased the bargaining power of local institutional entrepreneurs, who could refer to sustainability when advocating the ideas underlying the 'Rich Wetlands' to different stakeholders and when seeking support to establish a hub organization to coordinate the sustainable use of the wetlands.

The UN Man and Biosphere Reserve initiative, the development of its content, and the possibility of local communities being accredited as such reserves, introduced another change in the institutional framework at the international level, which increased the bargaining power of the same local institutional entrepreneurs.

These developments at various institutional framework levels provided new incentives that strengthened the positions of the institutional entrepreneurs in the case. Theoretical development could distinguish and clarify these different institutional levels and analyse how changes at one level influenced changes at others, that is, how changes at the international and national political levels provided incentives for new initiatives to build publicly initiated strategic networks. Institutional entrepreneurs at one level of the institutional framework thus induced changes that created opportunities for entrepreneurs at other levels.

Summary and conclusions

This chapter examines the establishment of a publicly supported hub organization that coordinates multiple uses of a natural resource, the wetlands of Kristianstad, Sweden. The case illustrates how some individuals established a hub organization, thereby informing and influencing public attitudes to the wetlands, and how they initiated collaborations and projects with various stakeholders. Few attempts have been made to analyse the establishment of hub organizations in theoretical terms. This chapter has demonstrated that a new theory of institutional change, based on the contributions of Douglass North, can be useful for this purpose.

The theoretical analysis suggests that two reasons for institutional change were increased scarcity and competition. Traditional wetlands use was diminishing in the 1970s and 1980s, when conservation and traditional cultivation interests were coming into competition with other interests, providing the starting point for institutional change. Institutional entrepreneurs acted with intentionality to influence attitudes and to establish a hub organization. One person in particular, Sven-Erik Magnusson, played a crucial role in this process. The hub-organization participants continually invested in knowledge and skills, shaping the evolving opportunities and choices that incrementally altered institutions. Increased public concern for environmental and conservation issues, together with the emergence of the 'sustainable development' and 'biosphere reserve' concepts, provided important new elements of the institutional framework, increasing the bargaining power of the institutional entrepreneurs. The process started in the 1970s with an exhibition at the local museum. This provided the basis for an outdoor museum, leading to an ecomuseum and a hub organization, which later became a Man and Biosphere Office in 2005. The process was incremental and path-dependent: new knowledge was built on earlier knowledge, and new initiatives and organizational solutions followed on earlier initiatives and solutions.

The theory of institutional change suggested by North extends new institutional economics by including institutional entrepreneurs and human belief systems, and by seeking to explain institutional change. The theory is promising for analysing how the hub organizations of strategic networks are established. Based on the case, further theoretical developments can be suggested. One observation is that 'concept innovations' created by institutional entrepreneurs can be important bearers of mental constructs between individual belief systems and institutions. In particular, the 'Rich Wetlands of Kristianstad' concept was instrumental in changing general views and attitudes. The entrepreneur also managed to load this concept with multi-interest proposals, attracting several actors with diverse interests. This illustrates how institutional entrepreneurs can develop methods to strengthen their bargaining power in a given institutional framework. Another observation is that institutional framework analysis can be developed in greater detail. Institutional entrepreneurs act at various institutional levels, and changes at one level provide new incentives for institutional entrepreneurs at other levels. Institutional entrepreneurs act at one end of relationships with other stakeholders, but how the network and the interactions per se arise is not analysed in this theoretical framework. For a more comprehensive analysis of strategic networks, the establishment of relationships and interactions needs further theoretical development.

References

R. Gulati, N. Nohria, and A. Zaheer, 'Strategic Networks', *Strategic Management Journal,* 21 (2000): 203–15.

T. Hahn, P. Olsson, C. Folke, and K. Johansson, 'Trust-Building, Knowledge Generation and Organizational Innovations: The Role of a Bridging Organization for Adaptive Co-management of a Wetland Landscape around Kristianstad, Sweden', *Human Ecology,* 34 (2006): 573–92.

J. C. Jarillo, 'On Strategic Networks', *Strategic Management Journal,* 9 (1988): 31–41.

B. Kogut, 'The Network as Knowledge: Generative Rules and The Emergence of Structure', *Strategic Management Journal,* 21 (2000): 405–25.

S.-E. Magnusson, 'The Changing Perception of the Wetlands in and around Kristianstad, Sweden: From Waterlogged Areas towards a Future Water Kingdom, Kristianstads Vattenrike Biosphere Reserve', *Annals of New York Academy of Sciences,* 1023 (2004): 323–7.

S.-E. Magnusson , K. Magntorn, E. Wallsten, H. Cronert, and M. Thelaus, *Kristianstads Vattenrike Biosphere Reserve.* Nomination form (Kristianstad: Municipality of Kristianstad, 2005).

C. Ménard (ed.), *Institutions, Contracts and Organizations: Perspectives from New Institutional Economics* (Cheltenham: Edward Elgar, 2000).

Ministry of the Environment, 'The National Strategy for Sustainable Development', (2002). Available online at http://www.sweden.gov.se (accessed 15 September 2010).

K. Möller and S. Svahn, 'Role of Knowledge in Value Creation in Business Nets', *Journal of Management Studies,* 43 (5) (2006): 985–1007.

D. C. North, 'Transaction Costs, Institutions, and Economic History', *Journal of Institutional and Theoretical Economics,* 140 (1984): 7–17.

D. C. North, *Institutions, Institutional Change and Economic Performance* (Cambridge: Cambridge University Press, 1990).

D. C. North, 'Institutions, Ideology and Economic Performance', *CATO Journal,* 11 (3) (1992): 477–89.

D. C. North, *Understanding the Process of Economic Change* (Princeton, NJ: Princeton University Press, 2005).

P. Olsson, C. Folke, and T. Hahn, 'Social–Ecological Transformation for Ecosystem Management: The Development of Adaptive Co-management of a Wetland Landscape in Southern Sweden', *Ecology and Society,* 9 (4) (2004). Available online at http://www.ecologyandsociety.org/vol9/iss4/art2 (accessed 15 September 2010).

P. Olsson, L. H. Gunderson, S. R. Carpenter, P. Ryan C. Folke, and C. S. Holling, 'Shooting the Rapids: Navigating Transitions to Adaptive Governance of Social–Ecological Systems', *Ecology and Society,* 11 (1): (2006). Available online at http://www.ecologyandsociety.org/vol11/iss1/art18 (accessed 15 September 2010).

Swedish EPA, *Biosphere Reserves for Man and Nature* (2006). Available online at http://www.naturvardsverket.se/en/In-English/Menu/Nature-conservation_and_wildlife_management (accessed 15 September 2010).

O. E. Williamson, 'The New Institutional Economics: Taking Stock, Looking Ahead', *Journal of Economic Literature,* 38 (2000): 595–613.

4

Interaction, the Innovative Milieu and Porterian Clusters: A Survey-Based Regional Assessment Illustrated with an Example of a Medical Technology Region in an Early Cluster Life-Cycle Stage

Claus Steinle, Holger Schiele and Kai Mietzner

Introduction: differentiating clusters by assessing the interaction in a regional-sectoral agglomeration

In the past decade, the cluster concept has become a fashionable subject, in particular in regional economics and economic geography. Hundreds of regional-sectoral agglomerations have been 'detected'. A meta-study, for instance, was able to collect and systematically capture more than 800 case studies on individual clusters (van der Linde 2003). Political bodies have widely adopted the cluster approach and have implemented strategies to foster their clusters, both on a regional as well as on a national level (Roelandt and den Hertog 1999; Dohse 2003; Garrett-Jones 2004; Fromhold-Eisebith 2007; Motoyama 2008).

The benefits clusters can offer to firms have been identified and include a greater degree of innovation (Baptista and Swann 1998; Molina-Morales and Martínez-Fernández 2003; Cainelli 2008) and higher productivity (Ciccone and Hall 1996; Baptista 2003; Cainelli 2008). As a consequence, firms anchored in clusters have been shown to be on average between 2 per cent and 4 per cent more profitable measured by return on investment, as compared to their isolated industry competitors (Fabiani and Pellegrini 1998; Hermes Lab 2000).

The problem, however, is that such advantages are not automatically derived from every agglomeration. On average, it is advantageous for a firm to be member of a cluster and for a region to host a strong cluster. But there are also cases of failed clusters, so one is able to differentiate between 'good' and 'bad' clusters (Grabher 1993; Hassink 1997; Suarez-Villa and Walrod 1997).

In order to distinguish between clusters, several variables have been proposed, such as the size (Folta *et al.* 2006) or age of a cluster, expressed in terms of a cluster life cycle (Audretsch and Feldman 1996; Tichy 2001; Bergman 2008; Menzel and Fornahl 2010). Another variable for differentiation, which has found initial empirical support (Bengtsson and Sölvell 2004; Gössling and Rutten 2007), is the 'climate' or the 'milieu' of a cluster, that is, the interaction taking place between the actors in an agglomeration. This paper will follow the latter path, exploring the interaction in a regional-sectoral agglomeration as a criterion for differentiation between clusters.

To assess the interaction of the actors in a regional agglomeration we draw on the 'school of thought which made the greatest contribution to understanding the process of innovation through the interplay between a situation and its surroundings' (Corpataux and Crevoisier 2007: 300) – the 'innovative milieu approach' (Fromhold-Eisebith 1995; Steinle *et al.* 1998; Franz 1999; Crevoisier and Camagni 2000; Fromhold-Eisebith 2004; Crevoisier 2004). Since the mid-1980s milieu research has developed into a stabilized conceptual framework. The innovative milieu approach focuses on the explanation of regional innovation systems, or, more precisely, 'explaining the success of regions that develop and the failure of those that become blocked' (Crevoisier 2004: 369). In the pursuit of explanations for excellence in innovation, the coordination mechanisms, that is, their interaction, between the local actors stand at the heart of the model. Therefore, this approach is well suited to our attempt to differentiate between regions based on the interaction between local actors. An interesting amplification of the concept of interaction can be found in the cluster-life-cycle thesis which argues that interaction is less pronounced in young clusters such as the one analysed here.

However, one fundamental challenge arises: how to measure the characteristics and the quality of the interaction in an agglomeration? The overwhelming majority of research in innovative milieus is qualitative in nature, relying on semi-directive interviews (Crevoisier 2004). In this paper, though, we propose a survey-based structure to capture the main elements of a regional milieu, assessing the interaction between the regional actors. More specifically, our contribution is

1. in developing the neglected concept of interaction in a cluster;
2. proposing and applying measurements for this interaction concept; and
3. by doing so, attaching a life-cycle perspective to the cluster concept.

The paper is organized as follows: the first part lays out our research concept by contrasting the traditional structure-oriented research on clusters with the interaction-oriented innovative milieu approach. Based on this conceptual basis we can then discuss the options for measuring interaction and illustrate our survey approach by applying it to a medical technology cluster. Finally, we are able to draw some conclusions on the method's applicability, the importance of assessing the interaction in a cluster and obtain additional insights by linking our findings to the cluster-life-cycle thesis.

Theory: merging the Porterian cluster approach and the concept of the innovative milieu

Porter's diamond of competitive advantage: describing a cluster's structure

The cluster concept is often associated with Michael E. Porter (Porter 1990). In the Porterian view a cluster can be described as 'a geographically proximate group of interconnected companies and associated institutions in a particular field, linked by commonalities and complementaries' (Porter 1998: 199). Although not without its critics (Moon *et al.* 1995; Waverman 1995; Davies and Ellis 2000), Porter's 'diamond of competitive advantage' is one of the most influential concepts on clusters. The diamond determines the key elements of a company's environment which influence its potential for international competitiveness (see Fig. 4.1).

The significance of the Porterian approach is the notion that all four determinants (structure of competition, structure of demand, linked industries, and factor conditions) form an interlinked and dynamic complex where each element is affected by the other three. The simultaneous presence of all factors and the bi-directional interdependencies between all determinants create an environment that promotes the formation of clusters. In the

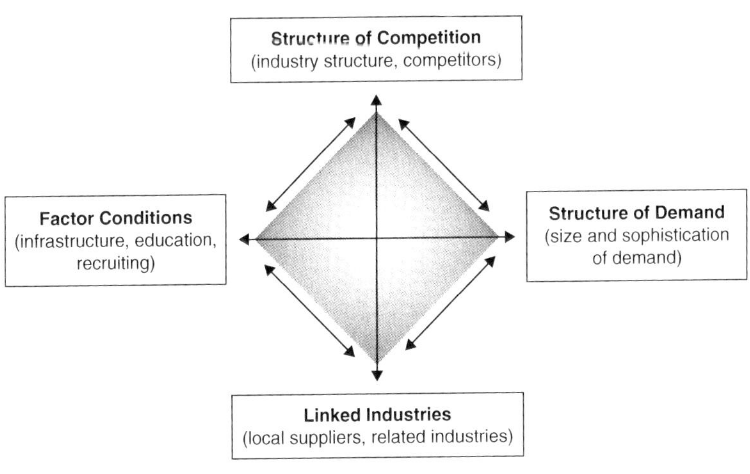

Figure 4.1 The diamond of competitive advantage
Source: Porter (1990, p. 72 ff.).

Porterian view, clusters can be confined to a region or appear on a national level as well.

There is a central criticism of Porter's approach: it neglects the process of interaction between the identified actors of a system, suggesting an almost 'automatic' cluster development, provided that all required actors are present. The diamond of competitive advantage, despite mentioning 'social glue', mainly focuses on the structure of an agglomeration. According to the diamond model, the particular success of firms in clusters largely relies on externalities. In a mostly competitive environment, where firms pursue their individual interests in a multitude of uncoordinated actions, cluster economies arise through a combination of chance and the law of large numbers (Steinle *et al.* 1998; Gordon and McCann 2000; Newlands 2003; Rugman and Verbeke 2003).

However, the Porterian approach is just an unilateral point of view, since 'clusters are not collections of individuals but interdependent set of businesses structured through network relationships' (DeBresson 1996: 161). In addition to the presence of potentially synergetic organizations and the associated externalities, the culture of an industry agglomeration, as well as the behaviour of its members towards each other – the 'software' of the cluster – also have been found to play an important role. In order to complement Porter's idea, the next section will concentrate on the interaction processes present in highly innovative systems.

The innovative milieu: explaining the interaction within regional agglomerations

A prominent approach which focuses on local interaction is the research on the innovative milieu. It was mainly coined by the Groupe de Recherche Européen sur les Milieux Innovateurs (GREMI) group. Since the mid-1980s, the GREMI has continuously endeavoured to explore the diverse aspects of innovation processes in regional economic milieus (Aydalot 1984; Ratti *et al.* 1997; Crevoisier 2000; Crevoisier 2004). A core assumption of the milieu approach is that socio-economic questioning cannot be understood independent of space and time (Colletis-Wahl *et al.* 2008). This assumption breaks with the Newtonian concept of homogeneous and isotropic space, i.e. the assumption that there is no qualitative difference between points in space or, put in a different way, space is reduced to a single point – and therefore not a distinguishing factor (Corpataux and Crevoisier 2007). Assuming contextuality in the sense of spatiality, the GREMI group was able to start to open the black box postulated by Aydalot's claim that there are factors localized on the regional level that can explain why some regions are more dynamic then others (Aydalot 1984).

An innovative milieu can be defined as 'the set, or the complex network of mainly informal social relationships in a limited geographical area, often determining a specific external "image" and a specific internal "representation" and sense of belonging, which enhance local innovative capability through

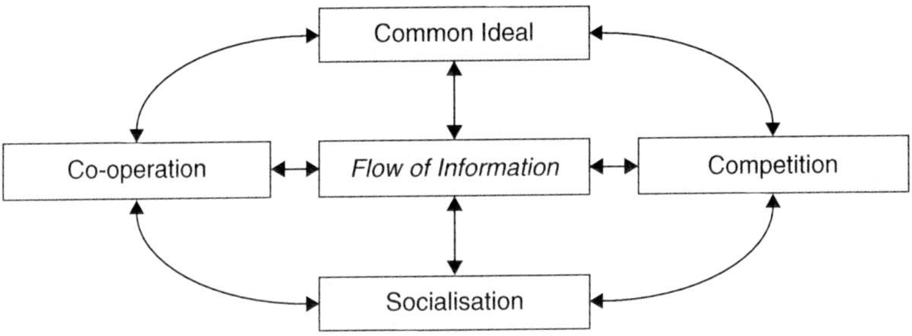

Figure 4.2 Linkages within an innovative milieu
Source: Steinle et al. (1998, p. 374).

synergetic and collective learning processes' (Camagni 1991: 3). In contrast to the implications of Porter's diamond model, the mere presence of a set of actors in a region is not sufficient to achieve innovative results unless these actors show an intensive interaction, thus taking advantage of proximity.

According to the GREMI school, an innovative milieu is a social network resulting from synergetic interaction and a collective learning processes. A basic characteristic is the simultaneous existence of cooperation and competition. This apparent antagonism becomes possible through intensive communication based on a homogenous socialization background and a region's common ideal (a 'Leitbild') (see Fig. 4.2).

- *Common ideal*: A common ideal, reflected by a conscious sense of belonging, constitutes the basic element of the milieu approach (Fromhold-Eisebith 2004). A collective region-related identity determines common goals of locality development and essential principles of collaboration. The common ideal also contributes to establishing the border of the milieu, which is precisely 'a collectivity endowed with a frontier' (Corpataux and Crevoisier 2007: 301). If the group of collective actors were borderless the coincidence of cooperation and competition might be endangered because no competitive advantage would derive. The members of a localized milieu can derive competitive advantages originating in their proximate environment as long as there are competitors who do not belong to the same 'club' and thus derive no benefits. On the other hand, the common ideal of belonging to a particular milieu fulfils the important function of defining milieu-specific norms to sanction antisocial behaviour.
- *Socialization*: The homogenous socialization background creates a coherent unity and facilitates a dynamic communication network and a trusting inter-firm cooperation. Shared norms of behaviour are thus established reducing transaction costs. In a local agglomeration actors may have gone through a common professional socialization, i.e. visited the same professional schools or universities. The practical consequence of this model is

that the value of specialized professional education is stressed, not only because of the working techniques it teaches but also because of the socialization aspect. Following the milieu approach, spatial proximity does not matter mainly in terms of reduction in physical distance and in the related transport costs but more in the similarity of cultural and psychological attitudes. It is worth highlighting that in a regional agglomeration with an innovative milieu the actors continuously go through a process of common socialization in the course of which they become increasingly similar to each other (Maillat 1990; Camagni 1994; Franz 1999).

- *Cooperation and competition*: A particularity of a milieu is the coincidence of collaboration and competition (Hansen 1992; Franz 1999). As discussed in the literature regarding the Porterian cluster model, local competitors can be the toughest competitors because they are easier to observe than remote competitors and they have precisely the same macroeconomic environment, thereby reducing the scope of excuses for managers in justifying their (lack of) performance. However, if a common Leitbild of collaboration exists which has been made possible by the shared socialization process of the members of a regional agglomeration, competition can be moderated, and forms of collaboration become possible which are not observed as often outside a cluster.
- *Flow of information*: Finally, an intense flow of information effectuates an open circulation of ideas, skills, and know-how and thereby boosts the pressure of competition between the local actors. Information exchange is the grease of a milieu. No Leitbild can develop and expand without information flow; no socialization is possible in isolation.

It is usually difficult to establish which of these elements develops first, but the milieu research indicates that in an innovative milieu they are all present simultaneously. To take this account into consideration, Figure 4.2 links all elements with arrows.

An illustrative example: in an agri-business cluster in Lower Saxony, the production facility of one firm burned down. The neighbouring competitor immediately stepped in to guarantee delivery (competition and cooperation). Managers and employees of both firms were linked to each other by shared social activities which not only promoted a common socialization but also ensured a continuous flow of information, even on an informal level. The cluster also shared the common ideal that 'if someone thinks about nutrition science and agro-technique he should think about the Oldenburger Münsterland' (Freisberg and Merx 2006: 63, our translation). To support the infrastructure of this agglomeration, the local firms have established a specialized university of applied sciences ensuring the professional quality of the workforce and further strengthening the socialization process.

The milieu approach complements Porter's cluster model by filling the gap left with regard to interaction. It also offers an explanation as to why some regional agglomerations are more successful than others – it may be the existence (or lack) of a local milieu. At the same time, the milieu approach could be considered as somewhat imprecise in terms of defining which actors would form a milieu and what roles they would play. Here, the Porterian cluster offers a much more comprehensive account. The idea, then, is to merge both approaches.

The concept of the innovative cluster: an integrative and holistic approach as a frame for analysis

Most models of regional-sectoral agglomerations tend either to concentrate on a cluster's structural characteristics in order to clarify which members constitute a successful agglomeration or on the way these actors interact to realize competitive advantages. In order to describe both the 'hardware' and 'software' of a cluster, the research at hand is based on the 'innovative cluster' approach, which combines the structure and the interaction-focused streams (Steinle *et al.* 1998; Schiele 2001). The name of this model reflects its two main roots: the *innovative* milieu and the Porterian *cluster,* the integrated form then is the *innovative cluster.*

The innovative cluster model arises from the synopsis of complementary cluster approaches and represents an ideal agglomeration that can be structurally described by the four facets of the diamond model but is additionally characterized by the intense interaction level of an innovative milieu. Figure 4.3 illustrates the constitutional characteristics of an innovative cluster by presenting the four main actors of Porter's cluster approach and their multiple linkages within a cooperative and competitive environment, indicated by arrows, and the underlying milieu. The illustration reflects

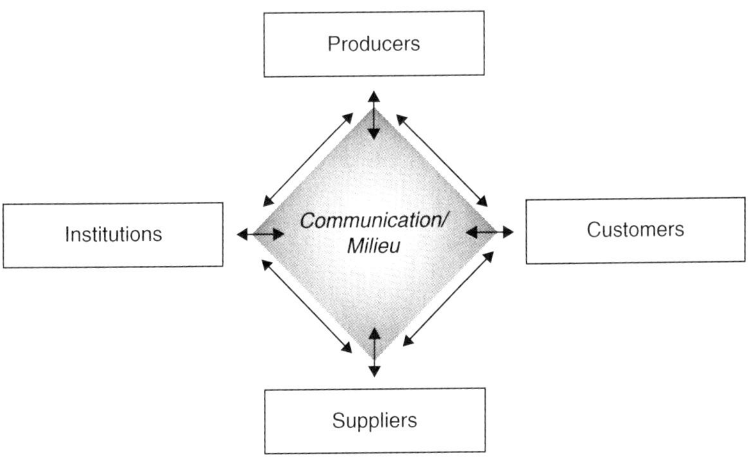

Figure 4.3 The 'innovative cluster'
Source: The authors.

the importance of considering both structure and interaction of a localized agglomeration. In fact, it places the existence of a milieu at the centre. The existence (or the lack) of a milieu establishes how customers and producers interact, the existence (or not) of simultaneous collaboration and competition between producers of the final goods, the way institutions are embedded, and so on.

An innovative cluster can be defined as 'a group of co-operatively and competitively interacting organisations from several steps of a value chain, located in an environment limited by a shared conscience and vision of conduct' (Schiele 1999: 180). It reflects an innovation and productivity-boosting system of several companies, their direct competitors, highly sophisticated and anticipatory key customers, a specialized supply chain, as well as cluster-specific institutions (structure) whose success results from an intensive flow of information between its actors who are linked within a cooperative and competitive milieu (interaction). Merging the Porterian cluster approach and the model of the innovative milieu allows for a more comprehensive accounting of this relationship. Importantly, it allows the observer to distinguish between agglomerations with a fully developed structure *and* interaction and those agglomerations where interaction is missing.

On the one hand, producers, customers, suppliers, and supporting institutions are interlinked elements of an innovative cluster. On the other hand, each of the groups has a particular role in a cluster. An ideal innovative cluster therefore includes:

- *Producers* of the particular good at hand: It is important to emphasize that ideally several producers of a good are present. Local competition has been found to be one of the key drivers of a cluster's innovativeness (Bengtsson and Sölvell 2004). Management has no macroeconomic justification for why a competitor next door is performing better.
- *Advanced customers* who anticipate global trends: some countries are lead markets in which demands develop earlier than in other countries (Beise and Gemünden 2004).
- *Suppliers:* considering that in modern industrial companies up to 70 per cent of turnover is purchasing volume directly paid to suppliers and that suppliers are also key contributors for innovations (Schiele 2006), their availability plays a pivotal role in many firms. Again, firms in an innovative cluster profit from the local availability of world-class suppliers (Jin 2004).
- *Supporting institutions* have been widely reported as key drivers of a cluster's performance, in particular when it comes to promoting collaboration between the members of a cluster. Associations, educational institutions, consultants – provided that they are specialized in the commodity of the cluster – constitute a final structural element of an innovative cluster. One of their key roles is to propel the interaction between the members of a cluster which is a precondition for collaboration.

- The presence of an *innovative milieu,* finally, makes the difference between a 'Porterian diamond' (described above, 1–4) and an innovative cluster. Only if the members of a cluster are aware of their membership in this cluster and therefore behave differently towards their fellow 'club members', intensively interacting on a local basis, can we speak about a fully fledged value-creating system (Steinle *et al.* 1998). This sense of belonging is therefore a constitutional element of an innovative cluster.

The innovative cluster approach as a tool for analysis provides further information on a cluster's character and its individual development stage. From the perspective of a single organization, it can be in any of the three following situations:

1. be a member of an 'innovative cluster', that is an agglomeration with a fully fledged structure and well-developed interaction;
2. be a member of a 'Porterian diamond', that is an agglomeration where many constituent organizations of a cluster are present, but which show little interaction and awareness, not yet having developed a milieu;
3. be in a 'peripheral situation', that is there is a cluster somewhere else, but the firm at hand does not belong to it (Steinle *et al.* 1998).

The challenge now is to operationalize the theoretical background, which is primarily rooted in economics and economic geography. The next section discusses suggestions on how to accomplish this task.

Assessing the interaction of an innovative cluster with a survey-based model

Methods of cluster analysis and their shortcomings: using the innovative cluster approach to surmount conceptual difficulties

It is generally possible to distinguish two essential steps of cluster analysis: (1) identification of a clustered region, for example, to verify the existence of a spatial agglomeration, and (2) analysis of the network relations within the cluster. Screening the literature on clusters reveals that there is no consistent and generally agreed procedure for their identification. The appropriate methodology is based on each individual case and depends on the specific research objective and the questions to be answered. At least four different techniques can be used for the identification of agglomerations: case studies, location quotients, correspondence analysis, and input–output analysis (Bergman and Feser 1999; Roelandt and den Hertog 1999).

In practice, a mixture of diverse procedures at different levels of aggregation is used to overcome the methodological limitations and the disadvantages which arise from using a single technique. The instruments presented above complement each other as they answer different questions, provide different kinds of information, and have specific advantages and drawbacks. Which methods are combined to analyse a regional-sectoral agglomeration will ultimately depend on the specific needs and the questions of the defined research objective.

Identifying the existence of a spatial agglomeration is the foundation of analysis and should be verified by exploring a cluster's interaction level. From an integrative point of view, network analyses ought to be added to investigate the quality of regional cluster formations and their individual development stages. Although it has long been used in social sciences, the network-analysis method is often disregarded in (economic) cluster studies (Krätke 2002). Network analyses can be carried out through company surveys and by assessing transaction and communication relations between the economic actors which are subsequently analysed graphically. Based on the direct recording of corporate relations they provide an exceedingly useful methodology for detecting and examining the interaction processes within the respective agglomeration. However, there are two inherent restrictions worth mentioning. Network-analysis procedures are highly limited by (1) the availability of data and (2) the lack of user-friendly software solutions that are necessary for managing and interpreting the complex set of information (Bergman and Feser 1999).

In consideration of the above-mentioned methodological shortcomings of 'classical' analytic concepts, this chapter introduces an integrative top-down approach that facilitates acquiring further information on the character of the agglomerations and their individual level of development. Based on the concept of the innovative cluster, a survey questionnaire sent to the entire population of a cluster can be used to obtain an overview of the region in question. There is another important consideration: in order to reflect both the structure of the agglomeration and the interaction that takes place between the actors, the hardware, and the software of the cluster have to be operationalized in the analysis. To keep the method as simple as possible, six dimensions of analysis are proposed: four determinants explored by the Porterian diamond in addition to explicit consideration of the communication and interaction taking place within the cluster by adding an innovation and a relationship dimension (Steinle *et al.* 2007). The existence of a local cluster initiative greatly favours this kind of research by providing a list of the cluster members and introducing the researchers.

In order to capture the four determinants of the Porterian diamond in the survey, firms located in the cluster are asked to indicate

1. the origin of their competitors (the region, the nation or international);
2. the specialization of their supplies (made for a particular product, made for an entire industry or very general supplies provided for all industries), as well as their origin;

3. the size and sophistication of local demand (would the home market anticipate international trends?); and
4. the importance and specialization of the local institutions along with a section which specifically concerns the local education and labour market.

In order to analyse the interaction taking place in the cluster, the elements depicted in Figure 4.3 are taken as indicators:

5. Firms are asked to indicate if there is a common ideal, that is, a sense of belonging to the cluster. Socialization is detected with two questions on where key employees have studied and where they have worked before. The firms are additionally asked questions on the intensity of interaction and on the level of trust with their partners in order to characterize the relationships, differentiating between regional, national, and international partners. An instrument adopted from Sako can be used for this purpose. She mapped relationships in a continuum between arm's length and obligational relationships (Sako 1992).
6. Finally, recognizing the importance of innovation in an 'innovative' cluster, the predominant type of innovation and the origin of the cooperation partners are captured. In the case of an occurrence of network innovations where several partners are involved in an innovative venture, local partners for innovation provide a great advantage (Steinle and Schiele 2002). Besides, collaborative processes of innovation are considered to be a typical manifestation of an innovative milieu.

Application case: identification of a medical technology cluster with limited interactions

In principle, clustering can be expected if a long value chain including multiple competencies is detected, if the market is volatile and therefore honours flexible reactions, and, finally, if innovation processes contribute to the reorganization of the system (Steinle and Schiele 2002). Medical technology is an industry sector that fulfils five of the six criteria considered to foster the formation of clusters. In particular, it has a long value chain requiring different competencies and it is highly innovative, with more than 50 per cent of the products on the market for less than two years (BMBF 2003). Not surprisingly, several agglomerations were documented, especially in the USA, the largest market for medical technology. No fewer than 35 cluster initiatives around the globe are trying to promote their medical technology cluster (Sölvell *et al.* 2003).

With a world market share of about 15 per cent and support from h&z business consulting, the German industry ranks second globally. In the region analysed, together with the local cluster initiative, 101 economic actors with a combined workforce of some 15,000 were identified. The delimitation

Table 4.1 Statistical delimitation of medical technology

Code WZ 93	Description
33.10.1	Manufacture of electric medical instruments and equipment
33.10.2	Manufacture of technical medical equipment
33.10.3	Manufacture of orthopaedic appliances
33.10.4	Dental laboratories
33.40.1	Manufacture of spectacle lenses, contact lenses, spectacle frames and frames fitted with lenses, whether or not the lenses are optically worked
35.43.0	Manufacture of invalid carriages

Note: Code WZ 93: German Code of Standard Economic Industry Classifications.

Source: German VAT Statistics 1997.

took place in accordance with the five-digit classification of the German economic sector classification system (see Table 4.1). From an initial structural perspective, a rather large cluster has been identified, considering the average cluster size identified in van der Linde's meta-study of about 10,000 employees (van der Linde 2003).

The analysis relied on a survey instrument of 23 questions, with at least two questions assigned to each of the six dimensions used to map the cluster:

1. competitors: local and international;
2. suppliers: specialization in medical technology, main origin of suppliers;
3. customers: size and anticipatory character of the German market;
4. institutions: specialization in medical technology and availability of nine types of institutions (specialized financial infrastructure, marketing agencies, consulting, research, political bodies, associations, applications such as clinics, education, entrepreneurs' associations);
5. interaction: intensity of knowledge exchange with and trust in suppliers and other partners, differentiated according to their geographical origin, as well as education of workforce and geographical origin of workforce and the sense of belonging to a cluster; and
6. innovation: type (network innovation, laboratory innovation, or inventor innovation (for this distinction, see Steinle and Schiele 2002) and origin of partners for innovation.

The questions were elaborated based on Schiele (2003), adding more details on the interaction (intensity of knowledge exchange and trust developed), in addition to collecting general data on the firm including performance indicators. The respondents were asked to classify their situation on a four-digit scale. Anchor phrases were used to ensure the reliability and compatibility of responses.

Out of the 101 companies identified as belonging to the cluster, 37 participated in the survey, after being contacted twice. This can be considered a good return rate. The results were validated by 10 semi-structured interviews in cluster firms and an in-depth analysis of a core firm (Steinle *et al.* 2007).

The questionnaire indicates medium mean scores for the dimensions analysed. Apparently, elements of a well-functioning cluster are present, in particular the infrastructure specialized in medical technology. However, regional suppliers and innovation partners are not abundant, that is, firms often have to rely on partners from other German regions to access these important resources. The analysis reveals that most competitors and suppliers from the surveyed firms come from other German locations, not from that particular region. The same is true of partners for innovation. On the other hand, only 35 per cent of the firms relied heavily on network innovations, while for 27 per cent the laboratory-type innovation model, which requires less cooperation, was most important. It can be concluded that most firms rely more heavily on partners external to the cluster for many of their activities, rather than primarily on local actors.

This impression is further underscored if the interaction between these firms is analysed in greater detail (Figure 4.3). A coincidence of cooperation and competition can be found in a fully developed milieu, mediated by an intensive flow of information. A common ideal of belonging to the region is present and supported by a shared socialization.

- *Common ideal*: an important indicator for the existence of an innovative cluster is the feeling of belonging to the region, that is 'cluster-awareness'. In this case, however, 40 per cent of the respondents were not aware of being located in a special cluster. In some firms it appears as if the notion of a cluster is not very widespread across all functions. In spite of that, a higher cluster awareness was identified within older firms.
- *Socialization*: ordinary socialization can form a basis for the particular relationship between the actors of a region. In the case analysed, however, only medium-average scores were reported by our indicators: the questions on whether the labour force had been recruited locally and whether most employees had completed their education in the region. Most staff had studied and worked throughout Germany, not exclusively in the region.
- *Cooperation and competition*: under 20 per cent of the firms had primarily local competitors so that the competitive area was generally Germany as a whole. In order to assess the cooperation aspect, the firms were then asked to rate the level of trust developed towards suppliers and other partners. A significant difference between domestic and international partners was identified. Trust in international suppliers and other international partners was appreciably lower. Again, no significant differences emerged between German partners and those anchored in the same region.

- *Flow of information*: finally, in order to assess the existence of an intensive information exchange, the firms were asked to rate their exchanges with suppliers and other partners, distinguishing between local, national, and international actors. In a fully developed innovative cluster, local interaction should be far more highly developed than exchange with partners from outside the region.

The evaluation of the intensity of knowledge transfer shows a rather homogenous picture: the majority of the companies surveyed meet with their suppliers only every now and again. Irrespective of the geographic origin of the respondents, knowledge transfer is characterized as overwhelmingly task-focused. Only every fifth company stated that personal relationships had developed on the basis of these regular meetings. No significant difference emerged between regional and national buyer–supplier interaction. The reluctance to develop personal relationships based on business contacts, it has been argued, could be a typical feature of German business behaviour.

The knowledge transfer with other regional partners other than suppliers is estimated to be slightly more intense. Again, no essential differences could be found between regional and national (German) partners. International partners, however, are involved to a considerably lower extent.

It may be concluded that there are clear indicators that the region analysed does not entertain a strong local milieu-type interaction. Indeed, the relatively weak basis for common socialization, a moderate level of local knowledge flow and no particular localized trust fit the observation of limited cluster awareness. The pattern observed in which there is a distinction between international and national partners was expected. Research in international buyer–seller relationships detected a similar phenomenon (Homburg *et al.* 2002). The absence of any significant differences of perception concerning regional and national relationships, however, can support the notion that a fully developed innovative cluster is not present.

A final question came up during the analysis: Why was there such a low level of interaction, even though the structure of the agglomeration was quite well developed? This issue was of particular interest in order to guide future cluster-development activities. The analysis, so far, had shown a dichotomy: the agglomeration analysed, from a purely structural point of view, resembled a fairly well-developed and rather large-sized cluster. From an interaction perspective, however, it still lacked important elements. Thus, a differentiation of a regional-sectoral agglomeration in terms of interaction was possible and valuable.

The final section of this paper proposes one possible explanation for the phenomenon of detecting only a Porterian diamond but no innovative cluster with full-fledged interaction: the cluster-life-cycle thesis. According to the cluster-life-cycle thesis, young agglomerations tend to show limited interaction patterns, that is, regional-sectoral agglomerations may start as Porterian diamonds and only later does a milieu materialize, the cluster then developing into an innovative cluster. In other words, both theory and our data suggest that agglomerations may start as a simple collection of organizations along a particular value chain. Only later do these organizations start to interact more intensively, eventually forming a fully fledged innovative cluster.

Discussion: interaction in a life-cycle perspective on regional clusters

The cluster-life-cycle thesis goes back to the classical product life cycle approach. A prominent figure linking the product life cycle to a regional dimension is Vernon, who argued that in the early phase of their life cycle, innovative products had a 'propensity to cluster in the home market' (Vernon 1979: 256). Meanwhile this idea has been differentiated, arguing that entire clusters may have a life cycle. In literature, four life-cycle phases for a cluster have been suggested (Menzel and Fornahl 2010), while most sources – including this paper – distinguish between three (Bergman 2008).

In the growth phase, a cluster develops by specializing in a particular industry (Tichy 2001). Also, at the beginning of a life cycle, proximity may foster the development of innovations. Later, lock-in phenomena can have a detrimental effect (Audretsch and Feldman 1996; Boschma 2005). There may be a size limit for clusters above which the benefits clusters provide to their members decline as congestion effects prevail (Folta *et al.* 2006).

On the other hand, there is an ongoing discussion as to whether the cluster view makes the product-life-cycle-concept obsolete (Norton 1992). This view is particularly stressed in the milieu approach which argues that agglomerations do have the capability to constantly reinvent themselves – if a fully developed innovative milieu is present (Crevoisier 2000, 2004). This latter point stresses the importance of the interaction aspect from a region's point of view, as a milieu may ensure sustainable development. Lauterbach suggests that the interaction in a region may be less developed in an early cluster life cycle and only matures later (Lauterbach 2005), which paves the way for linking our analysis on the interaction of an agglomeration with the life-cycle thesis.

The relatively moderate values concerning the milieu aspect have already been discussed above, in particular the limited interaction that was able to be detected. Concerning the region analysed, further indicators for classifying the region from a life-cycle perspective can be drawn from the survey: the process of specialization is not yet fully developed. Respondents were asked to assign their firm to any of nine subgroups of medical technology. No single segment was indicated as host to more than 20 per cent of the respondents. This indicates a vague sense of specialization in the region. The limited interaction and the lack of specialization both support the

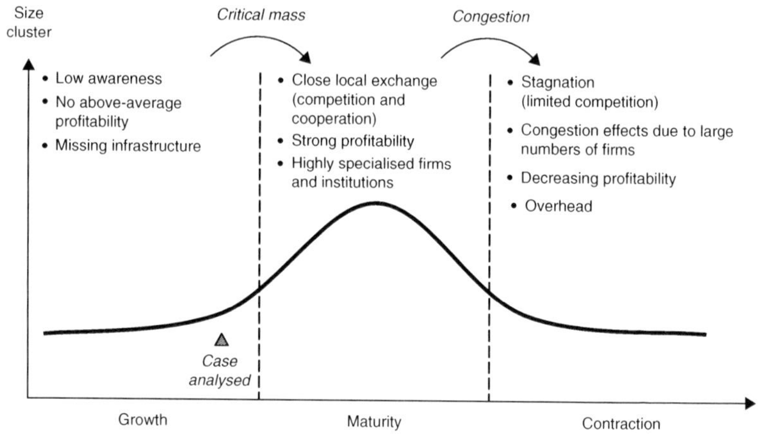

Figure 4.4 Life-cycle approach to clusters
Source: Depiction by the authors.

argument that the region analysed is still a cluster but in its early growth phase. This assertion is further substantiated when the age structure of the firms is taken into consideration: 60 per cent of the firms surveyed had been founded since 1990, with almost 20 per cent of those even having their origins outside the cluster and settling there only later. While there are some older firms, which actually score higher in the interaction questions, most firms in the cluster are rather young. Based on these findings, in Figure 4.4 – which on the one axis depicts cluster size and on the other the cluster's maturity (Menzel and Fornahl 2010) – we may classify this agglomeration as a young cluster in an early phase of the life cycle.

Such a classification has consequences with regard to suggestions for further cluster development. According to the life-cycle view, this cluster can benefit from further specialization. This requires some kind of 'cluster strategy' defining the direction of specialization. The cluster strategy may be initiated by local development bodies. The specialization could be further promoted by attracting new firms to the cluster, in particular firms working in that field of specialization. Finally, to speed up development and to ensure sustainable growth, the promotion of the local innovative milieu is given priority. This, however, is something that cannot be done by any one development or cluster authority alone but requires a dual approach, ensuring the comprehensive inclusion of local firms, as well as regional development bodies (Steinle *et al.* 2007).

It is possibly interesting to briefly sketch the reaction of the actors in the analysed cluster. The fact that it is a young cluster has had a substantial influence on the actors' reactions: the limited interaction was probably not due to a detrimental local culture that impeded collaboration but simply to the fact that the cluster was relatively new and members did not know about each other. The mayor of the county which hosts most of the firms was genuinely surprised by the results. It became clear to him that simply erecting a sign on the motorway that said 'Medical Technology Valley' would not make it so.

As many of the local firms did not have as a common ideal belonging to a regional cluster several measures were taken to create such awareness. In particular, two large cluster conferences were organized, the second with more than 200 participants. One of the best-known medical scientists in Germany gave the keynote address at the conference, and then the results of our analysis were presented and discussed. Finally, the participants were asked to join any of the several proposed workgroups on cluster development. Earlier, a responsible chairman, all from local firms or institutions, had been selected for each workgroup. The local authority's delegate for cluster development coordinated these groups and provided the infrastructure, but the major activities were carried out by the industries themselves. By linking the kick-off event with workgroup formation it was possible to use the initial energy to propel the continued evolution of the cluster.

One of the workgroups, for instance, implemented a local lecture series. Several firms in the region invite their neighbours to visit their facilities and to listen to a speech on a particular topic of common interest. The series of visits intends to increase the participants' awareness of belonging to the cluster by simply getting to know each other – and possibly lay a cornerstone for collaboration. As an example, during a visit one firm demonstrated its new testing facilities. One of the visitors was completely surprised to find out that such facilities existed almost next door. His firm needed to run the same type of tests performed at the local facility but had been sending their samples to a laboratory in the USA. It goes without saying that the owners of the testing facility were more than happy to leverage their investment by offering the service to the neighbouring firm. At the same time, this firm was able to derive substantial benefits by having the service almost within walking distance. Without interaction, though, they would possibly have continued to be unaware of the opportunities their cluster had to offer.

That development was so successful that the cluster has recently been awarded by the German Ministry of Education and Science as one of the top clusters with best growth potential.

Conclusion and further research: a survey-based interaction assessment and a life-cycle perspective

This paper has emphasized the need to distinguish between the structure of a cluster and the interaction that takes place between its actors. While the structure can be assessed by means of the Porterian diamond, the innovative milieu approach is helpful for categorizing the interaction. The combination of the two approaches results in the model of the innovative cluster model. Distinguishing between clusters with milieu-type interaction and agglomerations without strong internal exchange also helps to determine recommendations for firms that want to profit from their cluster (Schiele 2008). In terms of analytical rigor this view adds precision to the analysis. In the application case it became apparent that an agglomeration which – from purely a structural view – looks quite comprehensive may lack essential interaction elements. Thus, focusing on only either one or the other of the two elements describing an agglomeration, the structure and the interaction, may be misleading.

A further finding from this study was a methodological advancement in the analysis of regional clusters. Researchers struggle to evaluate the interaction in a region. The typical approach favoured by the research so far has been qualitative in nature. Here, we tested a survey-based approach. Results support the feasibility of such a procedure. This may pave the way for future research and encourage the development of more quantitative tools for the analysis of localized clusters.

Finally, employing the findings from a cluster-life-cycle perspective adds another layer of analysis. Though the life-cycle concept is still in development, with our case an application yielded practical indications on how to further develop the cluster at hand. The cluster-life-cycle idea could also provide a useful starting point for further research.

References

D. B. Audretsch and M. P. Feldman, 'Innovative Clusters and the Industry Life Cycle', *Review of Industrial Organization,* 11 (1996): 253–73.

P. Aydalot, *Milieux innovateurs en Europe* (*Innovative Milieus in Europe*) (Paris: Gremi, 1984).

R. Baptista and P. Swann, 'Do Firms in Clusters Innovate More?', *Research Policy,* 27 (1998): 525–40.

R. Baptista, 'Productivity and the Density of Regional Clusters', in J. Bröcker, D. Dohse, and R. Soltwedel (eds), *Innovation Clusters and Interregional Competition* (Berlin: Springer, 2003), pp. 163–81.

M. Beise and H. G. Gemünden, 'Lead Markets: A New Framework for the International Diffusion of Innovations', *Management International Review,* 44 (2004): 83–102.

M. Bengtsson and Ö. Sölvell, 'Climate of Competition, Clusters and Innovative Performance', *Scandinavian Journal of Management,* 20 (2004): 225–44.

E. M. Bergman and E. J. Feser, 'Industrial and Regional Clusters: Concepts and Comparative Applications', *The Web Book of Regional Science* (Morgantown, W.Va.: West Virginia University, 1999) online at http://www.rri.wvu.edu/WebBook/Bergman-Feser/chapter3.htm (accessed 1 October 2010).

E. M. Bergman, 'Cluster Life-Cycles: An Emerging Synthesis', in C. Karlsson (ed.), *Handbook of Research on Cluster Theory* (Cheltenham: Edward Elgar, 2008), pp. 114–32.

BMBF (Bundesministerium für Bildung und Forschung), *Kompetenzzentren für die Medizintechnik. Von der Forschung in die Praxis* (Competence Centres for Medical Technologies: From Research to Application) (Bonn: BMBF, 2003).

R. A. Boschma 'Proximity and Innovation: A Critical Assessment', *Regional Studies,* 39 (1) (2005): 61–74.

G. Cainelli, 'Spatial Agglomerations, Technological Innovations, and Firm Productivity: Evidence from Italian Industrial Districts', *Growth and Change,* 39 (3) (2008): 414–35.

R. Camagni, 'Introduction: From the Local "Milieu" to Innovation through Cooperation Networks', in R. Camagni (ed.), *Innovation Networks: Spatial Perspectives* (London: Belhaven Press, 1991), pp. 1–9.

R. Camagni, 'Space–Time in the Concept of "Milieu Innovateur"', in U. Blien, H. Herrmann and M. Koller (eds), *Regionalentwicklung und regionale Arbeitsmarktpolitik. Konzepte zur Lösung regionaler Arbeitsmarktprobleme?* (Regional Development and Regional Labour Policy: Concepts for the Solution of Labour Problems?) (Nuremberg, 1994), pp. 74–89.

A. Ciccone and R. E. Hall, 'Productivity and the Density of Economic Activity', *American Economic Review,* 86 (1) (1996): 54–70.

K. Colletis-Wahl, J. Corpataux, O. Crevoisier, L. Kebir, B. Pecqueur and V. Peyrache-Gadeau, 'The Territorial Economy: A General Approach in Order to Understand and Deal with Globalisation', in M. J. A. Querejacta, C. I. Landart and J. R. Wilson (eds), *Networks, Governance and Economic Development: Bridging Disciplinary Frontiers* (Cheltenham: Edward Elgar, 2008), pp. 21–9.

J. Corpataux and O. Crevoisier, 'Economic Theories and Spatial Transformations Clarifying the Space–Time Premises and Outcomes of Economic Theories', *Journal of Economic Geography,* 7 (3) (2007): 285–309.

O. Crevoisier, 'The Innovative Milieu Approach: Towards a Territorialized Understanding of the Economy?', *Economic Geography,* 80 (4) (2004): 367–79.

O. Crevoisier and R. Camagni, *Les Milieux urbains: innovation, systèmes de production et ancrage* (*The Urban Milieus: Innovation, Production Systems and Anchoring*) (Neuchâtel: Institut de Recherches Economiques et Régionales, 2000).

O. Crevoisier, 'Les Milieux innovateurs et la ville: une introduction' ('The Innovative Milieus and the Town: An Introduction'), in O. Crevoisier and R. Camagni (eds), *Les Milieux urbains: innovation, systèmes de production et ancrage* (Neuchâtel: Edes, 2000), pp. 7–32.

H. Davies and P. Ellis, 'Porter's Competitive Advantage of Nations: Time for the final Judgement?', *Journal of Management Studies,* 37 (8) (2000): 1189–213.

C. DeBresson, 'Why Innovative Activities Cluster', in C. DeBresson (ed.), *Economic Interdependence and Innovative Activity: An Input–Output Analysis* (Cheltenham: Brookfield, 1996), pp. 149–64.

D. Dohse, 'Taking Regions Seriously: Recent Innovations in German Technology Policy', in J. Bröcker, D. Dohse and R. Soltwedel (eds), *Innovation Clusters and Interregional Competition* (Berlin: 2003), pp. 372–94.

S. Fabiani and G. Pellegrini, 'Un'analisi quantitativa delle imprese nei distretti industriali italiani: redditività, produttività e costo del lavoro' ('A Quantitative Analysis of the Firms in Industrial Districts: Profitability, Productivity and Labour Costs', *L'Industria: Rivista di economia e politica industriale,* 19 (4) (1998): 811–31.

T. B. Folta, A. C. Cooper and Y. Baik, 'Geographic Cluster Size and Firm Performance', *Journal of Business Venturing,* 21 (2006): 217–42.

P. Franz, 'Innovative Milieus: Extrempunkte der Interpretation von Wirtschafts- und Wissenschaftssystemen' ('Innovative Milieus: Extreme Points in the Interpretation of Economic and Science Systems'), *Jahrbuch für Regionalwissenschaft,* 19 (2) (1999): 107–30.

A. Freisberg and S. Merx, 'Deutschlands heimliche Wirtschaftswunder' ('Germany's Secret Economic Miracles'), *Capital,* 45 (24) (2006): 62–71.

M. Fromhold-Eisebith, 'Bridging Scales in Innovation Policies: How to Link Regional, National and International Innovation Systems', *European Planning Studies,* 15 (2) (2007): 217–33.

M. Fromhold-Eisebith, 'Das "kreative Milieu" als Motor regionalwirtschaftlichr Entwicklung. Forschungstrends und Erfassungsmöglichkeiten' ('The "Creative Milieu" as a Motor for Regional Development: Research Trends and Modes of Assessment'), *Geographische Zeitschrift,* 83 (1) (1995): 30–47.

M. Fromhold-Eisebith, 'Innovative Milieu and Social Capital: Complementary or Redundant Concepts of Collaboration-based Regional Development?', *European Planning Studies,* 12 (6) (2004): 747–65.

S. Garrett-Jones, 'From Citadels to Clusters: The Evolution of Regional Innovation Policies in Australia', *R&D Management,* 34 (1) (2004): 3–16.

T. Gössling and R. Rutten, 'Innovation in Regions', *European Planning Studies,* 15 (2) (2007): 253–70.

I. R. Gordon and P. McCann, 'Industrial Clusters: Complexes, Agglomeration and/or Social Networks?', *Urban Studies,* 37 (3) (2000): 513–32.

G. Grabher, 'The Weakness of Strong Ties: The Lock-in of Regional Development in the Ruhr Area', in G. Grabher (ed.), *The Embedded Firm: On the Socioeconomics of Industrial Networks* (London, New York: Routledge, 1993), pp. 255–77.

N. Hansen, 'Competition, Trust, and Reciprocity in the Development of Innovative Regional Milieux', *Papers in Regional Science: The Journal of the Regional Science Association International,* 71 (2) (1992): 95–105.

R. Hassink, 'What Distinguishes "Good" from "Bad" Industrial Agglomerations?', *Erdkunde,* 51 (1) (1997): 2–11.

Hermes Lab, *Check-up economico finanziario dei distretti industriali. Rapporto esplorativo sui risultati economici dei distretti industriali italiani 1997–1998* (*Economic and Financial Check-Up of the Industrial Districts*) (Montebelluna: Club dei Distretti Industriali, 2000).

C. Homburg, H. Krohmer, J. P. Cannon, and I. Kiedaisch, 'Customer Satisfaction in Transnational Buyer–Supplier Relationships', *Journal of International Marketing,* 10 (4) (2002): 1–29.

B. Jin, 'Achieving an Optimal Global versus Domestic Sourcing Balance under Demand Uncertainty', *International Journal of Operations & Production Management,* 24 (12) (2004): 1292–305.

S. Krätke, 'Network Analysis of Production Clusters: The Potsdam/Babelsberg Film Industry as an Example', *European Planning Studies,* 10 (1) (2002): 27–54.

C. E. Lauterbach, *Regionale Wertschöpfungssysteme und Kernkompetenzen: Konzept, Empirische Untersuchung, Gestaltungsempfehlungen* (*Regional Value-Creating Systems and Core Competencies: Concept, Empirical Analysis, Recommendations*) (Munich: Rainer Hampp Verlag, 2005).

D. Maillat, 'Innovation and Local Dynamism: The Role of the Milieu', *Sociologia Internationalis,* 28 (2) (1990): 147–59.

M. Menzel and D. Fornahl, 'Cluster Life Cycles: Dimensions and Rationales of Cluster Evolution', *Industrial and Corporate Change,* 19 (1) (2010): 205–38.

F. X. Molina-Morales and M. Martínez-Fernández, 'The Impact of Industrial District Affiliation on Firm Value Creation', *European Planning Studies,* 11 (2) (2003): 155–70.

H. C. Moon, A. M. Rugman and A. Verbeke, 'The Generalized Double Diamond Approach to International Competitivness', *Research in Global Strategic Management,* 5 (1995): 97–114.

Y. Motoyama, 'What was New about the Cluster Theory? What Could It Answer and What Could It Not Answer?', *Economic Development Quarterly,* 22 (4) (2008): 353–63.

D. Newlands, 'Competition and Cooperation in Industrial Clusters: The Implications for Public Policy', *European Planning Studies,* 11 (5) (2003): 521–32.

R. D. Norton, 'Agglomeration and Competitiveness: From Marshall to Chinitz', *Urban Studies,* 29 (2) (1992): 155–70.

M. E. Porter, *On Competition* (Boston, MA: Harvard Business School Press, 1998).

M. E. Porter, *The Competitive Advantage of Nations* (London: Macmillan, 1990).

R. Ratti, A. Bramanti, and R. Gordon (eds), *The Dynamics of Innovative Regions: The GREMI Approach* (Aldershot: Ashgate, 1997).

T. J. A. Roelandt and P. den Hertog, 'Cluster analysis and cluster-based policy making in OECD countries: An introduction to the theme', in OECD (ed.), *Boosting Innovation: The Cluster Approach* (Paris: Organisation for Economic Co-operation and Development, 1999), pp. 9–26.

A. M. Rugman and A. Verbeke, 'Multinational Enterprises and Clusters: An Organizing Framework', *Management International Review,* 43 (3) (2003): 151–69.

M. Sako, *Prices, Quality and Trust: Inter-Firm Relations in Britain and Japan* (Cambridge: Cambridge University Press, 1992).

H. Schiele, 'How to Distinguish Innovative Suppliers? Identifying Innovative Suppliers as a New Task for Purchasing', *Industrial Marketing Management,* 35 (2006): 925–35.

H. Schiele, 'Location, Location: The Geography of Industry Clusters', *Journal of Business Strategy,* 29 (3) (2008): 29–36.

H. Schiele, 'Partnering Does Not Work Everywhere: The Advantages of Belonging to and a Method on How to Detect an "Innovative Cluster"', in S. Schruijer (ed.), *Multi-Organizational Partnerships and Cooperative Strategy* (Tilburg: Dutch University Press, 1999), pp. 179–84.

H. Schiele, *Der Standort-Faktor: Wie Unternehmen durch regionale Cluster ihre Produktivität und Innovationskraft steigern* (*The Location Factor: How Firms Increase Their Productivity and Power of Innovation through Regional Clusters*) (Weinheim: Wiley-VCH, 2003).

H. Schiele, *Strategisches Management in Wertschöpfungssystemen. Clusterbezogene Umweltanalyse – Gestaltungsempfehlungen – Anwendungsfall* (*Strategic Management in Value-Creating Systems: Cluster-Based Environmental Analysis – Recommendations – Case Study*) (Wiesbaden: Gabler, 2001).

Ö. Sölvell, G. Lindqvist, and C. H. Ketels, *The Cluster Initiative Greenbook* (Stockholm: Ivory Tower, 2003).

C. Steinle and H. Schiele, 'When Do Industries Cluster? A Proposal on How to Assess an Industry's Propensity to Concentrate at a Single Region or Nation', *Research Policy,* 31 (2002): 849–58.

C. Steinle, H. Schiele, and K. Mietzner, 'Merging a Firm-centred and a Regional Policy Perspective for the Assessment of Regional Clusters: Concept and Application of a "Dual" Approach to a Medical Technology Cluster', *European Planning Studies,* 15 (2) (2007): 235–51.

C. Steinle, M. Eickhoff, and H. Schiele, 'Zur Perspektivenerweiterung des Strategischen Management: Der "innovative Cluster" als Wertschöpfungssystem und die Entwicklung von Kernkompetenzen' (On the Broadening of Strategic Management's Perspective: The 'Innovative Cluster' as Value-Creating System and the Development of Core Competencies'), *Zeitschrift für Planung,* 9 (4) (1998): 367–90.

L. Suarez-Villa and W. Walrod, 'Operational Strategy, R&D and Intra-metropolitan Clustering in a Polycentric Structrure: The Advanced Electronics Industries of the Los Angeles Basin', *Urban Studies,* 34 (9) (1997): 1343–80.

G. Tichy, 'Regionale Kompetenzzyklen: Zur Bedeutung von Produktlebenszyklus- und Clusteransätzen im regionalen Kontext' ('Regional Competence Cycles: on the Importance of Product Cycle and Cluster Approaches in the Regional Context'), *Zeitschrift für Wirtschaftsgeographie,* 45 (3–4) (2001): 182–201.

C. van der Linde, 'The Demography of Clusters: Findings from the Cluster Meta-Study', in J. Bröcker, D. Dohse, and R. Soltwedel (eds), *Innovation Clusters and Interregional Competition* (Berlin: Springer, 2003), pp. 130–49.

R. Vernon, 'The Product Cycle Hypothesis in a New International Environment', *Oxford Bulletin of Economics & Statistics,* 41 (4) (1979): 255–67.

L. Waverman, 'A Critical Analysis of Porter's Framework on the Competitive Advantage of Nations', *Research in Global Strategic Management,* 5 (1995): 67–95.

5
Outcomes in Small-Firm Networks: A Quantitative Study in the Southern Brazilian Context

Jorge Renato Verschoore and Alsones Balestrin

Introduction

The small-firm networks have been the focus of increasing preoccupation in applied and academic debates. Interest on the theme has gained momentum through the reflections of authors who point to the structural and strategic transformations derived from the new competitive landscape. Castells (1996), among others, indicates that the traditional firm, operating in an individualized manner, experiences difficulties when facing such new challenges. In order to cope with a broad range of competitive requirements, such as continuous learning and innovation, Perrow (1992) points to the ascension of small-firm networks. Networks unite the flexibility and agility of small firms with the scale and power of conglomerates. A relevant reflection, provided by Thompson (2003), stresses that networks, due to their peculiar ambivalent characteristics, which unite competition and cooperation, scale and scope, and, foremost, hierarchy and market, respond better to competitive demands. 'The organization is then embedded in relationships with identifiable counterparts. This web of relationships can be called a network' (Håkansson and Snehota 1989: 191).

The network concept is not new; it has been employed by organizational theory since the beginning of the 20th century (Nohria 1992). However, the union of firms with the aim of achieving collective gains has received more attention in studies and organizational practices through the past decades (Oliver and Ebers 1998). A network central purpose is to bring together attributes that allow an adequacy of the competitive environment to a single structure, sustained by uniform actions, but decentralized, thus allowing scale gains without losing the flexibility of the associated firms. 'As noted, we have chosen to call this form the dynamic network to suggest that its major components can be assembled and reassembled in order to meet complex and changing competitive conditions' (Miles and Snow 1986: 64).

Firm networks present a new manner of facing competitive pressures, one in which the links among agents 'constitute a reflection and recognition of interdependence, as opposed to the autonomy postulated by the classic theory of the firm' (Thorelli 1986: 41). In these networks, the interaction among the players is more than a simple passive adaptation, since relationships encompass the standing against common difficulties and the search for joint solutions as a result of the individual capacities and those derived from collective synergy.

Collective gains, derived from synergy, are important elements in the delimitation of the network concept, which may be stated as 'long-term purposeful arrangements among distinct yet related profit-seeking organizations, allowing them to win or sustain competitive advantages before competitors who are external to the network' (Jarillo 1988: 32). This definition highlights the competitive character of networks. It means that cooperation among participants is strongly conditioned by the competition against firms that are not associated to the network. The collective gains can be achieved through self organized networks, called organic networks, or through policy-implanted networks, called Engineered Networks (Huggins, 2000).

In organically developed networks, cooperation emerges from occasional opportunities (Kreiner and Schultz 1993). In this case, firms perceiving collective gains create the conditions for the emergence of cooperation, in which the network consolidation depends mainly on the collective decision and managerial know-how without any external support. In engineered developed networks, leader firms or government representatives act as process advisers, defining rules, restrictions, rights, and duties that need to be followed. Typically, engineered networks are formally established and goal-directed rather than occurring serendipitously (Provan *et al.* 2007). The popularization of engineered networks, as a specific response to economic development issues, is highlighted by the growing policy interest in stimulating business cooperation in several countries (Huggins 2000). This study focuses on engineered networks, created and supported by the Government of Rio Grande do Sul State via a public policy named Cooperation Networks Program (CNP).

As cited, the network collective gains have been studied by scholars since the end of the 20th century. Human and Provan (1997) identified four network-outcomes categories through a qualitative study focused on organic small to medium-sized enterprise networks. Based on their findings and on other seminal contributions to the topic (Jarillo 1988; Perrow 1992; Powell 1998), allied to outcomes evidenced by some CNP case studies (Böhe and Silva 2004; Macadar 2004; Pereira 2004; Balestrin and Verschoore 2008), it was possible to distinguish five main categories of outcomes in small-firm networks in the southern Brazilian context:

1. Scale and Market Power;
2. Collective Solutions;

3. Learning and Innovation;
4. Cost and Risk Reduction;
5. Social Relationships.

These five categories of outcomes in small-firm networks will guide the empirical part of the quantitative research.

Two network characteristics are also analysed: time of existence and number of associates of the network. These characteristics are important because they are related to the network evolution. Some studies have shown that a large number of associated firms affect positively the degree of network sustainability (Huggins 2000). Others highlight that a relatively significant number of overall firm participants are by far more likely to achieve collective gains and the whole network success (Brüderl and Preisendörfer 1998). Taking into consideration the time of the existence, network evolution is often based on past, present, and future relationships. In other words, some say that the lifetime of the relationships in the network may modify its flow (Provan *et al.* 2007). Therefore, the time of existence segmentation allowed us to analyse the differences between networks with distinct relationship trajectories.

A deeper research on these five outcomes categories and these two network characteristics might contribute to a better understanding of the small-firm networks phenomenon, allowing managers and entrepreneurs to focus their efforts and also providing subsides for the development of public policies. Among other contributions, results presented herein will allow the evaluation of the impact of cooperation on the competitiveness of firms participating on networks created via the CNP. In order to achieve such goals, the paper is structured as follows: it starts with the discussion of the five outcomes categories, as well as their definitions, and the supporting theoretical framework; then, a summary of the methodology is presented, and the CNP is analysed. After, the main results are discussed together with implications and final considerations.

Outcomes in small-firm networks

Scale and market power

This category is defined as the set of outcomes obtained from the growth in the number of network players. The larger the number of firms, the larger the network capacity to obtain scale gains and market power. Network association creates scale economies because associated firms acquire, among other gains, a greater bargain power before partners and suppliers (Campbell and Goold 1999), a larger probability of creating better-recognized trademarks and greater public exposition (Lorenzoni and Baden-Fuller 1995). Scale gains allow the networks to enlarge their bargain power in various economic relationships and to close commercial deals involving exclusive conditions (Waarden 1992).

When one notices that deliberate use of market power is among the keys to the success of large firms (Perrow 1998) and that small firms cannot use such advantage (Best 1990), network formation becomes a tantalizing option for small firms seeking to enlarge their market power. While participating in a network, firms are distinctly perceived in their action areas besides receiving wider public recognition, a guarantee of greater legitimacy to their business activities and of a redimensioning of their institutional contexts (Dimaggio and Powell 1983). Also, there are possibilities for the establishment relationships with 'local universities, large suppliers, and state agencies, that smaller, individual firms could not establish' (Human and Provan 1997: 383).

Collective solutions

Part of the problems faced by a small firm can be overcome by the development of solutions generated inside the network in which the firm is inserted. Credit warranty services, prospecting and advertising of opportunities as well as accounting and technical support (Best 1990) can be collectively offered by networks, minimizing the obstacles posed to firms. Also, small-firm networks can supply the qualification needs of their firms through training and consulting, because they are better prepared to identify common weaknesses and to find collective suppliers. Moreover, a network can develop information systems for the electronic dissemination of solutions among its associates (Rockart and Short 1991). Therefore, the collective-solutions category relates to all services, products, and infrastructure that the network offers to its associates.

Network-provided solutions also support actions of wider amplitude, facilitating individual associate actions. The collective infrastructure materializes the individual's sense of belonging to a group (Olson 1971), strengthening interlinks and connections to the network (Handy 1997). Finally, it is important that associates perceive the game in which they are inserted as a positive sum game in order to render collective infra-structure a viable solution. 'Opening a market in a foreign country justifies in itself the presence of my firm in the network, even if my sales to that country were smaller than those of other network participants' (Balestro 2004: 63).

Learning and innovation

Learning possibilities in networks occur in different modes. For example, they can occur through interaction and routine cooperation practices (Powell 1998), through the development of collective competences and abilities, or through processes of joint adaptation to the market requirements (Kraatz 1998). Network cooperation provides firms with new concepts, methods, styles, and manners of approaching management, problem-solving and business development. It can also help firms to change their organizational approach (Polt 2001) and to develop abilities through competence synergy inside a productive chain (Wildeman 1998).

Actually, learning, innovation, and technological advances are key elements to the new competitive landscape and are ever more dependent on the structuring of collaborative arrangements and inter-firm networks. Small-firm networks allow the development of collective innovation strategies and a fast access to new technologies through their information channels – a considerable advantage. 'By enhancing the spread of information, they create the conditions for further innovation by bringing together different logics and novel combinations of information' (Powell 1987: 81). Another important innovation gain is the reduction of the gap between conception and execution since everyone is able to innovate in a small-firm network (Perrow 1992). Finally, one must mention the outcome derived from the approximation of firms, facilitating ideas-sharing, and the elimination of prejudices such as 'Not-Invented-Here syndrome, where innovation and ideas are rejected because they are not internally created and developed' (Lorenzoni and Baden-Fuller 1995: 151). Therefore, the Learning and Innovation category is defined as the sharing of ideas and experiences among associates and the innovative actions developed by them as a group.

Cost and risk reduction

This category refers to the advantage of sharing the costs and risks of certain actions and investments that are common to the participants. As any other organization, the associates of small-firm networks have internal and external costs, including for the establishment, maintenance, and management of their interdependencies (Ebers and Grandori 1997). Although it is not possible to eliminate them at all, the formation of small-firm networks considerably reduces the incidence of costs between the associates. This is due to the fact that a firm that participates in a network 'can enjoy lower costs because it captures economies of scale (or whatever source of efficiency) from its associated firms, that other competitors cannot obtain' (Jarillo 1988: 35). Therefore, the network cooperation, as a support to the performance of joint actions, allows the reduction of several costs, such as production, transaction, information, and problem-solving (Ebers and Grandori 1997; Human and Provan 1997). Another outcome of cooperation to the associated firms is to make the sharing of risks of complex actions between all participants feasible, dividing the costs and the results of collective efforts (Ebers 1997). As a consequence, the Cost and Risk reduction is one of the main motivating elements of network cooperation (Prahalad and Ramaswamy 2004). One possible way to achieve such gains is through complementarity (Richardson 1997). It is a crucial element, since complementarity allows the creation of networks designed to handle complex situations (Miles and Snow 1986). In other words, the small-firm networks facilitate the development of relationships that promote the access to non-existent resources in the firm, as well as combine such resources with those available in the network (Kay 1998). 'Through these relationships with other parties, resources and activities are made available and can be mobilized and exploited by the organization in order to enhance its own performance' (Håkansson and Snehota 1989: 193). Since there are several difficulties to generating resources in a small firm, and even greater difficulties to acquiring them externally, the adoption of alternatives to the hierarchy and to the market becomes one of the most attractive options (Barney 1999). The complementarity of resources between the partners is considered one of the main outcomes of network cooperation (Combs and Ketchen 1999).

Social relationships

The accumulation of trust and social capital by a given group of people increases the potential of the individual and collective capacity through collaborative practices (Coleman 1990). Thus, one of the major outcomes of small-firm networks is their capacity to promote, from within, the necessary conditions for the emergence of trust and social capital. The category Social Relationships is about the deepening of relations between individuals, the increase in trust, and the evolution of group relations beyond those merely economic ones. According to Perrow (1992), the organization of firms in a network is the most indicated organizational form to generate advantageous relationships, because it propitiates the occurrence of personal contacts between the entrepreneurs and allows the honest and open discussion of problems and opportunities that involve the participants' businesses.

Another positive point of Social Relationships is related to the limitation of opportunism, since 'A selfish individual can receive the benefits of another's altruism and not pay the welfare costs of being generous in return' (Axelrod 1990: 135). In the economic literature, the different opportunistic practices are fought by means of contractual safeguards or of the bureaucratic control established by hierarchical structures (Williamson 1985). Nevertheless, the high costs and the reduced efficiency transform these bureaucratic controls into new problems. Small-firm networks are an alternative to the reduction of opportunistic actions without the bureaucratic and contractual costs. This network characteristic is promoted both by endogenous safeguards, which generate social pressures in favour of the maintenance of relations (Ring and Van de Ven 1994) and by the risk of losing collective benefits, as a consequence of sanctions or network exclusion (Lado *et al.* 1997). Therefore, the cost of an opportunistic behaviour is higher for firms associated in networks (Gulati *et al.* 2000).

The analysis of the conceptual references made so far has led to the establishment of five outcomes in small-firm networks in the southern Brazilian context, which gather the set of categories that imply cooperation gains. Therefore, the theorizations summarized in Table 5.1 intend to guide the methodological procedures of the research, especially for the variables that should be observed in the empirical field, in order to achieve the objectives of the research.

Table 5.1 Summary of outcomes in small-firm networks

Outcome categories	Definition	Variables	References
Scale and Market Power	Gains obtained due to the growth of the number of network associates. The higher the number of firms, the higher the network capacity to obtain scale and market power gains.	Bargaining power; commercial relations; representativeness; credibility; legitimacy; market force.	Dimaggio and Powell 1983; Best 1990; Waarden 1992; Lorenzoni and Baden-Fuller 1995; Human and Provan 1997; Perrow 1998; Campbell and Goold 1999; Macadar 2004; Böhe and Silva 2004.
Collective Solutions	The services, products and infrastructure made available by the network for the development of its associates.	Training; consultancies; marketing; opportunity prospects; credit guarantee.	Olson 1971; Best 1990; Rockart and Short 1991; Handy 1997; Balestro 2004.
Learning and Innovation	The sharing of ideas and experiences between the associates and the innovative actions developed as a group by the participants.	Information dissemination; collective innovations; internal and external benchmarking; increase of added value.	Powell 1987, 1998; Lorenzoni and Baden-Fuller 1995; Kraatz 1998; Wildeman 1998; Polt 2001; Balestrin and Verschoore 2008.
Cost and Risk Reduction	The advantage of sharing the costs and risks of certain actions and investments that are common to the participants.	Shared activities; collective new investments; complementarity. transactional facility; productivity.	Miles and Snow 1986; Jarillo 1988; Håkansson and Snehota 1989; Ebers 1997; Ebers and Grandori 1997; Richardson 1997; Kay 1998; Barney 1999; Pereira 2004; Prahalad and Ramaswamy 2004.
Social Relationships	The deepening of relations between individuals, the increase in trust and the evolution of group relations beyond those merely economic ones.	Limitation of opportunism; increase in trust; accumulation of social capital; family bonds; reciprocity; internal cohesion.	Williamson 1985; Axelrod 1990; Coleman 1990; Perrow 1992; Ring and Van de Ven 1994; Human and Provan 1997; Lado *et al.* 1997; Gulati *et al.* 2000; Böhe and Silva 2004.

Research methodology

Since the outcomes in small-firm networks are distinguished (Table 5.1), the verification of the importance level of each category was made possible. In this case, importance means the relevance of the outcome for the business of the small firms associated to the network. Its hierarchical order propitiates broader knowledge about the firms and entrepreneurs involved in the networks, their interpretations, preferences, and opinions regarding the network aspects that contribute the most to the competitiveness of associated firms. In this sense, the conjoint analysis technique is the most adequate statistical method to achieve the proposed objectives. By using the conjoint analysis, it is possible to identify importance levels for a certain group of categories, thus allowing their hierarchical ordering and detailed analyses about the effective impact or the real use of the implicit variables in each category. According to some authors (Hair *et al.* 1998), the conjoint analysis is the only multivariate technique in which the researcher first builds the categories through the combination of variables and then presents them to the respondents.

After distinguishing the five network outcomes, we proceeded to the design of collection stimuli, which consist of cards presenting these five categories and a different importance level attributed for each category (low or high). When building the stimuli card, we adopted non-metric input data and a full-profile approach, in which complete profiles are created based on the group of categories. Usually, each profile is described separately on a profile card. In order to demonstrate it, two examples of profile stimulus cards are showed in Figure 5.1. Since the five categories would generate a high number of profiles, we performed a fractional factorial design using the Statistical Package for the Social Sciences (SPSS), reducing them to 12 profile-stimulus cards. According to authors, the fractional factorial design is considered to be the best method for establishing a subset of the total stimulus cards that can be analysed and will still provide the information needed for making precise and reliable part-worth estimates (Hair *et al.* 1998).

The survey data were collected in 2005 through personal interviews. The survey was conducted by the authors and their assistants, who were properly trained to apply the technique. The respondent group was randomly selected, based on the database of firms belonging to the CNP. During the interview, the respondents had to organize in hierarchal order the 12 profile-stimulus

Scale and market power	HIGH
Collective solutions	HIGH
Learning and innovation	LOW
Cost and risk reduction	LOW
Social relationships	HIGH

Scale and market power	LOW
Collective solutions	HIGH
Learning and innovation	LOW
Cost and risk reduction	HIGH
Social relationships	HIGH

Figure 5.1 Examples of profile stimulus cards

cards according to their preference or opinion about the relative importance of each category regarding the others. To measure the relative importance of the five categories we used a percentage scale, in which each one might take any value from 0–100 per cent, and the sum of all the categories would come up to 100 per cent. For example, if only one category were of full importance, that one would take 100 per cent, and the four remaining would take 0 per cent. On the other hand, if all the five categories carried the same weight of importance, each one would take 20 per cent.

We reached a sample unit of 443 respondents, which was considered satisfactory for the aims of this research. The small-firm networks were classified into two segments – time of existence and number of associates – to detail the result analysis, which was the next stage of the process. The main goal of the analysis was to identify the importance level attributed to the five presented categories by the respondents. First, the results were aggregately analysed. The aggregate analysis allowed a representative general view of the population of representatives from the firms organized into networks. Next, in order to complement it, a comparative analysis between the two segmented groups was performed, showing the differences between young and mature networks, and small, medium, and large networks.

Small-firm networks in the state of Rio Grande Do Sul

Based on the information provided by the Government of Rio Grande do Sul State, the main points of the CNP are highlighted here. This programme is responsible for the creation of more than 120 small-firm networks over the past seven years. The CNP stands out as a public policy focused on the promotion of a sustained development, based on the small firms and on the performance of actions oriented to the development of cooperation and to the overcoming of barriers to the formation and evolution of networks between firms. It is worth stressing that the networks formed by the CNP are comprised of small firms that:

1. are located geographically close;
2. operate in a specific market segment;
3. are related in a non-hierarchic and cooperative manner, prevailing the mutual aims;
4. are structured based on minimum contractual instruments, which assure basic governance rules.

The CNP was conceived based on three support pillars:

1. a method of formation, consolidation and expansion of small-firm networks;
2. a regionalized supportive structure for the implementation of the proposed network model
3. a state coordination.

Each pillar plays a crucial role in the challenge of creating and sustaining firm networks. The method of network formation is the operational support to the CNP. Its development aimed at promoting the best conditions to the creation of the networks, organizing the cooperation between the firms. It systematizes the main steps needed to make firms with similar characteristics able to understand joint actions with the aim to achieve common objectives. The stages of the methodology include, among others, the exposure of the idea, the definition of a joint action plan between the firms, the execution of the actions predicted in the network operational plan, and the long-term strategic planning. The second pillar of the CNP is the use of regional acting cores supported by partnerships with different universities, which play two relevant roles: the mediation between the local specificities and the state coordination of the cooperation networks governance. Finally, the third pillar is located on the state coordination. All CNP actions are organized by a specific structure maintained by the state government. It is responsible for providing an integrated sense of public policy focused on small firms and oriented towards the construction of an endogenous regional development.

The CNP started operating in 2000, through a pilot project that had the support of a university and seven skilled consultants, who met specific demands from groups of firms that were already expressing their desire to organize themselves into small-firm networks. This pilot project allowed enhancing the method and the training and follow-up process of the consultants. Over the following months, the stage of CNP dissemination started, in which other five universities became partners, 30 consultants were hired and trained, the mass-communication instruments and firm-persuasion techniques were developed, and events specifically focused on the small firms were held.

In December 2003, seven new partnerships with universities were signed, which increased to 45 the number of technicians involved with the CNP operation. A qualitative and quantitative leap of the networks was obtained by making improvements in crucial points, such as the method of network formation and the training of the technicians who supported the firms but without changing the basic acting assumptions. From its beginning in 2000 until 2007, 120 cooperation networks were formed, with the participation of more than 3,000 firms, generating and maintaining 30,000 jobs and representing a joint turnover of approximately US$2 billion. The CNP is therefore established as a unique supportive initiative to the economic development based on small firms and has been acknowledged by national awards.

Analysis of outcomes in small-firm networks

The analysis presented below comprehends the results of a conjoint analysis applied to representatives from the firms participating in the CNP.

Initially, it can be said that the research model adopted and the data collection were successful. No respondents had to be excluded from the statistical process, and there was no reversion in the importance ordering of the cards. Furthermore, according to the statistical processing, the significance of 0.0000 and the Pearson coefficient of 0.969 reduce the chance of sample errors and indicate a strong association between the variables. A brief appraisal of the results of the data-processing related to the outcome categories for the firms associated to the networks, according to the perception of the firm representatives, reinforces the importance of all outcomes categories defined by the researchers. The results of the statistical processing are presented in Figure 5.2.

The analysis of Graph 5.1 indicates a similar relevance between all outcomes categories listed by the researchers, since the difference between the less and more important categories does not reach ten percentage points.

Nonetheless, it is possible to identify in the perception of representatives from the firms participating in the small-firm networks a highlight to the outcome category Collective Solutions, which is composed of elements such as support infrastructure, courses and training, consultancies, and information technology. This high importance level, which reaches 26.29 per cent, shows a particular concern as to the availability of services that would hardly be accessed by the respondents' firms in an isolated manner. From a different analysis, the percentage obtained by Collective Solutions reveals the fact that the firms participating in networks tend to prefer short-term outcomes that may solve specific issues and difficulties or that may improve

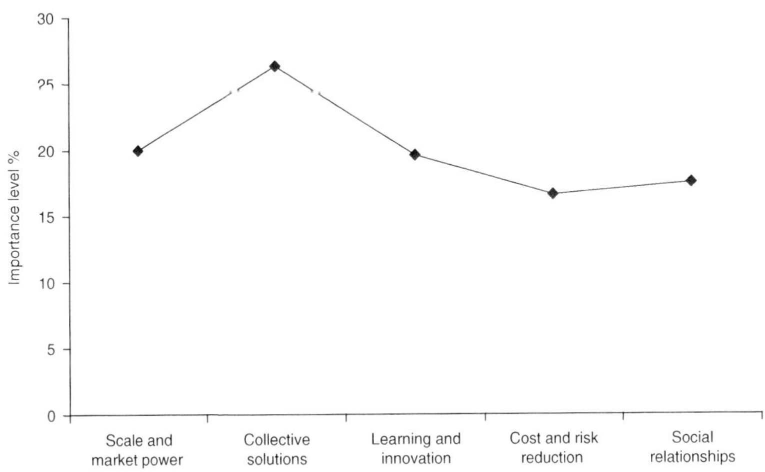

Figure 5.2 Result of the conjoint analysis of outcome categories in small-firm networks

the performance and competitiveness of the associates through instruments and services collectively generated.

The Scale and Market Power and Learning and Innovation categories are in an intermediate preference in relation to the other outcome categories. In the first case, the possibility that the firms have to obtain advantages from the scale in the relationship with suppliers and customers and conquer more credibility in their business environment is an outcome stressed by the respondents, reaching the percentage of 19.99 per cent. This high importance level reinforces the common sense that one of the major advantages of any type of union is the possibility to join forces and collectively to become something larger. From the organizational point of view, this force is translated into better negotiations, actions with a wide impact in the consuming markets, more institutional respectability and credibility. The importance granted by the representatives of the firms shows that, through a network, small firms are able to increase their Scale and Market power, thus becoming more competitive.

What is most striking is the relevance given to the outcome category Learning and Innovation by the representatives of the firms. Considering the fact that actions such as information-sharing and innovative practices, aiming to generate and spread improvements, are essential to the development of competitive differentials, the importance percentage of 19.60 per cent indicates the clear inclination of network participants towards this direction. Moreover, it represents another empirical confirmation of the theoretical postulates about the capacity of small-firm networks to promote a favourable environment for organizational learning and innovations. However, it is worth highlighting that the representatives of the firms indicated their constitutive elements as advantages as important as the routinely mentioned Scale and Market Power.

At a lower level was the category Social Relationships, with an importance of 17.51 per cent according to the sample unit. This value shows that aspects such as friendships, trust, and the formation of a social group are valued and perceived as outcomes with a high importance level by the representatives of the firms participating in networks. There are two possible considerations to be made as a consequence of such fact. First, it can be seen that, despite the firm organization presenting a priority focus on economic advantages and tangible outcomes, those involved value the small-firm networks as a source of personal relationships and intangible and non-economic outcomes. Second, the understanding of the representatives of the firms is directly associated with the reality experienced in their networks, which corroborates the idea that the participation in small-firm networks makes their associates able to develop permanent social relations and, as a consequence, to accumulate social capital, generate a community feeling, and create strong trust relationships between the members.

Finally, the category Cost and Risk Reduction stands out as the relatively less important outcome category. The 16.61-per-cent level attributed to it by the group of respondents shows the capacity of small-firm networks to reduce costs and risks for their associates. That is why aspects related to the increase in profitability of the firms through joint solutions were highlighted as outcomes that small-firm networks should not stop pursuing. Nevertheless, the lowest percentage of importance obtained by this category shows that the effective reduction of costs and risks through complementary actions is not so easy to be perceived and performed in networks formed by firms that belong to the same segment. It may also be explained due to the fact that, from the perception of the representatives of the firms, there are feasible ways to reduce costs and risks in an isolated manner, independently of the participation in a network. A consequence of this fact is the unequal comparison with the other outcome categories, which are hardly obtained without the participation in small-firm networks.

Aiming to perform a more detailed analysis of the categories that affect the management of small-firm networks, the sample unit was divided into two characteristic segments: time of existence and number of associates of the network. The segmentation allowed us to understand the differences in perception between networks with distinct characteristics. With regard to the time of existence, most respondents are part of small-firm networks with less than a year of existence (88.2 per cent). Out of the total, one respondent was classified in the scale between one and two years, and another one did not provide an answer. They were both excluded from the analysis, as can be seen in Table 5.2.

The following segmentation proved to be more disperse. Among the 442 respondents considered in the analysis, 49.8 per cent participate in networks with up to 16 associates and 43.4 per cent belong to networks with 16 to 30 associates. Since 23 firms are part of the networks from 31 to 100 members and seven respondents are members of networks with more than 101 associates, they were both grouped in the scale called 'more than 30 associates' (Table 5.3).

Table 5.2 Segmentation according to time of existence of the network

Segmentation	Frequency	Percentage	Valid percentage	Cumulative percentage
Valid				
1. Less than 1 year	389	60.2	88.2	88.2
3. More than 2 years	52	08.0	11.8	100.0
Total	**441**	**68.3**	**100.0**	
Missing				
2. Between 1 and 2 years	1	00.2		

Table 5.3 Segmentation according to the number of network associates

Segmentation	Frequency	Percentage	Valid percentage	Cumulative percentage
Valid				
1. Fewer than 16 associates	220	34.1	49.8	49.8
2. 16–30 associates	192	29.7	43.4	93.2
3. More than 30 associates	30	04.6	6.8	100.0
Total	**442**	**68.4**	**100.0**	

Table 5.4 Importance level of outcome categories and number of associates

Outcome category	Number of associates	Number of respondents	Mean importance
Scale and Market Power	Fewer than 16	220	21.8482
	16–30	192	18.5145
	More than 30	30	15.7177
	Total	442	19.9840
Collective Solutions	Fewer than 16	220	23.5339
	16–30	192	27.5848
	More than 30	30	38.4170
	Total	442	26.3038
Learning and Innovation	Fewer than 16	220	19.8625
	16–30	192	20.0730
	More than 30	30	14.9707
	Total	442	19.6219
Cost and Risk Reduction	Fewer than 16	220	17.8827
	16–30	192	15.5064
	More than 30	30	14.1053
	Total	442	16.5941
Social Relationships	Fewer than 16	220	16.8727
	16–30	192	18.3205
	More than 30	30	16.7870
	Total	442	17.4958

According to Table 5.4, the respondents' perception with regard to the outcome categories presents significant differences. It can be seen that the networks with fewer than 16 associates value the category Scale and Market Power more than the networks with a larger number of associates. This value is a consequence of the incapacity to obtain the scale gains due to the reduced size of the network and to the perception that the firms belonging to larger networks end up by effectively receiving the gains of the larger scale and market power. On the other extreme, the networks with more than 30 associates value the category of Learning and Innovation less than the smaller networks. Such differences indicate that the networks with more associates may present difficulties to join innovation efforts or even to generate a proper environment to learning when compared to middle-sized networks, since the highest relative importance of the outcome was perceived by the networks with 16 to 30 associates.

However, the most significant divergences are found in the category Collective Solutions. All three classifications of number of associates consider this a relevant outcome but the importance level changes according to the size of the network. Therefore, the small networks, which have fewer than 16 associates and still cannot offer them many solutions, present an average of 23.53 per cent. Middle-sized networks, from 16 to 30 associates, offer more solutions and an average of 27.58 per cent. Large networks, with more than 30 associates, are able to offer better solutions, reaching the highest average of the outcome, that is, 38.42 per cent. This direct relation between the size of the network and the importance attributed to Collective Solutions, along with the Scale and Market Power, shows that a considerable part of the outcomes obtainable through small-firm networks depends on the continuous growth of the number of network members.

Following the analysis about the respondents' view, it is essential to identify the peculiarities according to the time of existence of the network. Table 5.5 shows the convergence of the view between the two groups of respondents. In general, both the firms belonging to younger networks and

Table 5.5 Importance level of outcome categories and time of existence

Outcome category	Number of associates	Number of respondents	Mean importance
Scale and Market Power	Less than 1 year	389	19.5952
	More than 2 years	52	22.6360
	Total	441	19.9537
Collective Solutions	Less than 1 year	389	26.2321
	More than 2 years	52	26.0633
	Total	441	26.2122
Learning and Innovation	Less than 1 year	389	19.3204
	More than 2 years	52	22.2546
	Total	441	19.6664
Cost and Risk Reduction	Less than 1 year	389	17.4283
	More than 2 years	52	10.6725
	Total	441	16.6317
Social Relations	Less than 1 year	389	17.4236
	More than 2 years	52	18.3723
	Total	441	17.5355

the firms belonging to more mature networks verify a similar intensity in their competitive gains.

Despite this general similarity, small differences can be seen in the outcome categories Social Relationships, Scale and Market Power, and Learning and Innovation, whose relevance are more intensely perceived by the representatives of networks that have been active for longer than the representatives of networks with less than one year of existence. The greatest divergence, therefore, lies in the Cost and Risk Reduction outcome category, which has a higher degree of importance, from the respondents belonging to younger networks, when compared to the representatives of networks with more than two years of existence.

Such difference indicates that, as the network evolves, the outcomes related to the simple cost-reduction in the firms are being replaced by the Scale and Market Power and Learning and Innovation. These data indicate that the outcome categories of the firms become more complex as the network grows more mature.

Research implications

The predominant logic in small-firm networks is based on the fact that the cooperation relations result in gains for all parts involved; otherwise, none of them would cooperate. Therefore, the outcomes that may be reached by the networks shift from the traditional, essentially individualistic focus to a conception of collective results, influencing the actions and decisions made as a group. The engineered networks analysed in this paper have shown to be an alternative way to small firms, since cooperation between the associated firms have made possible the diffusion of experiences, knowledge, management practices, and also technologies. The same results might not be found while studying other types of networks. In this sense, the identification and hierarchal order of the network-outcome categories may drive researchers of the phenomenon towards a model for the management of such networks.

With regard to the results of this research, the possibility to increase the action power of a firm through the union with other firms is the most-cited outcome category by entrepreneurs when the issue is small-firm networks. Scale and Market Power, which have been stressed by the works of Lorenzoni and Baden-Fuller (1995), Human and Provan (1997), and Perrow (1998), were confirmed by this research as a desired and performed outcome category by the small-firm networks. In the aggregate analysis of the representatives of firms associated to networks, their percentages of importance stood out. Results show that the gains derived from that are widely perceptible, independently of the size or number of associates of the network. Concomitantly, Collective Solutions stands out as the most important category for network associates. The high percentage of this category indicates that the entrepreneurs perceive the network as a means to minimize their individual difficulties and at the same time reduce the difficulties of their network partners. The studies by Best (1990) and Waarden (1992) show that, in several cooperation initiatives, the Collective Solutions offered to the associates, in itself, is already a strong motivation to build the network.

One of the most significant findings of this research was the expressive relevance attached to the category Learning and Innovation by the representatives of the firms. The results showed that, in small-firm networks, the favourable environment to the organizational learning and the generation of innovations allow important outcomes that they are practically equal in preference to the Scale and Market Power, which were often identified. The empirical data thus corroborated the coherence of theoretical postulates by several authors, among them Powell (1998), Gulati (1998), Schibany and Polt (2001), and Hämäläinen and Schienstock (2001).

The possibility of reducing costs and risks through small-firm networks has been widely documented by the publications dealing with the issue (Jarillo 1988; Ebers and Grandori 1997; Prahalad and Ramaswamy 2004). This research contributed to the discussions on this topic, by demonstrating, based on the quantitative analyses, the importance of the category Cost and Risk Reduction for those involved in networks created through the CNP.

Although presenting lower levels of importance when compared to other outcomes, Cost and Risk Reduction is chased by network firms. The outcome Social Relationships was included in the list of categories studied as a consequence of the several theoretical works that show the impact of aspects such as trust and social capital in the socio-economic and organizational development (Gambetta 1988; Coleman 1990; Putnam 1993). The research demonstrated the capacity networks have to generate the necessary conditions to strengthen the relationship bonds between their participants, confirming the theoretical postulates by authors such as Perrow (1992), Human and Provan (1997), and Gulati *et al.* (2000).

The evidence related to the five outcome categories of the firms belonging to small-firm networks allow the understanding of the phenomenon based on two determining characteristics in any small-firm network: time of existence and number of associates of the network. According to the segmented analysis, it can be said that the outcome importance in small-firm networks is related to their age and size. The networks that have not been totally established, with few years of existence, have the priority to seek Cost and Risk Reduction and offer solutions to their associates. Some outcomes, such as scale and market power, and learning and innovation, are pursued by mature networks. Taking into account Collective Solutions, since the quantity and, more importantly, the quality of the solutions promoted by the network depends on the growth in the number of participants. The category

Social Relationships is much more important for the small and middle-sized networks than for the large ones.

Concluding remarks

The theoretical postulates and the empirical evidence presented in this research aim to contribute to the growing debates about the phenomenon of small-firm networks. The results of the research may even be considered a starting point for further investigations. With regard to the administrative practices, the article stressed the creation and growth of the small-firm network phenomenon in the Brazilian context. In relation to the public policies, the results showed that the promotion of cooperation through small-firm networks is a feasible way towards the development of local economies. With respect to small firm management, the research results indicate that the network cooperation may be an alternative to be considered in order to find and sustain competitive differentials.

Particularly with regard to the organizational theories, the results of this research allowed a better understanding of the categories that have a minor or major influence on competitiveness of firms organized into small-firm networks. The results obtained from the collected and statistically processed data pointed to a similar importance among the five outcome categories identified in the following order:

1. Access to Solutions;
2. Scale and Market Power;
3. Learning and Innovation;
4. Social Relationships;
5. Cost and Risk Reduction.

The sample segmentation made us advance in the understanding of the outcomes according to age and size of a given network.

Even if the results of this article present some limitations, especially because they are restricted to the context of small-firm networks developed in the state of Rio Grande do Sul, its empirical evidence suggests that networks can strengthen the firms in terms of competitive gains. Nevertheless, in order to have a solid confirmation of such evidence, the authors are deepening their researches, both in the Brazilian and in the international context, with the aim to complement the discussions and theorizations about the phenomenon of small-firm networks. Finally, it should be highlighted that the small-firm networks are awakening a growing interest in scholars, entrepreneurs, and politicians, particularly due to the possibility of sustaining the development and competitiveness of firms and regions. In this sense, there is a wide range of needs and research opportunities for the academic community.

References

R. Axelrod, *The Evolution of Cooperation* (London: Penguin Books, 1990).

A. Balestrin and J. R. Verschoore, *Redes de Cooperação Empresarial: Estratégias de Gestão na Nova Economia* (Porto Alegre: Bookman, 2008).

M. V. Balestro, 'Características Estruturais e Mecanismos de Governança em Redes de Cooperação: Apontamentos Conceituais', in J. R. Verschoore (ed.), *Redes de Cooperação: Uma Nova Organização de Pequenas e Médias Empresas no Rio Grande do Sul* (Porto Alegre: FEE, 2004).

J. B. Barney, 'How a Firm's Capabilities Affect Boundary Decisions', *Sloan Management Review,* 40 (3) (1999): 137–45.

M. H. Best, *The New Competition: Institutions of Industrial Restructuring* (Cambridge: Polity Press, 1990).

D. M. Böhe and K. M. Silva, 'O Dilema de Crescimento em Redes de Cooperação: O Caso da Panimel', in J. R. Verschoore (ed.), *Redes de Cooperação: Uma Nova Organização de Pequenas e Médias Empresas no Rio Grande do Sul* (Porto Alegre: FEE, 2004).

J. Brüderl and P. Preisendörfer, 'Network Support and the Success of Newly Founded Businesses', *Small Business Economics,* 10 (3) (1998): 213–25.

A. Campbell and M. Goold, *The Collaborative Enterprise: Why Links Across the Corporation Often Fail and How to Make Them Work* (Reading, MA: Perseus Books, 1999).

M. Castells, *The Rise of the Network Society* (Oxford: Blackwell, 1996).

J. S. Coleman, *Foundations of Social Theory* (Cambridge, MA: Harvard University Press, 1990).

J. G. Combs and D. J. Ketchen, 'Explaining Interfirm Cooperation and Performance: Toward a Reconciliation of Predictions from the Resource-based View and Organizational Economics', *Strategic Management Journal,* 20 (9) (1999): 867–88.

P. J. Dimaggio and W. W. Powell, 'The Iron Cage Revisited: Institutional Isomorphism and Collective Rationality in Organizational Fields', *American Sociological Review,* 48 (2) (1983): 147–60.

M. Ebers and A. Grandori, 'The Form, Costs and Development Dynamics of Inter-Organizational Networking', in M. Ebers (ed.), *The Formation of Inter-Organizational Networks* (Oxford: Oxford University Press, 1997).

M. Ebers, 'Explaining Inter-Organizational Network Formation', in M. Ebers (ed.), *The Formation of Inter-Organizational Networks* (Oxford: Oxford University Press, 1997).

D. Gambetta, 'Can We Trust Trust?', in D. Gambetta (ed.), *Trust: Making and Breaking Cooperative Relations* (Oxford: Basil Blackwell, 1988).

R. Gulati, 'Alliances and Networks', *Strategic Management Journal,* 19 (4) (1998): 293–317.

R. Gulati, N. Nohria, and A. Zaheer, 'Strategic Networks', *Strategic Management Journal,* 21 (3) (2000): 203–15.

J. F. Hair, R. E. Anderson, R. L. Tatham, and W. C. Black, *Multivariate Data Analysis* (Upper Saddle River, NJ: Prentice Hall, 1998).

H. Håkansson and I. Snehota, 'No Business Is an Island: The Network Concept of Business Strategy', *Scandinavian Journal of Management,* 5 (3) (1989): 256–70.

T. J. Hämäläinen and G. Schienstock, 'The Comparative Advantage of Networks in Economic Organisation: Efficiency and Innovation in Highly Specialised and Uncertain Environments', in Organisation for Economic Co-operation and

Development (ed.), *Innovative Networks: Co-operation in National Innovation Systems* (Paris: OECD Publishing, 2001).

C. Handy, 'The Virtual Organization', in D. S. Pugh (ed.), *Organization Theory: Selected Readings* (London: Penguin Books, 1997).

R. Huggins, 'The Success and Failure of Policy-Implanted Inter-Firm Network Initiatives: Motivations, Processes and Structure', *Entrepreneurship & Regional Development,* 12 (2) (2000): 111–35.

S. E. Human and K. G. Provan, 'An Emergent Theory of Structure and Outcomes in Small-Firm Strategic Manufacturing Network', *Academy of Management Journal,* 40 (2) (1997): 368–403.

J. C. Jarillo, 'On Strategic Networks', *Strategic Management Journal,* 9 (1) (1988): 31–41.

N. M. Kay, 'The Evolution of Collaborative Activity in the Firm', in M. G. Colombo (ed.), *The Changing Boundaries of the Firm: Explaining Evolving Inter-firm Relations* (London: Routledge, 1998).

M. S. Kraatz, 'Learning by Association? Interorganizational Networks and Adaptation to Environmental Change', *Academy of Management Journal,* 41 (6) (1998): 621–43.

K. Kreiner and M. Schultz, 'Informal Collaboration in R&D: The Formation of Networks across Organizations', *Organization Studies,* 14 (2) (1993): 189–209.

A. Lado, N. Boyd, and S. C. Hanlon, 'Competition, Cooperation, and the Search for Economic Rents: A Syncretic Model', *Academy of Management Review,* 22 (1) (1997): 110–41.

G. Lorenzoni and C. Baden-Fuller, 'Creating a Strategic Center to Manage a Web of Partners', *California Management Review,* 37 (3) (1995): 146–62.

B. M. Macadar, 'A Experiência Exportadora da Associação dos Fabricantes de Estofados e Móveis Complementares', in J. R. Verschoore (ed.), *Redes de Cooperação: Uma Nova Organização de Pequenas e Médias Empresas no Rio Grande do Sul* (Porto Alegre: FEE, 2004).

R. E. Miles and C. C. Snow, 'Organizations: New Concepts for New Forms', *California Management Review,* 28 (3) (1986): 62–73.

N. Nohria, 'Is a Network Perspective a Useful Way of Studying Organizations?', in N. Nohria and R. G. Eccles (eds), *Networks and Organizations: Structure, Form, and Action* (Cambridge, MA: Harvard University Press, 1992).

A. L. Oliver and M. Ebers, 'Networking Network Studies: An Analysis of Conceptual Configurations in the Study of Inter-organizational Relationships', *Organization Studies,* 19 (4) (1998): 549–83.

M. Olson, *The Logic of Collective Action: Public Goods and the Theory of Groups* (Cambridge, MA: Harvard University Press, 1971).

R. F. Pereira, 'Marketing em Redes de Cooperação: um Estudo de Caso na Redemac', in J. R. Verschoore (ed.), *Redes de Cooperação: Uma Nova Organização de Pequenas e Médias Empresas no Rio Grande do Sul* (Porto Alegre: FEE, 2004).

C. Perrow, 'Small-Firm Networks', in N. Nohria and R. G. Eccles (eds), *Networks and Organizations: Structure, Form, and Action* (Cambridge, MA: Harvard University Press, 1992).

C. Perrow, *Complex Organizations: A Critical Essay* (New York: McGraw-Hill, 1998).

W. Polt, 'The Role of Governments in Networking', in Organisation for Economic Co-operation and Development (ed.), *Innovative Networks: Co-operation in National Innovation Systems* (Paris: OECD Publishing, 2001).

W. W. Powell, 'Hybrid Organizational Arrangements: New Forms or Transitional Development?', *California Management Review,* 19 (4) (1987): 67–87.

W. W. Powell, 'Learning from Collaboration: Knowledge and Networks in the Biotechnology and Pharmaceutical Industries', *California Management Review,* 40 (3) (1998): 228–40.

C. K. Prahalad and V. Ramaswamy, *The Future of Competition: Co-Creating Unique Value with Customers* (Cambridge, MA: Harvard Business School Press, 2004).

K. G. Provan, A. Fish, and J. Sydow, 'Interorganizational Networks at the Network Level: A Review of the Empirical Literature on Whole Networks', *Journal of Management,* 33 (3) (2007): 479–516.

R. D. Putnam, *Making Democracy Work: Civic Traditions in Modern Italy* (Princeton, NJ: Princeton University Press, 1993).

G. B. Richardson, 'The Organisation of Industry', in N. Foss (ed.), *Resources, Firms and Strategies* (Oxford: Oxford University Press, 1997).

P. S. Ring and A. H. Van de Ven, 'Developmental Processes of Cooperative Interorganizational Relationships', *Academy of Management Review,* 19 (1) (1994): 90–118.

J. F. Rockart and J. E. Short, 'The Networked Organization and the Management of Interdependence', in M. S. Morton (ed.), *The Corporation of the 1990s: Information Technology and Organizational Transformation* (Oxford: Oxford University Press, 1991).

A. Schibany and W. Polt, 'Innovation and Networks: An Introduction to the Theme', in Organisation for Economic Co-operation and Development (ed.), *Innovative Networks: Co-operation in National Innovation Systems* (Paris: OECD Publishing, 2001).

G. F. Thompson, *Between Hierarchies and Markets: The Logics and Limits of Network Forms of Organization* (Oxford: Oxford University Press, 2003).

H. B. Thorelli, 'Networks: Between Markets and Hierarchies', *Strategic Management Journal,* 7 (1) (1986): 37–51.

F. Waarden, 'Emergence and Development of Business Interest Associations: An Example from The Netherlands', *Organization Studies,* 13 (4) (1992): 521–62.

L. Wildeman, 'Alliances and Networks: The Next Generation', *International Journal of Technology Management,* 14 (1–2) (1998): 96–108.

O. E. Williamson, *The Economic Institutions of Capitalism* (New York: The Free Press, 1985).

6

Email as a Communication Strategy in a Regional Strategic Network

Edith Andresen, Anette Bergman and Lars Hallén

Introduction

Regional strategic network initiatives

Firms cooperating in various arrangements with other private and public sector actors, for example, other business firms, organizations, state agencies, or universities, are generally believed to reap benefits from such cooperation. Regional strategic networks (RSNs) financed from public or private sources serve as tools to support regional development by promoting such cooperation. They are intended to strengthen the competitive advantage of participating firms and organizations and thereby the region in which they operate. With this in mind, efforts have been made to create relationships between firms in order to obtain synergy to support innovation, new businesses, and job opportunities. As defined by Jarillo (1988), strategic networks are purposefully designed cooperation ventures, mainly between small and medium-sized enterprises (SMEs), a definition that also describes RSNs. Strategic networks are considered to embody opportunities for member companies to coordinate resources, reduce uncertainty, increase capacity, and obtain greater flexibility (Child and Faulkner 1998).

RSNs are created as distinct entities with a formalized structure. They are not hierarchical organizations, as their members remain independent autonomous entities with the ability to exit at any time (Lundberg 2008). Still, RSN boundaries are clearly defined, for example, by a membership list. Although some RSNs are set up as legally incorporated entities, for example, member-owned companies with overall responsibility for the results, most are more loosely organized as voluntary associations.

RSN establishment is stimulated by the allocation of targeted financial resources, which may derive from EU regional development funds, financial means made available by national, regional, or local governments, private funds, or any combination of these sources. These funds are normally made available for a specified project period, and the activities are expected to produce effects persisting beyond this time (Lundberg 2008).

The facilitator or centre in charge of governing RSN operations is often called a hub. It may consist of several people working with the RSN, often part-time together with other local administration or private-sector assignments. The hub may also include a company or group of companies, a public agency, or another organization. The hub's tasks include designing the RSN, working to fulfil its aims, and taking responsibility for the use of resources provided by external actors or collected through membership fees. As leader, rule setter, and capability builder, the hub is expected to contribute to structuring, strategizing, and value-creation processes (Lorenzoni and Baden-Fuller 1995).

Managing regional development processes is a complex task, as the involved units are independent, formal authority is missing, actor commitment is uncertain, and expectations, goals, and demands are varied and incoherent (Christensen and Kempinsky 2003). This is reflected in the requirements placed on RSN management.

The limited lifespan of RSNs implies that they can be characterized as projects or temporary organizations with specific aims to be achieved within a predetermined time. This enhances the role of the hub as the project leader and of the activities chosen by the hub. In the case study comprising the empirical basis of the present paper, an email-based communication strategy supported by a web portal was used by the hub as its central tool to achieve the RSN's aims. When the RSN was set up, email communication was already widely used in parts of society, but only marginally in SMEs like those which were the members of the studied RSN.

Purpose

The purpose of this chapter is to describe and analyse the development of email communication over time in an RSN with an explicit communication strategy in which email is designated the preferred means of communication. To achieve this, a model is developed that specifies descriptive dimensions of the communication pattern together with factors that affect this development.

The empirical basis comprises the incoming and outgoing emails of the RSN hub manager. Three samples were drawn from the dataset, which comprised the 1999–2001 period when the RSN was active. Each sample consists of one month's email communication and was selected to represent each of the three identified RSN development phases.

This chapter opens by reviewing, first, the development phases of temporary organizations and, second, the use of communication media with a focus on email. Previous studies of the appropriateness of various communication media are presented and used as inspiration for a communication pattern model. After a section on methodology, the findings are presented, followed by concluding remarks summarizing the findings and suggesting theoretical and practical implications.

Conceptual background

Temporary organizations and projects

RSNs as temporary organizations

As RSNs are often financed by project-related grants and are expected to fulfil their aims within a predetermined time frame, they can be seen as temporary organizations sharing the characteristics of ongoing projects (Lundberg 2008). There are similarities between the development phases of RSNs and phases describing the development of projects and temporary organizations.

Projects are often considered to pass through four phases: goal-setting, planning, implementation, and evaluation. Critics have argued that the assumed temporal linearity, strict phase delimitation, and clear set of assignments in each phase do not comply with the fundamental operational uncertainty of projects (Christensen and Kreiner 1997: 31–2; Maaninen-Olsson 2007: 17). A different perspective that takes this uncertainty into account can be arrived at by also considering the role of action. In temporary organizations, specialized actions are performed to achieve goals (Lundin and Söderholm 1995: 437–8). This implies a focus on *why* and *how* actions are performed, unlike the traditional project perspective centred on *what* is done (Maaninen-Olsson 2007).

When analysing action in temporary organizations, Lundin and Söderholm (1995: 440) identify time as a key aspect. Time is regarded as a sequence divided into phases, which differ with regard to the kind of action needed. These phases are identified as action-based entrepreneurship, fragmentation for commitment building, planned isolation, and institutionalized termination.

The phase structure according to the traditional project perspective and the action-based perspective of temporary organizations is summarized in Table 6.1.

Table 6.1 The phases of projects and temporary organizations

Time sequence	Projects	Temporary organizations
Initiation	Goal-setting	Action-based entrepreneurship
	Planning	Fragmentation for commitment building
	Implementing	Planned isolation
Conclusion	Evaluation	Institutionalized termination

Source: Adapted from Maaninen-Olsson (2007) and Lundin and Söderholm (1995).

RSN development can also be seen as passing through phases. After an initial design phase there is an operational phase, after which the RSN either is terminated or passes into a long-term stage called the transitional phase. RSN phases can be related to those of projects and temporary organizations by treating the first two phases of projects or temporary organizations as equivalent to the RSN design phase, after which the third and fourth phases correspond to phases 2 and 3 of RSNs, as detailed below.

Goal-setting and action-based entrepreneurship: the design phase of RSNs

Goal-setting is seen as the first phase of projects. In this phase, the project leader – often together with project team members or financiers – decides what is to be accomplished in terms of project-related goals. The focus of this phase is on goal fulfilment using available resources and on motivating project participants, for example, by communicating a vision that mobilizes commitment, resources, and passion (Christensen and Kreiner 1997). Goal-setting and communication that aim to create legitimacy for the operation are important activities in this phase (Maaninen-Olsson 2007).

According to the terminology of temporary organizations, action-based entrepreneurship, that is, the first phase, is characterized by an entrepreneur who initiates and provides the impetus for creating the temporary organization (Lundin and Söderholm 1995: 445). This phase may be based on experience from previous projects.

As a purpose of RSNs is to support regional development by fostering cooperative relationships between the RSN members, the development stages of RSNs can be characterized in terms of internal integration. In the first RSN phase, the design phase, integration is low. Increased integration depends on entrepreneurial action as specified in the terminology of temporary organizations. The task of the hub, which often acts as the initiator, is to start-up and design the operations and to motivate participation by identifying opportunities, approaching financiers, determining goals, and choosing a strategy to facilitate cooperation and communication. The RSN name and concept is disseminated to attract the interest of potential members and financiers.

Planning and fragmentation for commitment building: continuation of the RSN design phase

In traditional project terminology, planning is the second phase in which the focus is on how to act to achieve the goals. This phase includes the planning and development of relevant strategies. Plans serve an important symbolic function in the project development process, as does communication that facilitates interaction (Christensen and Kreiner 1997). However, fixed goals and plans may prevent learning when adaptation is required to changes in the environment.

In the terminology of Lundin and Söderholm (1995), the second phase of temporary organizations is fragmentation for commitment building. In this phase, the project is detached from other projects, and decisions are made as to what assignments should be fulfilled, how this should be done, and who should be in charge and involved. The start-up and closing stages are also defined in this phase (Lundin and Söderholm 1995; Maaninen-Olsson 2007).

The first two phases as defined in the terminology of projects and temporary organizations often coincide in time in the case of RSNs and are managed simultaneously by the hub. The RSN design phase covers both goals and activity planning. In RSNs, as in projects, communication is central. Activities such as deciding when to start the RSN, defining the purpose and overarching goals, identifying and determining the composition of potential actors, and formulating possible performance-related strategies (which are included in the phase fragmentation for commitment building) are all important elements of the design phase.

Implementation and planned isolation: the RSN operational phase

Performance is in focus in the implementation phase of projects. In projects, this phase concerns exploring project-related opportunities, which requires proactive management (Christensen and Kreiner 1997). In temporary organizations, this phase is termed 'planned isolation'. Isolation, which refers to the balance between openness and closedness (Lundin and Söderholm 1995), may be needed for independent acting. Modes of action to be followed by the project group must be created and communicated. If performance could be disturbed by external involvement, action may have to be taken against this. However, the lack of interaction or involvement with other actors could lead to an unrealistic view of the project in the minds of participants, thus hampering development and learning (Maaninen-Olsson 2007).

The implementation and planned isolation phases can be seen to correspond to the operational phase of RSNs, in which network activities are performed jointly with members. In projects, interaction with outsiders may be kept low to achieve results, but in RSNs, expanded interaction and communication could instead be the task in this phase. RSN integration increases as members become acquainted both professionally and socially. Supporting the development of relationships between the members becomes an important task of the hub.

Evaluation and institutionalized termination: the RSN transitional phase

A project often concludes with an evaluation in which goal fulfilment and the process of doing so are measured and discussed. Evaluation and assessment of project results, processes, and applicability to other contexts are the focus (Christensen and Kreiner 1997). The institutionalized termination phase of temporary organizations concerns both the wrapping-up of the project and its 'recoupling' to an organizational context. Recoupling may take place when the parts of the project are terminated and is done through bridging activities. These activities aim to integrate project-related knowledge in its organizational context (Maaninen-Olsson 2007).

Application of the term 'transitional phase' to RSNs instead of 'institutionalized termination' stresses the recoupling aspect. Central to RSN project completion is the continued use of project-related knowledge and adaptation to the surrounding business network, as RSN relationship-building processes are expected to continue. The transitional phase differs from institutional termination as it encompasses a more extended time perspective. In the transitional phase, operational financing comes to an end, but the RSN's goals normally indicate that the relationships established should not be dissolved but either continue without organizational support or are included in another organizational form in which the RSN hub function gradually fades out.

Not all RSNs pass through all three phases. In some cases, the RSN may become stuck in the first phase. In other cases, the members may already have established relationships before the start of the RSN, which consequently moves directly into the operational phase. The hub's task may thus vary between RSNs. A common feature, however, is that RSNs share many characteristics of projects and temporary organizations. The predetermined lifespan affects the efforts devoted to the RSN, as does the fact that the RSN project is just one of many projects competing for the attention of RSN members. The possibilities of isolation against external involvement are small and may be seen to contradict RSN goals.

Communication in RSNs

Communication strategies

Establishing a communication strategy is often a challenge for the RSN hub. Such a communication strategy may be either informal or formally codified in a written statement, where preferences regarding communication media is an important aspect. The introduction of email as a medium for business-related communication has changed communication routines, and many RSNs, especially big ones with geographically dispersed member companies, have turned to electronic communication media such as email. The informal character of email allows easy and unpretentious communication (Wiesenfeld *et al.* 1999), well suited to the modes of action in many RSNs. Email as a tool for intra-organizational coordination is believed to increase personal and organizational productivity (Markus 1994), but as this may occur at the expense of face-to-face meetings or personal phone calls, it could have other effects on the interaction between companies and relationship development (Monge and Eisenberg 1987).

How communication media are used is not only a matter of communication technology but also of the social definition of the media (Yates *et al.* 1999). The hub is the focal communicator in RSNs, so its communication behaviour may influence the communication of others and RSN performance. User familiarity with the communication medium influences the quality and frequency of task-related communicative interaction (Papa and Papa 1992); familiarity also influences the willingness to adopt email (Bengtsson *et al.* 2007). Insights into actual communicative interaction are important, as information about the communicative workflow and norms of accepted and desired communicative interaction are needed for the design of a communication strategy (De Moor and Weigand 2005).

Email as a communication medium

Email is a medium described as 'using computer text-processing and communication tools to provide a high-speed information exchange service' (Sproull and Kiesler 1986). It is an effective system for quickly and simultaneously involving numerous recipients (multiple addressability), in different time zones, in complex interaction performed any time around the clock. The transmission speed of email may be regarded as instantaneous, but the response time depends on recipient behaviour. Email is not always considered the most convenient medium, as it implies typing out messages, which can be time-consuming and awkward. The advantage, however, is that these messages can be saved and retrieved for later reference.

Like regular mail, email is a written and asynchronous communication medium. However, it is faster than paper-based written communication, which brings it closer to synchronous media. Features such as computer-searchable memory and multiple addressability provide email with capabilities not found in traditional media. In this respect, email rivals and exceeds traditional communication media such as the telephone, which, however, has advantages in transmitting social cues.

In a stream of research called information-richness theory (Daft *et al.* 1987), in which achieving a match between the potential of various communication channels and the information-processing requirements is seen as essential for organizational success, email is perceived as a 'lean medium'. It is seen as 'lean' as it does not support the communication richness associated with, for example, face-to-face meetings, because email filters out important cues such as body language and tone of voice and lacks the capacity for direct feedback. There are studies demonstrating that people take longer to form impressions of one another when conversing electronically, because it is time-consuming to decode social cues in such communication (Sproull and Kiesler 1986). Ideas and impressions of others and the amount and character of relational communication are hence influenced by electronic communication (Walther 1995). It has been claimed that the use of email entails consequences such as less trust, less commitment, and less openness in the interaction (Leek *et al.* 2003).

However, Lee (1994) states that richness or leanness is not an inherent property of the communication media but an emergent property of the medium in its organizational context. Richness is obtained by the active participation of the receiver. The most appropriate medium for a particular communication transaction therefore depends on the manager's familiarity with and existing skills in using the medium and the manager's willingness, opportunities, resources, and support (Lee 1994).

As a rapid communication medium with multiple addressability, email has characteristics that make it suitable for connecting actors in an RSN. However, email also limits the possible outcomes, as it gives the sender more control over what to reveal. These limitations are further reinforced by the fact that the communicating parties do not see each other.

In studies of business communication between two engineering firms, Leek and Mason (2006) analyse the appropriateness of a communication medium in terms of how well it provides efficient and effective communication for actors in a dyadic business relationship. They incorporate McGrath and Hollingshead's (1993) task media fit model, which states that there is an optimal communication medium for a specific task. The communication media studied are formally arranged face-to-face meetings, everyday face-to-face interaction, email, formal written documents, and informal written notes. The measured tasks are idea generation, information exchange, problem-solving, negotiation and adaptation, and crisis insurance. Information exchange is the main function of the interaction. The most used method of communicating is face to face, but email tends to be used if the communication involves concrete information. Written media are used for important tasks.

A communication pattern model

The components of the model

By relating contextual factors to the task media fit model identified by McGrath and Hollingshead (1993) and to Leek and Mason's (2006) media-appropriateness model, a model can be obtained describing the communication pattern of email use in an organization such as an RSN. The model focuses on the communicating actors (message senders and recipients), communication direction (inside or outside the RSN), communication frequency, and kind of information exchanged.

These variables, which are used to describe the communication pattern, are regarded as influenced by conditions that characterize the RSN as a temporary organization. The individual communication preferences of the involved actors, their geographic location, the existing relationship atmosphere between the loosely coupled members, and the characteristics of the task to be performed are identified as determinants of the variables constituting the communication pattern.

Individual communication preferences concern the actors' propensity to use email. The RSN's temporary character implies that the communication strategy cannot be imposed, and the project character of the RSN also implies that communication within the RSN competes with other tasks that are important to its members. Individual preferences can therefore be expected to be important.

The location of the actor influences the need to use long-distance communication techniques. Whether or not email is seen to fulfil such a function can be expected to affect the direction of communication towards partners in the immediate vicinity or towards partners who are more distant.

As email is seen as a lean medium, that is, a medium that does not convey social cues in the same way as does face-to-face contact, the relationship atmosphere is believed to influence how frequently it is used, as this determines the conditions for informal communication.

Finally, the characteristics of the task, for example, requirements for complexity, speed, and confidentiality, are believed to influence the content of the messages for which email is chosen as the medium.

The model is summarized in Figure 6.1.

A communication pattern is supposed to describe how group members 'communicate to and from all members of the group', how they 'send messages to and receive messages from individuals and groups outside the group', how they 'have access to a number of bodies for information or knowledge

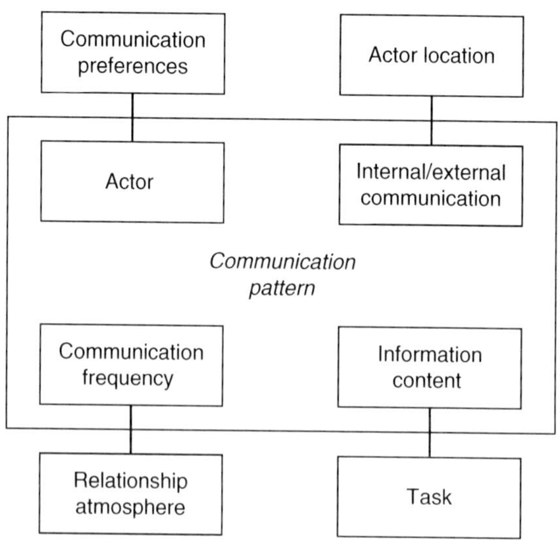

Figure 6.1 Determinants and indicators of communication patterns

outside the group', and how they 'receive task information and make task responses' (McGrath and Hollingshead 1993: 80). Most of these aspects are captured by the model.

The four variables used to describe the communication pattern (namely, actors, internal/external direction, frequency, and content) are measured in the data available in the present study. The determinants – the factors depicted outside the frame enclosing the communication pattern descriptors – are not measured in the study but are used to discuss the findings. The reasons for including these determinants are provided below.

Communication preferences

Communication behaviour is influenced by individual propensity to use certain communication media. These communication preferences are related to technical, social, and individual factors. From a technical viewpoint, the availability of suitable facilities such as computers and internet access are fundamental. From a social viewpoint, it is a matter of expected and accepted modes of communication in the relevant business environment. Individual factors, such as the degree to which an actor is accustomed to using computers, are also important.

Anxiety related to computer use may also affect an individual's propensity to use email. Sending and receiving messages and obtaining, processing, and interpreting information requires an understanding of and the ability to use computer-mediated communication systems (Jablin and Sias 2001). Managers of small companies, who often constitute the membership base of RSNs, do not always have such competence. Moreover, as communication behaviour may be guided by cognitive scripts that are unconsciously triggered by situational cues, it is difficult to influence such behaviour through strategic plans.

As responsiveness in medium use is socially determined, it is important to consider receiver preferences. It is beneficial to have a universal-access medium by which anyone in the organization can be reached (Markus 1994). This makes it necessary to consider system ability to adapt to the tasks to be accomplished (McGrath and Hollingshead 1993; Leek and Mason 2006), actor ability to use computer-mediated communication systems (Jablin and Sias 2001), and actor commitment and willingness to act (Sharma *et al.* 2006).

Actor location

The actor-location dimension refers to the influence that geographic distance or vicinity may exert on the actor's communication. Geographical distance between actors has been found to influence media choice (Trevino *et al.* 1987). Email and telephone are suitable for spanning great distances, whereas face-to-face meeting is favoured if the actors are located in each other's immediate vicinity.

The direction of communication in RSNs can be defined as intra-hub (between hub members), intra-RSN excluding the hub (directly between RSN members), and external (with actors outside the hub). The RSN's internal communication consequently concerns both closely cooperating actors, such as hub members, and actors who are at least initially more loosely coupled, such as member companies.

Relationship atmosphere

Relationship atmosphere refers to the attitudinal setting of business interaction (Williamson 1975). More specifically, the atmosphere can be described as the feelings, intentions, will, and interest of both parties (Hallén and Sandström 1991). It affects and is affected by the kind of bonds the communicating actors have with each other, for example, regarding trust and commitment, as well as by how the actors perceive and communicate with each other.

Actors who have relationships with each other in a trusting climate share activities that are more interdependent and can be expected to demand higher communication frequency (Mohr and Nevin 1990). The strength of relationships changes as mutual activity coordination is tightened up or loosened, as reciprocal adaptations in resources are made, and as actors engage in interaction with others (Ford 2002). Through interaction, the actors get to know each other and to gain an understanding of each other's sets of values. By cooperating to achieve a common goal, shared values may develop, which in turn may contribute to creating trust and commitment between the actors (Morgan and Hunt 1994). Only a little communication is required to maintain the contact between two actors, but more frequent interaction might be needed to secure coordination and strengthen relationships (Mohr and Nevin 1990).

The relationship atmosphere is dependent on perceived satisfaction as an outcome of interaction. Satisfying interaction or perceived benefits from interaction will increase the level of trust and commitment among actors (Morgan and Hunt 1994; Leek and Mason 2006). Relationship development is time-consuming, requires frequent communication, and generally occurs only after many years of interaction (Håkansson and Snehota 1995).

The choice of medium might also have an impact. Too many messages conveyed via an inappropriate medium may harm the chance to develop trusting relationships (Leek *et al.* 2003).

Thus, in an RSN, the communication frequency can be seen to influence the characteristics of the relationship atmosphere, which in turn is an outcome of the interaction processes between the members.

The task

Monge and Eisenberg (1987) argue that the tasks an organization performs influence its patterns of communication. The information content of messages exchanged in a communication process indicates the kind of tasks performed by the communicating parties. The function of an RSN hub manager can, like any management task, be considered to deal with directing behaviour towards a purpose and with pooling the actions of more than one individual (Snehota 1990). The tasks that are to be accomplished may concern idea generation, information exchange, problem-solving, assessment, negotiation, or social relationships (McGrath and Hollingshead 1993; Leek and Mason 2006).

Thus, managing an RSN resembles managing a firm. It concerns coordinating many companies and individuals, but the absence of formal authority contributes to the complexity and ambiguity of the task.

Method

The RSN case study

The RSN studied here started in 1998 as a project supported by eight municipalities in metropolitan Stockholm. The idea of setting up a large-scale RSN was based on interviews with about 100 companies in the region that had expressed interest in collaboration. The stated purpose of the RSN was to create business opportunities and growth for regional SMEs in the manufacturing and engineering industries. Cooperation between subcontractors as well as between the subcontractors and their customers was supposed to be brought about by implementing structured procedures for product development and innovation. The RSN project was financed by government agencies, EU regional development funds, and one of the main operators of telecommunication services in Sweden.

The RSN design process started by identifying a target group of 400 companies, followed by a recruitment campaign in the autumn of 1999. The potential member firms were contacted by phone, visited, and invited to information meetings. At the outset, the RSN comprised 50 companies, and, two years later, it had expanded to 130 member companies. Although these companies operated in the same region, most were unknown to each other and had neither business nor social relationships. The project was transformed into a cooperative association in 2001, though by then the number of member companies had decreased to 60.

The RSN was managed by a hub composed of a manager, an administrator, and a marketer working full time on the assignment. The hub's main task was to manage the RSN and to coordinate its activities. This task included communicating with RSN members and providing information. The hub was also supposed to maintain contacts with influential actors outside the RSN, for example, in order to obtain additional financial resources for the RSN.

The RSN manager compared his job to that of a business manager. He found his task quite demanding due to the RSN's size, the lack of sufficient managerial tools, and the lack of spontaneous commitment on the part of the member companies. He also mentioned the administrative burden related to publicly financed projects: this was time-consuming and took time from personal meetings with RSN members.

The RSN was set up as a virtual organization, in the sense that it was to be based on a web-based communication portal. An important initial task was to design the web portal and to implement it as a communication tool. Another purpose of the website was to support the development of a joint identity among RSN members.

At an early stage, the RSN board decided that email should be used as the main communication medium in the RSN. It was assumed that at least 150 and preferably 200 companies would be needed to make this solution suitable.

Approximately 2 million Swedish crowns were invested in designing and implementing the web portal, which, despite considerable effort, never became fully operational. By 2001, the hub manager realized that electronic communication alone was insufficient for getting RSN members involved in cooperative projects. The members probably had to meet face to face to get to know each other. Promises made by the team responsible for designing the portal, as well as promises made by the telecommunication supplier regarding technical equipment performance and education activities, had created expectations that were not fulfilled. This disappointment contributed to a loss of confidence in and reduced commitment to the RSN on the part of its members.

As to the RSN's product development ambitions, ten new products were developed from 1998 to 2003 through cooperation activities involving members. This was many fewer than expected at the outset.

By analysing interviews with key informants, the RSN process could be divided into development phases. The design phase was identified as running from the autumn of 1998 to the end of 1999. This phase focused on financial planning, recruiting member companies, and business-plan formulation, as well as on setting up the web portal and organizing the team responsible for it. In this phase, membership increased to 50 companies.

The turning point when planning as a dominant activity was replaced by actual RSN operations was marked by the launch of the web portal in January 2000, which indicated the beginning of the operational phase. At this time, the business plan and a set of rules of conduct had been formulated. The hub was focused on organizing activities and projects, administration, and recruiting additional member companies. The number of members increased from 50 to 130 companies.

An RSN can be said to have entered its transitional phase when its specially designated financing expires. This occurred in June 2001, as the RSN shifted from being a kind of virtual organization financed by public actors to a cooperative association financed by the participating companies' membership fees. At that time, recruitment had to start all over again, as only 24 member companies had joined the new association.

Data collection and sampling

To map the communication pattern over time, samples were drawn from the email messages sent and received by the hub manager. The samples consist of his email communication in three one-month periods, selected to represent the three RSN development phases. The samples include the complete email communication of these periods, meaning that some private and confidential emails also remained in the dataset. According to the manager, nothing had been deleted.

The criterion for selecting the sample months was to pick periods when there was high communication activity. This can be characterized as purposive non-probability sampling, where extreme cases were selected as findings from these can provide an understanding of more typical cases (Saunders *et al.* 1997). December 1999 was chosen to represent the design phase, and October 2000 and October 2001 were selected to represent the operational and transitional phases. The samples include a total of 365 ingoing and outgoing emails; however, 46 were excluded from the analysis, as one of the information content categories was not used as specified in the section 'Communicating actors'. That left a total of 319 emails: 85 from the design phase, 101 from the operational phase, and 124 from the transitional phase. These figures do not include mass emails, which chiefly comprise mass outgoing emails from the hub (mostly invitations to RSN activities), handled by the hub administrator. These mass emails were part of the information exchange within the RSN.

Data were also collected through interviews with the hub's manager, administrator, and marketer and with staff in two member companies (one from each one). The interviews were conducted by two researchers in 2002 at the RSN headquarters and at the member companies by means of an open-ended questionnaire.

Communication dimensions

The emails were read and their contents interpreted to establish a set of categories and to register how many emails fell into each category (Silverman 2006). The category definitions were created by initially coding a small sample (Weber 1990). The obtained categories were based on a review of 100 emails sent or received by the hub manager. These categories were then tested on another 100 emails, to confirm the functionality of the categories. Both samples were randomly selected from the entire dataset and analysed independently by two researchers.

The categories derived are summarized in Table 6.2.

Information content was registered in terms of content items, that is, topics covered per email. As most emails concerned several topics, the number of registered content items is greater than the number of analysed emails.

Table 6.2 Classification categories of email communication

Communicating actors	**Direction of communication**	**Communication frequency**	**Information content**
Hub (administrator and marketer) *Board and reference group* (actively managing RSN operations) *Member companies* *Authorities* (interested parties or financers) *Trade and industry* (interested, cooperating, or supporting partners) *Consultants* *Others* (private contacts and automatic answers from the web server)	*Intra-hub* *Intra-RSN (excluding intra-hub)* *To/from external actors*	*Number of incoming emails* *Number of outgoing emails*	*RSN project organization* (coordination and organizing) *Project collaboration* (cooperation with external actors) *RSN information* (information about RSN operations) *Strategic management issues* *Operative information* *IT communication and development* (communication strategy and web portal) *Sales* (product and service offers) • *outgoing sales* (from the manager) • *incoming sales* (from other actors) *Establishing social contacts* *Private emails* (unrelated to the RSN)

Findings

Communicating actors

The incoming and outgoing emails during the three phases are mapped in Table 6.3. The figures refer to the number of emails, indicating how frequently email was used for communication to and from the identified groups of actors. The email senders and recipients are grouped into six of the seven defined categories, as the 'others' category (private contacts and automatic answers from the web server) is excluded. The exclusion of these 46 emails gives a dataset of 319 emails as a basis for the analysis.

The total number of emails to and from the manager increased from 85 in the design phase to 110 in the operational phase, when more extensive activities gave rise to more email communication. The number of emails increased slightly in the transitional phase to 124 emails, indicating continued activity by the manager of the hub as the RSN was re-established as a cooperative association.

Table 6.3 Number of emails sent and received by the hub manager in the three RSN phases

	Design phase			Operational phase			Transitional phase			Total sum
	Inbox	Outbox	*Sum*	Inbox	Outbox	*Sum*	Inbox	Outbox	*Sum*	
Sum: Intra-hub	–	*1*	*1*	–	*2*	*2*	–	*2*	*2*	*5*
Board and reference group	15	1	16	8	3	11	27	27	54	81
Member companies	2	6	8	3	7	10	4	2	6	24
Sum: Intra-RSN (excl. intra-hub)	*17*	*7*	*24*	*11*	*10*	*21*	*31*	*29*	*60*	*105*
Authorities	2	2	4	10	13	23	4	4	8	35
Trade and industry	11	12	23	10	14	24	8	12	20	67
Consultants	23	10	33	21	19	40	22	12	34	107
Sum: External actors	*36*	*24*	*60*	*41*	*46*	*87*	*34*	*28*	*62*	*209*
Total sum	*53*	*32*	*85*	*52*	*58*	*110*	*65*	*59*	*124*	*319*

The figures in Table 6.3 also indicate that 306 of the manager's 319 emails (96 per cent) were sent to or received from the RSN's member companies or external actors. The hub members hardly used email at all to communicate with each other: they could easily communicate face to face, as they were situated in the same office.

About a third of all external emails were sent to or from RSN members (33 per cent), primarily the board and reference group. Email communication with this category was quite low in the design and operational phases but increased markedly in the transitional phase. The transformation of the RSN into a cooperative association probably brought to the fore many issues to be dealt with in the board and reference group.

Overall, email communication with member companies was infrequent, although the RSN had a communication strategy focusing on email. Email communication with member companies did not increase over time, accounting for 9 per cent of the incoming and outgoing emails to and from the manager in the design phase, 10 per cent in the operational phase, and 5 per cent in the transitional phase. However, it should be kept in mind that the hub manager devoted a lot of energy to other issues such as designing the RSN.

In addition, the hub administrator communicated with RSN members by email, sending about two emails per month to them. As the dataset consists of the emails in the inbox and outbox of the RSN's hub manager, these mass emails are not included in the analysis.

Table 6.3 also shows that consultants constitute the category with highest email communication frequency in the design and operational phases. This can be understood against the background of implementing the web portal and other IT-related issues in these phases.

In the transitional phase, most of the email communication involved the board and reference group. The consultants were still frequently involved in email communication, but less than before as other issues than the web portal were the focus of RSN attention.

Frequent contacts with trade and industry in all phases indicate work on regional development. The same issues concern communication with authorities, which, however, was infrequent in all phases. This may at first seem surprising for an RSN, as it is a project partly financed by governmental organizations and the EU, but other media than email may be more appropriate for official contacts.

The hub manager received more emails than he sent. For example, there were many incoming emails from sellers; many of these did not require answers, nor did the automatic messages from the web server. The latter, however, are not included in the dataset.

Information content

Several emails included content from more than one information category, so the number of content items in the dataset is greater than the number of emails in the selected periods. The number of both emails and content items increased from the design to the operational phase, after which both decreased. As indicated in Table 6.4, the number of content items per email is rather stable, indicating that the general structure of the email messages remained the same over time.

In Table 6.5, the specific content items of incoming and outgoing emails are presented according to the empirically derived content categories.

Table 6.4 Number of content items per email in the three RSN phases

	Design phase			Operational phase			Transitional phase			Total sum
	Inbox	Outbox	Sum	Inbox	Outbox	Sum	Inbox	Outbox	Sum	
Content items	106	52	153	115	80	195	110	87	197	545
Emails	53	32	85	52	58	110	65	59	124	319
Content items per email	2.0	1.6		2.2	1.4		1.7	1.5		1.7

Table 6.5 Number of content items in the hub manager's incoming and outgoing emails

	Design phase			Operational phase			Transitional phase			
Information content	**Inbox**	**Outbox**	***Sum***	**Inbox**	**Outbox**	***Sum***	**Inbox**	**Outbox**	***Sum***	***Total sum***
RSN project organization	*17*	*5*	*22*	*10*	*6*	*16*	*27*	*19*	*46*	*79*
Project collaboration	*5*	*1*	*6*	*6*	*2*	*8*	*6*	*13*	*19*	*33*
Strategic management	16	4	20	12	10	22	32	15	47	89
Operative information	13	11	24	16	13	29	18	15	33	86
Seminars and lectures	9	8	17	3	8	11	3	2	5	33
Sum: RSN information:	*38*	*23*	*61*	*31*	*31*	*62*	*53*	*32*	*85*	*208*
IT communication and development	*21*	*1*	*22*	*42*	*9*	*51*	*15*	*15*	*30*	*103*
Incoming sales	19	10	29	13	18	3	9	5	14	74
Outgoing sales	–	–	–	–	–	1	–	1	1	1
Sum: Sales	*19*	*10*	*29*	*13*	*18*	*4*	*9*	*6*	*15*	*75*
Establishing social contacts	*6*	*12*	*18*	*13*	*14*	*27*	–	*2*	*2*	*47*
Total sum	*106*	*52*	*153*	*115*	*80*	*195*	*110*	*87*	*197*	*545*

Information concerning the RSN comprised a substantial part of the manager's email communication, accounting for 40 per cent of the content items in the design phase, 32 per cent in the operational phase, and 43 per cent in the transitional phase. Strategic management issues and operative information accounted for most of the RSN information items, following an increasing trend. However, information about RSN seminars and lectures decreased over time, accounting for 11 per cent of the content items in the design phase, 6 per cent in the operational phase, and 3 per cent in the transitional phase.

Work on the web portal was time-consuming, as reflected in the hub manager's emails, where 19 per cent of the content items dealt with this. The many content items dealing with IT in the operational phase (26 per cent of content items) reflect the efforts to launch the web portal.

Items dealing with the hub's coordinating function represent 14 per cent of the total. This share rose to 23 per cent in the transitional phase, reflecting the ongoing role of the hub in the formal transformation of the RSN into a cooperative association.

In all, 9 per cent of all content items were classified as concerning social contacts. There were some emails dealing with such content in the design and operational phases, but hardly any in the transitional phase. At that stage, the manager had probably already established the contacts needed via face-to-face contact or other more direct media. Information items regarding project collaboration increased over time but still remained rather few.

Salespeople approached the manager in all phases. Their efforts peaked in the operational phase, when 14 per cent of all content items concerned sales contacts. However, both sales and social contacts were likely handled via other media.

Discussion and implications

The role of email and the RSN

Electronic communication has been developing rapidly. Email is now in wide use in business, and private individuals tend to take another step by leaving email in favour of so-called social media. In 1998, when the RSN studied here was launched, email was already widely used in parts of society, particularly in universities, research organizations, and IT companies. It was also being used by big companies for commercial communication and by many people for private communication. Still, it had not yet spread to all parts of society. In 1994, just a few years before the RSN of this case study was set up, the heavily publicized sending of an email by Swedish Prime Minister Carl Bildt to US President Bill Clinton was considered a newsworthy event, indicating that the new communication medium had for the first time been used for communication between heads of government.

Thus, at the time when the RSN was launched, many parts of society could be considered still to be untouched by the alleged benefits of simple, swift, and efficient email communication. In SMEs, there seemed to be potential for productive email use that had not been fully exploited, and many companies were eager to offer IT solutions to remedy that. This helped emphasize email as a communication strategy in the minds of the decision makers involved in regional development and RSN design.

Therefore, regional development initiatives such as the studied RSN could make it a top priority to provide computer facilities to RSN members and to increase the computer literacy of managers of member firms, to make them accustomed to using email. The value of using email for business purposes was more or less seen as axiomatic by the decision makers.

By formally prioritizing email as a communication strategy, it was hoped that two objectives could be reached. As email communication in itself was seen as an efficient way of communicating, it was assumed it would facilitate RSN management. Moreover, encouraging RSN member firms to start using email was expected to benefit these firms as they became acquainted with and, it was hoped, interested in modern communication methods.

Implementing such a communication strategy in a temporary organization with a predetermined lifespan, such as an RSN, entails specific problems. Is there time enough to implement the communication system – technically and socially – within the available time? Is it possible to motivate members to use the system, when their top priorities are other matters, such as running their day-to-day business operations? Do the ambitions of the experts involved in the project – the hub members and IT consultants – coincide with the best interests of RSN members?

The present analysis of email communication in an RSN answers some of these questions, but not all. Doing that would call for more extensive analysis of the RSN. The present analysis is based on the hub manager's outgoing and incoming email messages. Although he was the key RSN actor, and although what was saved in his inbox and outbox probably constituted the lion's share of total email communication in the RSN, there were still other emails exchanged within the RSN. The mass emails (about two per month) sent from the hub to the RSN members, communicating invitations to various RSN activities, were not sent by the hub manager but by the administrator. However, the absence of these emails from the analysed dataset does not change the general communication pattern.

The absence of direct email communication between RSN members might be of greater importance, as one purpose of the RSN project was to stimulate such contacts. In this case, however, this can be assumed not to have affected the overall pattern to any great extent, as copies of RSN-related contacts between members that were handled by email would probably have been sent to the hub in most cases. The interviews with hub actors and a few member companies indicate that business contacts between RSN members were normally handled in other ways, for example, by phone or personal meetings. Thus, the emails contained in the inbox and outbox of the hub manager probably provide a satisfactory image of the email-based communication pattern of the RSN.

The email communication pattern in the three RSN phases

Generally, communication in the design phase of an RSN is required to support activities such as initiating and driving a motivating dialogue with participants and financiers. The purpose is to identify and reach consensus regarding opportunities, strategies, goals, and commitment building, all of which may create legitimacy for the hub and for the RSN in general. In this early phase, RSN members are often only loosely connected to each other, and the hub has to work as an active driver.

The studied RSN corresponded to this general situation. The manager used email mainly to organize technical IT solutions with consultants, and he received quite a few sales offers. This outward focus of his email communication coincides with what could be expected in the design phase, particularly as email was not the standard means of communication for RSN members. In addition, the manager's frequent communication with members of the board and the reference group about operative and strategic management issues is in line with expectations.

In the operational phase, the RSN's focus was expected to shift to activities such as how to act to achieve goals, who should be in charge of what, who should be involved, and how deeply participants should be involved. The amount of email communication rose in the operational phase, due to more extensive contacts with external actors such as IT consultants and contacts making sales offers. An important activity in this phase was the launch of the web portal, an activity that required IT support. Email contacts with RSN member companies remained low.

In the transitional phase, activities are supposed to deal with evaluation, assessment of results, and knowledge adoption and integration. The hub may also become involved in initiating a new RSN design process. The transformation of the present RSN into a cooperative association can be seen as such a redesign activity.

The manager's email communication remained at about the same level as previously but shifted to increased contacts with the RSN board and reference group. Strategic management issues concerning the new cooperative association had to be addressed, and the RSN hub remained involved in this although it formally meant that the RSN ceased to operate in its previous form.

In all phases, there were contacts with trade and industry people to support the RSN's business ambitions. These contacts remained at the same level over the three periods, so there is no indication that email acquired a more important role as far as such contacts were concerned.

Email communication with RSN member companies remained insignificant in all three phases. Although another hub member, the administrator, was also involved in communication with member companies, this did not change the general pattern: email never became the main means of communication within the RSN.

Implications

The hub manager and RSN board members believed strongly in email communication, whereas the managers of the member companies often initially neither had access to proper equipment nor knowledge of how to use the new communication medium. The decisions regarding the communication strategy were made by actors who had individual preferences for email. The emerging communication pattern reflects these preferences, and the launch of the web portal hardly contributed to increased use of electronic media. As the individual and social preconditions for changed communication behaviour were not there, it is hardly surprising that the expectations that the web portal would create a shared identity amongst the members (Wiesenfeld *et al.* 1999) were not fulfilled.

An RSN communication strategy must meet individual and social expectations in addition to technical prerequisites. This means that RSN managers must adapt to the preferences, settings, and abilities of member companies. A communication tool cannot be introduced in isolation from other means, such as personal meetings.

The ensuing communication pattern in the case was clearly influenced by individual communication preferences.

The hub members sat in the same office, whereas the members of the board and reference group and the managers of member companies were spread out in the region. Although distances are short in metropolitan Stockholm, where the RSN operated, it was still time-consuming to travel between the locations where the members were based.

The hub members did not use email much when communicating with each other, as it was easy for them to speak directly face to face. However, email was used frequently to communicate with the members of the board and reference group. They were based elsewhere, and, particularly in the operational phase, when the RSN was transformed into a partnership-owned cooperative association, there were many issues for the board and reference group to handle.

However, email communication with member companies remained infrequent, although it could have been an appropriate tool for communication between the hub and members, particularly considering the RSN's email-based communication strategy. However, the distance factor did not compensate for the different communication preferences of the members, and, in practice, it seems that the hub management acknowledged this. The RSN manager dedicated considerable time to applying for resources and lobbying to receive them, leaving little time to use email in contacts with members in order to symbolize adherence to the communication strategy. In any case, such emails would – as indicated by information from the interviews – often have been complemented with phone calls informing the recipient that he had received an email.

When the technical and social conditions were right for email communication, actor location was found to influence the communication pattern in terms of whether or not email was used. This is illustrated by the infrequent email communication within the hub and the more frequent communication with the board and reference group members. However, when these conditions were not met, as in the case of email communication with member companies, distance was not a sufficient condition to make email communication attractive.

Email is a lean communication medium, that is, it cannot transfer social cues to the same extent as can a rich medium, such as face-to-face meetings. Phone calls are also better for conveying social cues than is email. This means that the leanness of email must be compensated for by other relationship characteristics, such as personal closeness, trust, commitment, and interdependence, as well as other qualities generally related to the atmosphere of the relationship between the communicating parties. The closer the relationship in terms of its atmosphere, the more easily and frequently email can be expected to be used.

There was little email communication between the hub and the member companies. Information from the interviews indicates a similar pattern regarding direct email communication between RSN member companies. The business relationships that actually existed between some member companies were handled outside the email system, and the members did not become sufficiently acquainted with each other to start using email informally in their contacts with each other or with the hub. Thus, the potential effect of the relationship atmosphere was insufficient to overcome the obstacles deriving from the communication preferences of the members.

However, the relationship atmosphere prevailing between the hub manager, IT consultants, board members, and reference group probably facilitated the use of email, despite its low capacity for conveying social cues. Their shared interest in IT solutions and in the RSN as an opportunity for business development probably created an atmosphere of commitment to both the idea of an email communication strategy and to the RSN project as such.

Relationship atmosphere can thus be seen as a factor that contributed to the communication pattern that emerged.

Information content is influenced by the task to be performed. Assessing the RSN based on the information content of the hub manager's email communications suggests that the RSN itself – organizing it, managing it, and implementing its IT strategy – was the manager's major task. Indeed, there were emails concerning sales and building social contacts between RSN members, but their share of the total number of information content items is much smaller.

However, the information content of the emails does not necessarily reflect the composition of tasks performed in the RSN. Email was used for communication for which it was suitable and practicable. Other types of communication media might have been used for activities such as facilitating relationship development and interaction leading to the business development of member companies. However, the focus on IT communication might have distracted attention from those tasks.

The communication pattern model developed in this chapter, which includes the communicating actors, the direction of their communication, their communication frequency, and the information content of their messages, provides a tool with which to map email communication in an RSN. The analysis, focusing on how individual, social, and technical factors, specified as actor preferences and location, the atmosphere of actor relationships, and the tasks to be performed, indicates that all these aspects must be considered in designing a communication strategy subject to the time constraints of an RSN as a temporary project.

References

M. Bengtsson, T. Mullern, A. Söderholm, and N. Wåhlin, *A Grammar of Organizing* (London: Edgar Elgar, 2007).

J. Child and D. Faulkner, *Strategies of Cooperation: Managing Alliances, Networks and Joint ventures* (Oxford: Oxford University Press, 1998).

L. Christensen and P. Kempinsky, *Vad kräver arbetet med regionala utvecklingsprocesser?* (*What Is Required for the Work with Regional Development Processes?*), Dahménforum, 3, 2003.

S. Christensen and K. Kreiner, *Projektledning: att leda och lära i en ofullkomlig värld* (*Project Management: Managing and Learning in an Imperfect World*) (Lund: Academia Adacta, 1997).

R. L. Daft, R. H. Lengel, and L. K. Trevino, 'Message Equivocality, Media Selection, and Manager Performance: Implications for Information Systems', *MIS Quarterly*, 11 (3) (1987): 355–66.

A. De Moor and H. Weigand, 'Communication Pattern Analysis in Communities of Practice', Paper presented at the Language Action Perspective in Communication Modelling conference, Kiruna (2005).

D. Ford, 'The Development of Buyer–Seller Relationships in Industrial Markets', in D. Ford (ed.), *Understanding Business Marketing and Purchasing* (London: Thomson Learning, 2002).

H. Håkansson and I Snehota, *Developing Relationships in Business Networks* (London: Routledge, 1995).

L. Hallén and M. Sandström, 'Relationship Atmosphere in International Business', in S. J. Paliwoda (ed.), *New Perspectives on International Marketing* (London: Routledge, 1991) pp. 108–25.

F. M. Jablin and P. M. Sias, 'Communication Competence', in F. M. Jablin and L. L. Putnam (eds.), *The New Handbook of Organizational Communication: Advances in Theory, Research and Methods* (Thousand Oaks, Calif.: Sage Publications, 2001) pp. 819–64.

J. C. Jarillo, 'On Strategic Networks', *Strategic Management Journal,* 9 (1) (1988): 31–41.

A. S. Lee, 'Electronic Mail as a Medium for Rich Communication: An Empirical Investigation using Hermeneutic Interpretation', *MIS Quarterly,* 18 (2) (1994): 143–57.

S. Leek and K. Mason, 'An Investigation into the Utilisation of Communication Methods in a Business to Business Relationship', Paper presented at the 22nd IMP Conference, Milan (2006).

S. Leek, P. T. Turnbull, and P. Naudé, 'How is Information Technology Affecting Business Relationships? Results from a UK Survey', *Industrial Marketing Management,* 32 (2) (2003): 119–26.

G. Lorenzoni and C. Baden-Fuller, 'Creating a Strategic Web of Partners', *California Management Review,* 37 (3) (1995): 146–63.

H. Lundberg, 'Geographical Proximity Effects and Regional Strategic Networks', Doctoral dissertation, Uppsala University, Department of Business Studies, 2008.

R. A. Lundin and A. Söderholm, 'A Theory of the Temporary Organization', *Scandinavian Journal of Management,* 11 (4) (1995): 437–55.

E. Maaninen-Olsson, 'Projekt i tid och rum: Kunskapsintegrering mellan projektet och dess historiska och organisatoriska kontext' ('Projects in Time and Space'), Dissertation, Uppsala University, Department of Business Studies, 2007.

L. M. Markus, 'Electronic Mail as the Medium of Managerial Choice', *Organization Science,* 5 (4) (1994): 502–27.

J. E. McGrath and A. B. Hollingshead, 'Putting the Group Back in Group Support Systems: Some Theoretical Issues about Dynamic Processes in Groups with Technological Enhancements', in L. M. Jessup and J. S. Valacich (eds), *Group Support Systems: New Perspectives* (New York: MacMillan, 1993), pp. 78–96.

J. Mohr and J. R. Nevin, 'Communication Strategies in Marketing Channels: A Theoretical Perspective', *Journal of Marketing,* 54 (4) (1990): 35–51.

P. R. Monge and E. M. Eisenberg, 'Emergent Communication Networks', in F. M. Jablin, L. L. Putnam, K. H. Roberts, and L. W. Porter (ed.), *Handbook of Organizational Communication: An Interdisciplinary Perspective* (Newbury Park, CA: Sage Publications, 1987), pp. 304–42.

R. M. Morgan and S. B. Hunt, 'The Commitment–Trust Theory of Relationship Marketing', *Journal of Marketing,* 58 (3) (1994): 20–38.

W. H. Papa and M. J. Papa, 'Communication Network Patterns and the Re-invention of New Technology', *Journal of Business Communication,* 29 (1) (1992): 41–61.

M. Saunders, P. Lewis, and A. Thornhill, *Research Methods for Business Students* (London: Pitman Publishing, 1997).

D. Sharma, L. Young, and I Wilkinson, 'The Commitment Mix: Dimensions of Commitment in International Trading Relationships in India', *Journal of International Marketing,* 14 (3) (2006): 64–91.

D. Silverman, *Interpreting Qualitative Data: Methods for Analyzing Talk, Text and Interaction* (London: Sage Publications, 2006).

L. Sproull and S. Kiesler, 'Reducing Social Context Cues: Electronic Mail in Organizational Communications', *Management Science,* 32 (11) (1986): 1492–512.

I. Snehota, 'Notes on a Theory of Business Enterprise', Doctoral dissertation, Uppsala University, Department of Business Studies, 1990.

L. K. Trevino, R. H. Lengel, and R. L. Daft, 'Media Symbolism, Media Richness, and Media Choice in Organizations', *Communication Research,* 14 (1987): 553–74.

J. B. Walther, 'Relational Aspects of Computer-Mediated Communication', *Organization Science,* 6 (2) (1995): 196–203.

B. M. Wiesenfeld, S. Raghuram, and R. Garud, 'Communication Patterns as Determinants of Organizational Identification in a Virtual Organization', *Organisation Science,* 10 (6) (1999): 777–90.

O. E. Williamson, *Markets and Hierarchies: Analysis and Antitrust Implications* (New York: Macmillan/The Free Press, 1975).

R. P. Weber, *Basic Content Analysis,* 2nd edn (Newbury Park, CA: Sage Publications, 1990).

J.-A. Yates, W. J. Orlikowski, and K. Okamura, K, 'Explicit and Implicit Structuring of Genres in Electronic Communication: Reinforcement and Change of Social Interaction', *Organization Science,* 10 (1) (1999): 83–103.

7

Cluster Membership, Knowledge and SMEs' Internationalization

Snejina Michailova and Sylvie Chetty

Introduction

Several streams of literature have acknowledged the increasing importance of knowledge in firms' internationalization. Knowledge is considered to be fundamental to the firm's commitments to foreign markets in the framework of the process model of internationalization (Johanson and Vahlne 1990). Knowledge is treated as an enabling resource in the international new venture literature (McDougall *et al.* 1994; Oviatt and McDougall 1997; Autio *et al.* 2000). Knowledge facilitates the processes of identifying and exploiting opportunities abroad according to the international entrepreneurship approach (Zahra *et al.* 2000; Zahra 2005). Knowledge is also emphasized as an important factor leading to international engagement in the literature on managerial determinants of international behaviour (Bloodgood *et al.* 1996; Reuber and Fisher 1997). The importance of both planning-based knowledge (Yip *et al.* 2000) and experiential knowledge (Johanson and Vahlne 1990; Michailova and Wilson 2008) is recognized for driving internationalization of large, as well as small and medium-sized enterprises (SMEs). The importance of SMEs has been growing, and at present they account for approximately 30 per cent of exports and 10 per cent of foreign direct investment globally (Organisation for Economic Co-operation and Development [OECD] 2006).

Firms place a greater emphasis on increasing their knowledge base through interacting with the market compared with information obtained through public or private information services (Denis and Depelteau 1985). For instance, firms overcome their lack of foreign market knowledge by collaborating with others (Eriksson and Chetty 2003), and these network strategies expedite the firms' internationalization process (Chetty and Campbell-Hunt 2003). Indeed, a large amount of internationalization activity is associated with networking as it involves building relationships with foreign intermediaries, customers, suppliers, and alliance partners (Eriksson *et al.* 1997). Collaboration provides firms with the opportunity to overcome limitations in their capabilities and resources to conduct business in a particular market (Madhok 1996): collaboration facilitates accessing and acquiring knowledge, which, in turn, lead to firm internationalization.

In recognition of the benefits of collaboration various structural interorganizational configurations have emerged. Of particular interest to researchers have been regional clusters. A regional cluster is 'a geographically proximate group of interconnected companies and associated institutions in a particular field, linked by commonalities and complementarities' (Porter 2000: 16). In an earlier work, Porter (1998: 78) pointed out that rather than being unique, clusters are 'highly typical – and therein lies a paradox: the enduring competitive advantages in a global economy lie increasingly in local things – knowledge, relationships, motivation – that distant rivals cannot match'. Cluster members are embedded within a network of relationships within a specific industry, and they are involved in both cooperation and competition (Astley and Fombrun 1983; Bresser 1988). Regional clusters are defined as 'examples of advantage-generating "superfirm" groups inside industries, within which member firms simultaneously share and differentiate sources of competitive advantages' (Tallman *et al.* 2004: 259).

This chapter focuses on the links between cluster membership, knowledge processes, and SMEs' internationalization. In particular, we examine how SMEs access and acquire knowledge within a regional industry cluster. We also study whether certain knowledge types are better suited to be accessed in the cluster and whether there are others that are more appropriate in terms of knowledge acquisition. We combine the knowledge-based perspective (Grant 1996) with the internationalization literature (Johanson and Vahlne 1977; Eriksson *et al.* 1997; Eriksson and Chetty 2003) to develop a conceptual model and propositions that relate to the above questions. We use the New Zealand boat-building cluster to illustrate the concepts and verify the links we are proposing.

Regional industry clusters and cluster firms' internationalization

Geographical proximity, clusters, and firm internationalization

Geographical proximity refers to 'spatial separation and relations in terms of distance' (Lemarie *et al.* 2001: 67). Close geographical proximity enables firms to exchange knowledge among each other (Ibert 2007; Waxell and Malmberg 2007). In fact, industry cluster researchers highlight the importance of sharing informal information, which is facilitated by geographical proximity. The close geographical proximity of firms in an industry cluster encourages face-to-face communication which helps develop relationships with other firms in the cluster (Malmberg and Maskell 2006; Waxell and Malmberg 2007; Bönte 2008; Morrison 2008). As Harrison (1992: 477) states, 'proximity promotes the "digestion" of experience which leads to trust'. This encourages them to continue doing business together and to share a common support infrastructure, which eventually promotes regional growth. Organizations within an industry cluster, therefore, have the advantage of developing their collective knowledge, partially because of their close geographical proximity. Andersson and Karlsson (2007) state that since knowledge is often intricate with complex elements, it is subsequently only accessible through interactions with networks that are bounded by geographical proximity. In addition, Leamer and Storper (2001) argue that the transmission of complex uncodifiable messages necessitates a contact between the sender and receiver that cannot be acquired through the Internet and propose that the Internet does not replace the desire for proximity. Buckley and Carter (2004), too, highlight that geographical distance is a barrier to knowledge acquisition. They argue that geographical distance and time differences make it difficult to communicate. Distance also decreases 'mutual awareness so that groups which are "out of sight" also remain "out of mind"' (Buckley and Carter 2004: 9).

Other researchers, however, have challenged the relevance of geographical proximity. For instance, Tallman *et al.* (2004) argue that occasional face-to-face contact supported by information and communications technology may negate the need for geographical proximity. Similarly, Davenport's (2005) study of New Zealand firms found that in a case of a small domestic market, firms internationalize quickly, so their sources of knowledge become their international rather than their local relationships. Ganesan *et al.* (2005) argue that distance does not matter as knowledge seekers use electronic communication, which is timely and inexpensive compared to face-to-face interaction. They also argue that strong relationships with important knowledge sources are more important for the firm than whether the geographical proximity of these organizations is close or distant.

Firms, governments, and policy-makers alike realize the value of regional clusters in creating opportunities for knowledge acquisition and subsequent internationalization. In Denmark, Sweden, Australia, and New Zealand, among others, policy-makers have acted as catalysts for cluster formation by encouraging firms, in particular SMEs in a similar industry, and which are geographically close, to collaborate in a more structured way to boost exports. In some cases, for example in Denmark and New Zealand, industry networks were intentionally formed as export promotion initiatives to increase specific industries' international sales and competitive advantages (Neergaard and Ulhoi 2006; Chetty and Agndal 2008). Studies from other countries, too, provide empirical support for the role of regional clusters in firm internationalization. For example Gellynck *et al.* (2007) noted in their study of innovation in Belgian food firms that the firms which are active in international markets gain from regional networking. Eraydin and Armatli-Køroğlu (2005) studied three Turkish industrial clusters and emphasized the importance of local and national networking as well as global linkages. They also found that despite the weakening role of nation-states and boundaries through globalization, national linkages are still important and that most economic and social relations are bounded by national space.

Social embeddedness within clusters

Since geographical proximity of firms within a cluster encourages more frequent interaction, firms become more socially embedded in the cluster (Harrison 1992; Audretsch 1998). This frequent interaction through close geographical proximity amongst firms also helps to build trust (Harrison 1992; Etzioni and Etzioni 1999) and long-term relationships. Sharing norms and having mutual trust encourages cluster members to share information (Harrison 1992; Rosenfeld 1997) and exchange knowledge with each other in the cluster. Such collaborative relationships help knowledge to be shared more easily. In her study of alliances, Norman (2004) proposes that this happens because knowledge exchange is a socially embedded process and requires individuals to interact openly with others. Indeed, it is important for a firm to have frequent social interactions in order to access more easily its partner's knowledge (Lane and Lubatkin 1998; Yli-Renko *et al.* 2001). When a firm acquires this knowledge it opens up new opportunities for the firm (Penrose 1959). Tsai and Ghoshal (1998) in their study of product innovations emphasized the importance of informal social interactions to encourage the exchange and combination of knowledge in order to create innovative products. The existing social networks of a firm tend to determine the opportunities available in a particular period (Johanson and Vahlne 2006), some of which occur unexpectedly through serendipitous events. It is the knowledge that firms acquire through their business relationships that enables them to recognize these serendipitous events as opportunities. Consequently, the more relationships a firm has, the more diverse the knowledge it acquires and the more opportunities are recognized and created. Furthermore, such diversity of relationships increases the breadth, depth, and speed of a firm's knowledge acquisition (Zahra *et al.* 2000), which can facilitate firm internationalization.

The firm's network of relationships is regarded as a source of information for the firm (Nahapiet and Ghoshal 1998; Yli-Renko *et al.* 2002; Inkpen and Tsang 2005; Rycroft 2007). Through frequent interaction and joint activities partners can exchange information and acquire new knowledge (Nahapiet and Ghoshal 1998). The more interaction there is amongst partners in a network, the more knowledge is acquired. A network that has strong linkages, trust, reciprocity, and mutual commitment creates the foundation for such interaction to occur and for knowledge acquisition to increase.

Strong and weak ties (Granovetter 1973) play different roles in acquiring knowledge. Hansen (1999) argues that since weak ties are less costly to maintain, having a network of predominantly weak ties is more efficient for projects that require mainly explicit knowledge. A network of strong ties leads to more knowledge acquisition in general (Uzzi 1997; Hansen 1999; Levin and Cross 2004), and a cluster provides the opportunity to provide such strong ties. Ganesan *et al.* (2005) argue that valuable knowledge is more likely to be transferred through a strong tie than through weak ones while Levin and Cross (2004) state that weak ties provide more helpful knowledge than strong ties.

These social networks take time and effort to build and maintain (Granovetter 1973; Ganesan *et al.* 2005). Ganesan *et al.* (2005) challenge the assumption in cluster theory (for example, Porter 1998) that proximity leads to the development of strong ties. They conclude that face-to-face communication is less effective than electronic communication in obtaining new product-related knowledge. Ganesan *et al.* (2005) also argue that relationship ties within the cluster have to be maintained and cannot be taken for granted. They argue that in order to understand knowledge acquisition in a cluster one needs to consider both geographical and relational closeness.

Knowledge governance in industry clusters

Firms within a cluster develop a specific stock of knowledge that will differentiate them from other industries (Tallman *et al.* 2004). This knowledge is the tacit understanding of the members about the norms and functioning of the collaboration. It includes their comprehension of reciprocity, interdependencies, connectedness, and how to cooperate and compete with each other and share knowledge. According to Jones *et al.* (1997), network governance in industry clusters is characterized by informal social systems rather than by bureaucratic structures within firms and formal contractual relationships between them. It involves 'a select, persistent, and structured set of autonomous firms (as well as nonprofit agencies) engaged in creating products or services based on implicit and open-ended contracts to adapt to environmental contingencies and to coordinate and safeguard exchanges' (Jones *et al.* 1997: 914). Exchange conditions marked by demand uncertainty, high level of task uncertainty, and human-assets specificity are especially favourable for network governance vis-à-vis other governance structures (Jones *et al.* 1997). In the core of collaborative network governance we find that social mechanisms, such as restricted access to the collaboration, macro-cultures and norms for behaviour in the network, collective sanction and protection of individual organizations' reputation are efficient means for safeguarding the exchanges in the collaboration.

Network governance is able to coordinate complex products or services in competitive and uncertain environments (Ring and Van de Ven 1992). Following Kogut (2000), there is a greater 'variety generation' in networks, which means that there is a greater diversity of knowledge in a network than in a firm. In order for the network to be effective at knowledge management, it must create principles that encourage coordination among specialized firms (Kogut 2000).

The social networks formed in a cluster have a downside pertaining to the risks involved and the investment in time and costs associated with forming, monitoring, sustaining, and developing social networks. In some cases, the quality of relationships within them can be problematic. The disadvantage of exchanging knowledge through social networks is that it can constrain the development of knowledge (Inkpen 1998). For instance, if one partner has acquired a substantial amount of knowledge, this can limit the value of the other partners' knowledge. Business partners' potential opportunistic behaviour (for example, withholding information for their own strategic advantage instead of sharing it with others) is a possible additional obstacle (Buckley and Carter 2004).

In an 'open network', firms have less access to social networks, they seem to be less tightly connected, and the norms and information about behaviour are more loosely defined and more slowly disseminated. In such a situation it is hard to keep opportunistic behaviour in check. Nahapiet and Ghoshal (1998) argue that some aspects of social networks can hinder interaction and thus constrain rather than enhance knowledge exchange. They argue that while social norms and identity have a positive effect on group performance, these attributes may also hinder the group's receptiveness to new information and to seek other methods of doing things. The firm can suffer from being part of what Uzzi (1997) refers to as an over-embedded network where very close relationships block out external information from other sources. Consequently, a firm in such a closed network will fail to recognize new and better opportunities. Indeed these 'ties that bind' can lead to 'ties that blind' (Grabher 1993: 24). In this situation it is important for the firm to also have weak ties so that it can enter other networks and thus expose itself to new knowledge and opportunities (Granovetter 1973). In contrast to an 'open network', in a 'closed network' members are well connected to each other and have well defined and well established and accepted norms that govern the code of conduct (Walker *et al.* 1997).

Cluster membership, knowledge processes, and cluster members' internationalization

We suggest that combining the knowledge-based view and the firm internationalization literature can result in some important insights about how knowledge access and knowledge acquisition in regional industry clusters influence the internationalization of cluster member firms. We argue that cluster membership facilitates the exchange of different types of knowledge (that is, component and architectural knowledge), which, respectively lead to different kinds of knowledge processes, namely knowledge access and knowledge acquisition, both of which can lead to cluster members' internationalization. The proposed links are illustrated in Figure 7.1.

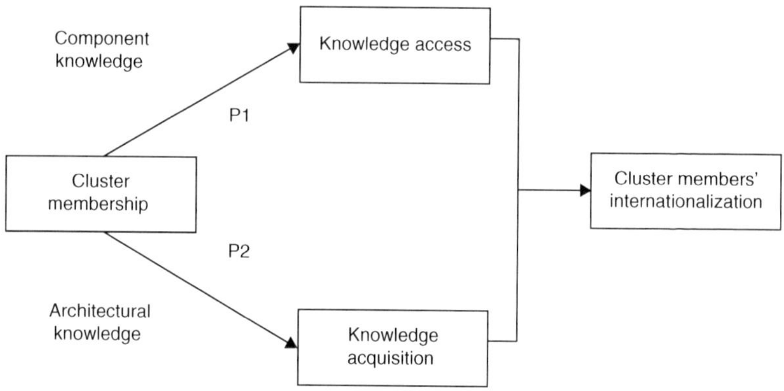

Figure 7.1 Cluster membership, knowledge processes and cluster members' internationalization

Knowledge types and processes

Using work previously done by Henderson and Clark (1990) and Matusik and Hill (1998), Tallman *et al.* (2004) examined knowledge and competitive advantage in regional clusters by referring to component knowledge and architectural knowledge as two distinctive knowledge types. Tallman *et al.* (2004) defined component knowledge as consisting of specific knowledge resources, skills, and technologies that relate to identifiable parts of an organizational system rather than the whole. Component knowledge is typically linked to the technology used in the industry, and it is transferable (as well as subject to leakage) as it can be understood by informed recipients in the industry. If firms share their experiences, they are more likely to increase their mutual absorptive capacities, and thus it becomes easier to get involved in mutual transfers of component knowledge. According to Tallman *et al.* (2004: 264), 'component knowledge ranges in nature from straightforward technical (simple, tangible, explicit) know-how through highly systemic (complex, intangible, tacit) scientific knowledge'.

Architectural knowledge, on the other hand, 'relates to an organization as an entire system and the structures and routines for coordinating and integrating its component knowledge into patterns for productive use and for developing new architectural and component knowledge' (Tallman *et al.* 2004: 265). Architectural knowledge tends to be complex, intangible, and tacit. It is also organization-specific, ambiguous, and private because it is path-dependent, embedded in organizations, and it has a holistic and evolutionary character (Nelson and Winter 1982; Reed and DeFillippi 1990; Matusik and Hill 1998) – features that make it difficult to transfer. The cluster creates its own architectural knowledge from the interdependencies of firms within the cluster, shared interests, and geographical identity of the individual firms (Tallman *et al.* 2004).

Using an earlier conceptualization by Winter (1987), Garud and Nayyar (1994) identified three distinctive knowledge dimensions, namely tacit vs. articulable, simple vs. complex, and independent vs. systemic. While it is difficult to argue that tacit, complex, and systemic knowledge are dimensions that are typical for architectural knowledge and articulable, simple, and independent knowledge are more characteristic of component knowledge, we would contend that on a continuum between the two extremes one can observe the dominance of some dimensions as compared to others. Tacitness of knowledge is a source of ambiguity (Reed and DeFillippi 1990). The inability to articulate it (Polanyi 1962; Nelson and Winter 1982) and its personal nature (Polanyi 1962; Nonaka and Takeuchi 1995) are the two main characteristics of tacitness put forward in the literature. While the first characteristic is associated with the articulation procedures, the second one relates to the articulation principles (McEvily and Chakravarthy 2002). Tacit knowledge is difficult to express in writing (Polanyi 1962), and those who possess it are unaware that they even have it, which makes it difficult to imitate (Winter 1987; Reed and DeFillippi 1990). Tacit knowledge is best transmitted through personal contact (for example, face-to-face interaction and apprenticeship-based teaching and learning) rather than through codification means. In industry clusters, tacit knowledge is usually obtained through face-to-face interaction (Rosenfeld 1997; Porter 1998; Ganesan *et al.* 2005). Since knowing the knowledge source is of crucial importance when knowledge is predominantly tacit (Levin and Cross 2004), the social embeddedness in a cluster facilitates this process, as it allows firms to get to know the knowledge source better and to obtain the capability to recognize their competence.

The second dimension is a continuum that has simple and complex knowledge as polar opposites. Complexity is usually defined according to dimensions that increase the difficulty of comprehending how a system (that is, organization, organism, and device) functions or produces some output (McEvily and Chakravarthy 2002: 289). In his work 'The Architecture of Complexity', Simon (1962) defined a complex system as consisting of many distinct and interacting elements, which have equally important individual effects as well as joint effects on the outcomes produced by the system and its performance. Complex knowledge evokes more causal uncertainties as compared to simple knowledge. Consequently, whereas simple knowledge can be captured with little information, the description of complex knowledge requires a larger amount of information (Garud and Nayyar 1994: 370). This makes complex knowledge more difficult to imitate when compared to simple knowledge (MacMillan *et al.* 1985).

The third dimension is the distinction between independent and systemic knowledge. While independent knowledge can be described by itself, systemic knowledge needs to be described in relation to other knowledge vectors (Winter 1987; Garud and Nayyar 1994). Hence, systemic knowledge implies a higher level of specificity.

Besides the component/architectural continuum, we also distinguish between knowledge access and knowledge acquisition as two separate knowledge processes. Grant and Baden-Fuller (2004) defined knowledge access as the process of sharing solutions to a specific problem in the receiver end while the knowledge and capacity to develop the solution stays with the source. According to these authors, knowledge acquisition is sharing the knowledge about how to solve the problem and thereby enabling the receiver to become independent of the source in the future. Whereas knowledge access is associated with partners tending to remain specialized and their knowledge bases remaining differentiated (Grant and Baden-Fuller 2004), a constellation based primarily on knowledge acquisition risks being unstable as partners start to absorb each other's knowledge. Thus we develop the following two propositions:

P1: Cluster membership facilitates access primarily to component knowledge.
P2: Cluster membership facilitates acquisition primarily of architectural knowledge.

As mentioned earlier, several researchers have stated that knowledge plays a central role in the process of firm internationalization (Johanson and Vahlne 1977; Eriksson *et al.* 1997; Johanson and Vahlne 2009). In their seminal article, Johanson and Vahlne (1977) argued that as a firm gains more knowledge about its market it becomes more committed to that market. So, how do firms learn about internationalization? This question has been the centre of much research on learning and internationalization (for example, Barkema and Vermeulen 1998; Autio *et al.* 2000; Forsgren 2002; Elango and Pattnaik 2007). For example, in their study about learning and internationalization of new ventures, Zahra *et al.* (2000) focus on knowledge about products, technology, and markets (similar to component knowledge) and on knowledge about organizations (similar to architectural knowledge).

According to Johanson and Vahlne (2009), the business environment is a web of interconnected relationships, which they refer to as networks, and these networks are fundamental for firms to learn about internationalization. Networks increase the knowledge base of the firm, as well as allow both the firm and the network to create new knowledge. Clusters also consist of webs of interconnected relationships (Astley and Fombrun 1983; Bresser 1988) through which firms learn (Ibert 2007; Waxell and Malmberg 2007) and internationalize. Hence we suggest the following proposition:

P3: Knowledge access and knowledge acquisition within a cluster influence cluster members' internationalization.

In the following section we present the case of the New Zealand boat-building cluster to illustrate the arguments we have put forward and to verify the conceptual model we have proposed.

The New Zealand boat-building cluster

Government support

The New Zealand government initiative in encouraging the growth of industry clusters was instigated when Michael Porter and his team conducted a study on 'Upgrading New Zealand's Competitive Advantage' (Crocombe *et al.* 1991). Various industry associations with financial assistance from government were catalysts for industry collaborations in various guises and with varying degrees of commitment (Ffowcs Williams 1996). The main aim of these collaborative schemes was to encourage members within the same industry to cooperate in running their businesses. Thus, industry clusters in New Zealand evolved in various stages. The New Zealand Trade Development Board, now called New Zealand Trade and Enterprise (NZTE), a government-funded export-promotion organization, introduced the concept of industry clusters to New Zealand. NZTE recognized that members within the same industry competed with each other in the domestic market and decided to encourage firms to 'collaborate to compete internationally'. One scheme NZTE applied was to provide funds at a national level for a cluster facilitator to act as a catalyst to set up and facilitate a cluster initiative. Thus, networks evolved mainly as a government initiative to encourage SMEs to export (Ffowcs Williams 1996). NZTE eventually reduced its involvement in cluster development as it expected industry clusters to become self-managing and self-funding within a short period of time. Consequently, some newly formed clusters that were just starting to grow lost their financial support, thus curtailing their activity. Some local governments picked up on the cluster initiatives started by NZTE and now partially fund the development of selected regional industry clusters to boost regional growth. In other words, industry cluster initiatives started at a national level with the main objective to boost exports but are now primarily used at a local level to boost regional growth.

The boat-building industry cluster is an example of a successful cluster. It won the 1999 Trade New Zealand Export Award in the 'Cooperating to Compete' section. The cluster initiative at national level in the boat-building industry was mainly through the Marine Industry Association (MIA). An organization called Marex (now known as New Zealand Marine; NZMarine) was established with NZTE funding in 1992 to boost exports in the boat-building industry and to encourage boat builders to collaborate so that they can learn from one another as well as develop new knowledge which would help them to compete successfully in international markets.

This boat-building cluster consists of boat builders, boat suppliers, boat designers, sail makers, boat repairs, chandlers, consultants, trade associations, universities, training institutes, and government institutions. This cluster is characterized by a close geographic proximity: 80 per cent of boat builders in New Zealand are located within a 20-kilometre radius. It is also a networking cluster as it allows information to be exchanged amongst members through boat shows, meetings, and seminars. It encourages members to work together to promote their products at international boat shows. To some extent, cluster members obtain government assistance to attend these boat shows and to present New Zealand as a boat-building nation. This helps cluster members to share costs and resources as well as allowing them to learn from each other's experiences. During these cluster-based activities members learn about new markets, new opportunities, technologies, and the benefits of working together.

Research method

We collected data for this study by conducting semi-structured interviews with respondents belonging to 18 organizations from the New Zealand boat-building cluster.[1] Ten firms were from the core of the cluster, and eight were cluster-supporting institutions. The ten core firms were small to medium-sized companies with five to 215 employees. All but one (B3) of these firms sell their products or services to international markets and have international sales ranging from 18 per cent to 100 per cent of total sales. B3 is indirectly involved in internationalization as most of its customers have international sales. All ten firms are owner-managed businesses with the founding members actively involved in the day-to-day running of the business. Respondents were chosen largely because they were members of the MIA and they were willing to participate in the study. For core firms, the chief executive officers were interviewed because they were the key decision-makers in terms of their firm's involvement in the cluster as well as in internationalization.

The eight cluster-supporting institutions included MIA, New Zealand Marine Export Group (NZMARINE), City Council, Economic Development Agency (EDA), NZTE, a university, a technical college, and a management consultancy in the boat-building industry. Each of these organizations plays a specific role in the cluster. For instance, MIA focuses on training, NZMARINE on marketing and exports, economic-development agencies on marketing and facilitation, city councils on infrastructure, and educational institutes on different types of training and academic courses relating to the boat-building industry, and the consultancy provides business advice to the industry.

---

[1] To maintain anonymity the names of some of these organizations and respondents will not be disclosed.

Table 7.1 Firms' international sales, scope of knowledge and engagement in knowledge sharing

Firm	% of international sales	Geographic scope	Process linkages of knowledge sharing
B1	90	Local or global	Social network main source of industry information.
		Local	Marex facilitates knowledge sharing.
B2	31	Local	Marex facilitates knowledge sharing.
B3	None	Global	Global social network good source of global marine industry information.
B4	80	Local	Local social sailing. Network facilitates cooperation, which in turn allows for better product development).
		Local	Kiwi firms 'work together to develop a total product'.
B5	50	Local	Long-term friendships, often from sailing, encourages knowledge sharing.
B6	90	Local	Social side of sailing allowed greater sharing of ideas.
		Local	High level of vertical co-specialization a medium for transfer of ideas.
		Local	Operating in niches often allows Kiwi marine firms to share technology.
		Global	Many workers leave for higher wages overseas, and few, but some workers return from overseas with new skills.
		Local	Marex facilitates technology sharing.
		Local	Cooperation on America's Cup regattas developed further innovations to beat international competition.
B7	90	Local	Passion for sailing a source of knowledge. Social network encourages knowledge sharing.
		Local	Auckland University a source of knowledge.
		Local	Joint projects involve much sharing of knowledge.
B8	99	Local	Marex's functions are a source of information regarding overseas markets.
B9	100	Local	Information sharing through Marex and social networks through sailing.
B10	100	Global	Information sharing through global networks industry.

Access to the network is restricted to members only. The members of the cluster initiative have to abide by the rules and regulations set by the boat-building cluster. There are also unwritten rules, norms, and values for behaviour within the cluster. Opportunistic behaviour is kept in check by group monitoring and by ostracizing those who behave in such a way. Members who damage the reputation of the cluster are forced to withdraw.

The information in Tables 7.1 and 7.2 provides an illustration of the arguments we have put forward to develop our propositions relating to knowledge access and knowledge acquisition within a regional cluster. Our respondents were pretty clear regarding the percentage of their firms' international sales, the geographic scope of the knowledge they worked with, and what knowledge-sharing processes they were involved (Table 7.1). Using the interviewees' descriptions of knowledge and their specific references to, for instance, market knowledge, product knowledge, technical knowledge, business knowledge, formal academic knowledge, etc., we classified the knowledge type as either component or architectural knowledge (Table 7.2). By far most of the respondents referred to either access or acquisition of knowledge, and in a few instances both terms were used – a fact reflected in the last column in Table 7.2. When these specific terms were not used during the interviews, we carefully analysed the descriptions they gave and the examples they provided in order to specify the particular knowledge process.

Cluster members' internationalization

Previous work on clusters has focused mainly on the clusters' ability to foster competitive advantage of member firms and to support and encourage member firms' internationalization (Schmitz 1995; Porter 1998, 2000; OECD 2000). We would like to point out that a reverse link exists, too: namely, from firm internationalization to becoming part of a regional cluster. Such a link is documented in a study by Chetty (2004) which suggested that the experience of entering international markets initiated the complex processes of cluster development. Once the firms she studied started to enter international markets, they realized that they could learn more about building boats (knowledge access) and about international markets and business practices (knowledge acquisition) by collaborating with local firms in the industry. Thus, internationalization changed the relationships between local competing firms from one of 'win-lose' competition to one of 'win-win' cooperation and mutual dependency. When these firms started to gain international experience they recognized the strategic benefits of working together with other cluster members and subsequently became more committed to the cluster. The growing focus and specialization of firms in this cluster has contributed to their international success as firms build distinctive reputation and knowledge assets in their chosen niches and the market assets of the cluster. Since there is technology and product specialization in

Table 7.2 Coding of knowledge types and knowledge processes

Description of knowledge	Knowledge type	Access/ acquisition
Sharing of market and product information in the cluster lifts the level of everyone's professionalism (Company 1).	C (Market, product)	Access
They love boat building and have the technical skills for that, but their business knowledge is weak, so they lose money and fail in business (Company 1).	C	
A lot of New Zealand boat designers are self taught and have no academic qualifications. In places such as America and Europe boat designers are academically qualified but tend to lose their creative edge as they are focused on a narrow path and do not look at innovative ways of doing things (Company 1).	A (formal academic)	Acquisition
Boat building it's not something you can learn in a year. Traditionally it's been a five or a six-year apprenticeship and you pretty much need all of that. It's something that you're not born with it and you need a lot of time to be taught the skills (Company 1).	A (Experiential)	Acquisition
Many boat builders have good technical skills, but lack business skills. Trade New Zealand, the Business Development Board, informal mentors and others from the industry provide good business advice (Company 2).	C (Business)	Access
We interact closely with our customers to identify what their needs are and then adapt the material and technology to suit the customer's requirements. The cluster has helped us to identify the needs of the industry and how to overcome the problems. [...] If you don't understand the issues that the builders got, you'll tend to develop a technology that doesn't work [...] Without the cluster we would have been trying to force upon the industry or our customers technologies that just wouldn't flow (Company 2).	C (Market)	Access
There is a company which is the leader in the materials technology in the industry. Others come to learn from them about this technology (Company 2).	C (Technology)	Acquisition

Continued

Table 7.2 Continued

Description of knowledge	Knowledge type	Access/ acquisition
Information through informal networks is useful, but one has to consider the facts as there is some rumour and gossip (Company 2).	C (Information)	Access
Our problem is that we need skilled design engineers and craftsmen and we're such a specialized field that we don't have education systems that are targeted at our technology. You learn about engineering or you learn about naval architecture, but you don't learn about composites for the marine industry. So, if we take on a graduate or two or three, we've got to start with training them from scratch (Company 2).	C and A	Acquisition
We have a good relationship with a university and research institutes for access to knowledge. We learn about international trends through exposure by visiting markets and talking to customers (Company 2).	C (Technical, market)	Access
We go to international boat shows, so we can meet up with customers. By wandering around a show with them, we get a far better idea of what their needs and requirements are (Company 3).	C (market)	Access
Informal communication is important, especially amongst people who have common debtors. Communication among us is very important because there's a lot of risk in the market. The industry is very small worldwide, so you get to know a lot of people from right round your centre. They say: 'You've been coming to these shows a lot, do you know who this guy is? He wants to buy my products – is he reputable?' (Company 3).	C	Access
A lot of people who are running businesses in this industry, apart from learning how to physically build a boat, have never had any commercial training, or have never worked in a commercial environment. As our companies get bigger, we're getting other people involved that can help us with our management [...] to make sure we are planning and thinking right (Company 3).	C (managerial)	Access and acquisition

Continued

Table 7.2 Continued

Description of knowledge	**Knowledge type**	**Access/ acquisition**
We've gone very well in the super yacht industry because we've had those same groups of people from the racing background come into the super yacht industry and we could work together to develop a total product (Company 4).	C, A	Access and Acquisition
We acquire information from boat shows and designers in order to be aware of what is happening in the industry (Company 4).	C	Access
We have brought in people with no marine experience but who have good management skills, such as human-resource management, planning and project management skills. We still need people with yachting experience to sell the product. As the company has started to grow, we need these management skills (Company 4).	C (managerial)	Access and acquisition
One actually has to learn most of the things in the marine industry through sailing or through being involved in the sport, it's not quite as easy as reading it in a book (Company 5).	C and A	Acquisition
The people who get involved in boat building are people who started out sailing in little wee boats when they were kids. Later on they went to bigger boats and they they've been sailing in the America's Cup. Then they decide to start their business (Company 5).	A	Acquisition
The industry in the past was pretty much backyard boat building, so you've generally got boat builders running boat builders and no one ever takes any time off to learn the management skills (Company 6).	C (managerial)	Access and acquisition
People go and work overseas and come back with new ideas (Company 5).	C and A	Access and acquisition
We are all fairly competitive and we have settled into our own little niche areas within the industry. We often share or compare notes on different aspects of the business, whether it's accounting software, or time-clock tracking mechanisms. There is often times when we can share that technology because we don't directly compete with each other (Company 6).	C (Technology)	Access

Continued

Table 7.2 Continued

Description of knowledge	Knowledge type	Access/ acquisition
There is an awful lot of knowledge that is shared within the boat-building industry through the social aspect of our industry. This is probably quite specific to this industry. The social aspect also brings skills back into the industry because others are playing with the very things we build (Company 6).	C	Access
The America's Cup is a direct result of a lot of effort outside the cluster that has educated and brought together a whole bunch of skills and taken them offshore to basically beat all the international syndicates that were out there. From the very first challenge that New Zealand participated in, we were making America's Cup history. The industry produced innovative fibreglass boats and mast shapes that challenged existing products. [...] The talent and that depth of skill wasn't created overnight, it has evolved. [...] We're sailing these boats and constantly looking for that edge [...] by being innovative with the boats that we produce (Company 6).	A	Acquisition
Industry New Zealand gave us a grant for $200,000 through the Boat Industry Association (BIA) to help develop the apprenticeship workbooks and the training kind of things to cross train people into boat building out of other industries and that sort of thing (Company 6).	C (Government support)	Acquisition
We go out there and we look at our competitors and try and build on what we do already and make it better (Company 6).	A and C	Acquisition
We look, learn, and listen when we attend boat shows. We realized that we had great innovations when we attended these shows and compared our boats to others in the market (Company 6).	C	Access
Members in the cluster may share the same interior designers. This means that knowledge in the industry is shared which is beneficial (Company 6).	C	Access
Entering international markets has been a hard learning curve (Company 6).	A (Experiential)	Acquisition

Continued

Table 7.2 Continued

Description of knowledge	**Knowledge type**	**Access/ acquisition**
The [boat-building] company founders were sailors first and then went into boat building. As they have been professional sailors competing in the major yachting races, they know more about sailing than their customers (Company 7).	A	Acquisition
An important part of keeping a business successful is seeing the members of staff sailing with the best. [...] One of the prerequisites for being a designer in our company is a sailing CV. This is just as important as the technical work experience (Company 7).	A (Experiential)	Acquisition
The innovation and new ideas is what it's all about and that's what has got them [the boat builders] to where they are. They are open to new ideas. [...] Some of them won't employ people who haven't come through the same route as they have. They simply won't do it. I think potentially that could be a hindrance to the ongoing success of their business (Company 7).	A	Access and acquisition
There's a very strong bias towards people needing to have practical skills and being very technically sound. In regards to training, this used to occur slowly through experience and learning, but now they cannot produce boat builders fast enough. So, they are working with the Marine Industry Association on training programmes through an apprenticeship (Company 7).	C	Acquisition
We keep up to date with technology by working with customers, suppliers, and the University of Auckland. We collect information through the Internet, customers, boat shows, sailing regattas, and social networks in the cluster (Company 7)	C (Information)	Access
Marex is an excellent networking group. Within the group there is a lot of information sharing regarding overseas markets (Company 8).	C (Information)	Access

Continued

Table 7.2 Continued

Description of knowledge	Knowledge type	Access/ acquisition
We share the costs of acquiring knowledge, such as purchasing an expensive market report, with other cluster members (Company 8).	C	Access (although interviewee talks about acquisition)
We keep up to date with what is going on through feedback from distributors worldwide (Company 8).	C	Access
The New Zealand Marine group is very cohesive. People are prepared to go out and seek large projects and if they do not have the capabilities [for these projects], they are prepared to work with their competitors. [...] The cluster members have a lot of international exposure so they are aware of new innovations and opportunities and they are adaptable to change (Company 8).	C and A	Access and acquisition
We collect a lot of information through our subsidiary. We changed our distribution mode as our previous distributor was filtering information. Now we have our own subsidiary abroad (Company 8).	C and A	Access
We produced products for a multinational, so we had to lift our standards. This was a huge learning curve for us, but we benefited from this by winning another contract with another multinational (Company 9).	A	Acquisition
Boat building is so complex that unlike a lot of other industries it's got to grow slowly (Company 9).	C and A	Acquisition
I built my first boat in New Zealand at the age of 14. [...] We have set up our own apprenticeship programme. The first year was expensive, the second year we started making money, and then we have got people trained exactly how we wanted them to do it (Company 10).	C and A	Acquisition
We attend at least three boat shows a year to get business and to keep up to date with the technology. When we go to the shows, we normally take four or five people in-house with us and they go through other boats and they get different ideas [...] We come back and we have a meeting and we pool them all together for the next boats.	C (Technology)	Access

the cluster this illustrates knowledge access as the knowledge and capacity to develop the solution stays with the source.

Consistent with Dhanaraj *et al.* (2004), the firms in our study realized that it is easier to acquire tacit knowledge such as management and marketing skills through social interactions with business partners embedded in networks. By being embedded in this cluster, members are more likely to benefit from sharing each other's experiences in international markets and learning from their successes and failures. This type of foreign-market knowledge is usually tacit as it cannot easily be codified and made explicit. As Table 7.1 illustrates, most of the architectural knowledge in this cluster was acquired at the local cluster level. Table 7.2 provides several internationalization examples on the basis of access and acquisition of respectively component and architectural knowledge. This table shows that it was important for these firms to attend international boat shows to learn about competitors, customers, and the latest technology developments. By attending international boat shows and other events together, cluster members strengthened their relationships and informally shared knowledge. Through these frequent social interactions, cluster members developed trust and learned to communicate openly, thus easing access and acquisition of knowledge. They acquired (typically tacit) foreign-market knowledge through listening and observing how their peers interact and do business in foreign markets. This facilitated collaboration in this co-specialization alliance and subsequently encouraged individual members' internationalization.

Table 7.2 also verifies our theoretical propositions that, with some exceptions, knowledge access is mostly related to component knowledge whereas knowledge acquisition is typically related to architectural knowledge. For example, sharing of market and product knowledge provides cluster members with access to component knowledge, thus increasing the knowledge of the cluster as a whole. Another example is the long period of time that it takes to learn boat-building skills because this architectural knowledge cannot be acquired overnight as it is usually complex, intangible, and tacit. The trust built in social networks within this cluster leads to the informal accumulation of both component and architectural knowledge which results in economic benefits for the firm. Through these social networks, information and knowledge are diffused rapidly and group absorptive capacity is developed, which makes it easier to access and acquire knowledge within the cluster. In fact, the glue that holds this boat-building cluster together is sailing. There are several examples in Tables 7.1 and 7.2 illustrating that through their links with sailing these boat builders form social networks with each other and subsequently access and acquire knowledge.

Consistent with Gulati (1998) and Ellis (2000), these social networks also lead to formation of strong relationships and the subsequent accumulation of social capital, which allows them to learn and internationalize. These social networks often have a long history as they were formed when members, who are now middle-aged, sailed together in their youth. Through these social networks boat builders build trust, learn to identify new opportunities, find out and decide who to work with within the cluster, and share knowledge about technological developments and international markets. For example, while sailing the boat, they discuss the technical features of the boat and what aspects to improve, as well as organizational issues such as international distributors, customers, and markets (component knowledge and architectural knowledge).

Conclusion

In this chapter we have proposed a conceptual model to explain how cluster membership based on close geographical proximity facilitates access to component knowledge and acquisition of architectural knowledge within the cluster. We then use these two categorizations – of types of knowledge and of knowledge processes – to examine how the latter, namely knowledge access and knowledge acquisition, accelerate firm internationalization. We used the New Zealand boat-building cluster to illustrate these concepts and to verify the proposed links.

For the sake of the clarity of our theoretical arguments, we positioned component and architectural knowledge types as opposite poles. In reality, however, what one cluster member may perceive to be component knowledge can appear as architectural knowledge to another cluster member. Nevertheless, our illustrative case study confirms that access to knowledge is more frequently associated with component knowledge whereas knowledge acquisition is typically associated with architectural knowledge. We also argued and provided evidence for the idea that cluster membership provides a number of advantages for member firms for both knowledge access and knowledge acquisition and, consequently, for members' internationalization. In addition, we highlighted the involvement of the New Zealand government to take initiatives at both national and regional level to facilitate the development of clusters to boost SME internationalization. This shows that policy-makers recognize the value of clusters in creating opportunities for knowledge access and knowledge acquisition and subsequent internationalization. It also indicates that governmental support is crucial for internationalization of SMEs.

References

M. Andersson and C. Karlsson, 'Knowledge in Regional Economic Growth: The Role of Knowledge Accessibility', *Industry and Innovation*, 14 (2007): 129–49.

W. Astley and C. Fombrun, 'Collective Strategy: Social Ecology of Organizational Environments', *Academy of Management Review*, 8 (1983): 576–87.

D. B. Audretsch, 'Agglomeration and the Location of Innovative Activity', *Oxford Review of Economic Policy*, 14 (1998): 18–29.

E. Autio, H. J. Sapienza, and J. G. Almeida, 'Effects of Age at Entry, Knowledge Intensity, and Imitability on International Growth', *Academy of Management Journal,* 43 (5) (2000): 909–24.

H. G. Barkema and F. Vermeulen, 'International Expansion Through Start-up or Acquisition: A Learning Perspective', *Academy of Management Journal,* 41 (1) (1998): 7–26.

J. M. Bloodgood, H. J. Sapienza, and J. G. Almeida, 'The Internationalization of New High-Potential U.S. New Ventures', *Entrepreneurship Theory and Practice,* 20 (1996): 61–76.

W. Bönte, 'Inter-Firm Trust in Buyer–Supplier Relations: Are Knowledge Spillovers and Geographical Proximity Relevant?', *Journal of Economic Behavior & Organization,* 67 (3–4) (2008): 855–70.

P. J. Buckley and M. J. Carter, 'A Formal Analysis of Knowledge in Multinational Enterprises', *Journal of International Business Studies,* 35 (2004): 371–84.

R. Bresser, 'Matching Collective and Competitive Strategies', *Strategic Management Journal,* 9 (1988): 375–85.

S. Chetty and H. Agndal, 'Role of Inter-Organizational Networks and Interpersonal Networks in an Industrial District', *Regional Studies,* 42 (2008): 175–87.

S. Chetty, 'On the Crest of a Wave: Evolution of the New Zealand Boat Building Cluster', *International Journal of Entrepreneurship and Small Business,* 1 (2004): 313–29.

S. Chetty and C. Campbell-Hunt, 'Explosive International Growth and Problems of Success amongst Small Firms', *International Small Business Journal,* 21 (2003): 61–81.

C. T. Crocombe, M. J. Enright and M. E. Porter, *Upgrading New Zealand's Competitive Advantage.* (Auckland: Oxford University Press, 1991).

S. Davenport, 'Exploring the Role of Proximity in SME Knowledge-Acquisition', *Research Policy,* 34 (2005): 683–701.

J. E. Denis and D. Depelteau, 'Market Knowledge, Diversification, and Export Expansion', *Journal of International Business Studies,* 16 (1985): 77–89.

C. Dhanaraj, M. A. Lyles, H. K. Steensma, and L. Tihanyi, 'Managing Tacit and Explicit Knowledge Transfer in IJVs: The Role of Relational Embeddedness and the Impact on Performance', *Journal of International Business Studies,* 35 (5) (2004): 428–42.

B. Elango and C. Pattnaik, 'Building Capabilities for International Operations Through Networks: A Study of Indian Firms', *Journal of International Business Studies,* 38 (4) (2007): 541–55.

P. Ellis, 'Social Ties and Foreign Market Entry', *Journal of International Business Studies,* 31 (2000): 443–69.

A. Eraydin and B. Armatli-Køroğlu, 'Innovation, Networking and the New Industrial Clusters: The Characteristics of Networks and Local Innovation Capabilities in the Turkish Industrial Clusters', *Entrepreneurship & Regional Development,* 17 (2005): 237–66.

K. Eriksson and S. Chetty, 'The Effect of Experience and Absorptive Capacity on Foreign Market Knowledge', *International Business Review,* 12 (2003): 673–95.

K. Eriksson, J. Johanson, A. Majkgard, and D. Sharma, 'Experiential Knowledge and Cost in the Internationalization Process', *Journal of International Business Studies,* 28 (1997): 337–60.

A. Etzioni, and O. Etzioni, 'Face-to-Face and Computer-Mediated Communities: A Comparative Analysis', *Information Society,* 15 (1999): 241–8.

M. Forsgren, 'The Concept of Learning in the Uppsala Internationalization Process Model: A Critical View', *International Business Review,* 11 (3) (2002): 257–78.

F. Ffowcs Williams, 'Hard and Soft Networks: Helping Companies Cooperate for Export Growth', *New Zealand Strategic Management*, 2 (1996): 30–6.

S. Ganesan, A. J. Malter, and A. Rindfleisch, 'Does Distance Still Matter? Geographic Proximity and New Product Development', *Journal of Marketing*, 69 (2005): 44–60.

R. Garud, and O. Nayyar, 'Transformative Capacity: Continual Structuring by Intertemporal Technology Transfer', *Strategic Management Journal*, 15 (1994): 365–85.

X. Gellynck, B. Vermeire, and J. Viaene, 'Innovation in Food Firms: Contribution of Regional Networks within the International Business Context', *Entrepreneurship & Regional Development*, 19 (2007): 209–26.

M. Granovetter, 'The Strength of Weak Ties', *American Journal of Sociology*, 78 (1973): 1360–80.

G. Grabher, 'Rediscovering the Social in the Economics of Interfirm Relationships', in G. Grabher (ed.), *The Embedded Firm: On the Socioeconomics of Industrial Networks* (London and New York: Routledge, 1993), pp. 1–31.

R. M. Grant, 'Toward a Knowledge-based Theory of the Firm', *Strategic Management Journal*, 17 (1996): 109–22.

R. M. Grant and C. Baden-Fuller, 'A Knowledge Accessing Theory of Strategic Alliances', *Journal of Management Studies*, 41 (2004): 61–84.

R. Gulati, 'Alliances and Networks', *Strategic Management Journal*, 19 (1998): 293–317.

M. T. Hansen, 'The Search–Transfer Problem: The Role of Weak Ties in Sharing Knowledge across Organizational Subunits', *Administrative Science Quarterly*, 44 (1999): 82–111.

B. Harrison, 'Industrial Districts: Old Wine in New Bottles?', *Regional Studies*, 26 (1992): 469–83.

R. Henderson and K. B. Clark, 'Architectural Innovation: The Reconfiguration of Existing Product Technologies and the Failure of Established Firms', *Administrative Science Quarterly*, 35 (1990): 1–30.

O. Ibert, 'Towards a Geography of Knowledge Creation: The Ambivalences between "Knowledge as an Object" and "Knowing in Practice"', *Regional Studies*, 41 (2007): 103–14.

A. C. Inkpen, 'Learning and Knowledge Acquisition through International Strategic Alliances', *Academy of Management Executive*, 12 (1998): 69–80.

A. C. Inkpen and E. W. K. Tsang, 'Social Capital, Networks, and Knowledge Transfer', *Academy of Management Review*, 30 (2005): 146–65.

J. Johanson and J.-E. Vahlne, 'The Internationalization Process of the Firm', *Journal of International Business Studies*, 8 (1977): 23–32.

J. Johanson and J.-E. Vahlne, 'The Mechanism of Internationalization', *International Marketing Review*, 7 (1990): 11–24.

J. Johanson and J.-E. Vahlne, 'Commitment and Opportunity Development in the Internationalization Process: A Note on the Uppsala Internationalization Process Model', *Management International Review*, 46 (2006): 165–78.

J. Johanson and J.-E. Vahlne, 'The Uppsala Internationalization Process Model Revisited: From Liability of Foreignness to Liability of Outsidership', *Journal of International Business Studies*, 40 (2009): 1411–31.

C. Jones, W. S. Hesterly, and S. P. Borgatti, 'A General Theory of Network Governance: Exchange Conditions and Social Mechanisms', *Academy of Management Review*, 22 (4) (1997): 911–45.

B. Kogut, 'The Network as Knowledge: Generative Rules and the Emergence of Structure', *Strategic Management Journal*, 21 (2000): 405–26.

P. J. Lane and M. Lubatkin, 'Relative Absorptive Capacity and Interorganizational Learning', *Strategic Management Journal*, 19 (1998): 461–77.

E. E. Leamer and M. Storper, 'The Economic Geography of the Internet Age', *Journal of International Business Studies,* 32 (2001): 641–65.

S. Lemarie, V. Mangematin, and A. Torre, 'Is the Creation and Development of Biotech SMEs Localized? Conclusions Drawn from the French Case', *Small Business Economics,* 17 (2001): 61–76.

D. Z. Levin and R. Cross, 'The Strength of Weak Ties You Can Trust: The Mediating Role of Trust in Effective Knowledge Transfer', *Management Science,* 50 (2004): 1477–90.

I. MacMillan, M. McCaffery, and G. Van Wijk, 'Competitors' Responses to Easily Imitated New Products: Exploring Commercial Banking Product Introductions', *Strategic Management Journal,* 6 (1) (1985): 75–86.

A. Madhok, 'Know-How-, Experience- and Competition-related Considerations in Foreign Market Entry: An Exploratory Investigation', *International Business Review,* 5 (1996): 339–66.

A. Malmberg and P. Maskell, 'Localized Learning Revisited', *Growth and Change,* 37 (1) (2006): 1–18.

S. Matusik and C. W. Hill, 'The Utilization of Contingent Work, Knowledge Creation and Competitive Advantage', *Academy of Management Review,* 23 (1998): 680–97.

P. P. McDougall, S. Shane, and B. M. Oviatt, 'Explaining the Formation of International New Ventures: The Limits of Theories from International Business Research', *Journal of Business Venturing,* 9 (6) (1994): 469–98.

S. K. McEvily and B. Chakravarthy, 'The Persistence of Knowledge-Based Advantage: An Empirical Test for Product Performance and Technological Knowledge', *Strategic Management Journal,* 23 (2002): 285–305.

S. Michailova and H. I. M. Wilson, 'Small Firm Internationalization through Experiential Learning: The Moderating Role of Socialization Tactics', *Journal of World Business,* 43 (2008): 243–54.

A. Morrison, 'Gatekeepers of Knowledge within Industrial Districts: Who They Are, How They Interact', *Regional Studies,* 42 (6) (2008): 817–35.

J. Nahapiet and S. Ghoshal, 'Social Capital, Intellectual Capital, and the Organizational Advantage', *Academy of Management Review,* 23 (1998): 242–66.

R. Nelson and S. Winter, *An Evolutionary Theory of Economic Change* (Cambridge, MA: Belknap Press of Harvard University, 1982).

H. Neergaard and J. P. Ulhoi, 'Government Agency and Trust in the Formation and Transformation of Interorganizational Entrepreneurial Networks', *Entrepreneurship Theory and Practice,* 30 (2006): 519–39.

I. Nonaka and H. Takeuchi, *The Knowledge-Creating Company: How Japanese Companies Create the Dynamics of Innovation* (Oxford: Oxford University Press, 1995).

P. M. Norman, 'Knowledge Acquisition, Knowledge Loss, and Satisfaction in High Technology Alliances', *Journal of Business Research,* 57 (2004): 610–19.

New Zealand Trade and Enterprise, NZTE website on cluster initiatives, http://www.nzte.govt.nz/section/11962.aspx (accessed 3 October 2008).

M. Polanyi, *Personal Knowledge: Toward a Post-critical Philosophy* (New York: Harper Torchbooks, 1962).

OECD (ed.), Bologna Italy, 14–15 June Workshop 2: SME Conference Business Symposium (2000).

OECD, *SMEs and Entrepreneurship* (Organisation for Economic Co-operation and Development 2006). Available online at http://www.oecd.org.document (accessed 14 November 2008).

B. M. Oviatt and P. P. McDougall, 'Challenges for Internationalization Process Theory: The Case of International New Ventures', *Management International Review,* 37 (2) (1997): 85–99.

E. Penrose, *The Theory of the Growth of the Firm* (Oxford: Blackwell, 1959).
M. Porter, 'Location, Competition, and Economic Development: Local Clusters in a Global Economy', *Economic Development Quarterly,* 14 (2000): 15–34.
M. E. Porter, 'Clusters and the New Economics of Competition', *Harvard Business Review,* November–December (1998): 77–90.
R. Reed and R. J. DeFillippi, 'Causal Ambiguity, Barriers to Imitation, and Sustainable Competitive Advantage', *Academy of Management Review,* 15 (1990): 88–102.
A. R. Reuber and E. Fisher, 'The Influence of the Management Team's International Experience on the Internationalization Behaviors of SMEs', *Journal of International Business Studies,* 28 (4) (1997): 807–25.
P. S. Ring and A. H. Van de Ven, 'Structuring Cooperative Relationships between Organizations', *Strategic Management Journal,* 13 (1992): 483–98.
S. A. Rosenfeld, 'Bringing Business Clusters into the Mainstream of Economic Development', *European Planning Studies,* 5 (1997): 3–23.
R. W. Rycroft, 'Does Cooperation Absorb Complexity? Innovation Networks and the Speed and Spread of Complex Technological Innovation', *Technological Forecasting and Social Change,* 74 (2007): 565–78.
H. Schmitz, 'Small Shoemakers and Fordist Giants: Tale of a Super Cluster', *World Development,* 23 (1995): 9–28.
H. A. Simon, 'The Architecture of Complexity', *Proceedings of the American Philosophical Society,* 106 (1962): 467–82.
S. Tallman, M. Jenkins, N. Henry, and S. Pinch, 'Knowledge, Clusters, and Competitive Advantage', *Academy of Management Review,* 29 (2004): 258–71.
W. Tsai and S. Ghoshal, 'Social Capital and Value Creation: The Role of Intrafirm Networks', *Academy of Management Journal,* 41 (1998): 464–76.
B. Uzzi, 'Social Structure and Competition in Inter-Firm Networks: The Paradox of Embeddedness', *Administrative Science Quarterly,* 42 (1997): 35–67.
G. Walker, B. Kogut, and W. Shan, 'Social Capital, Structural Holes and the Formation of an Industry Network', *Organization Science,* 8 (1997): 109–25.
A. Waxell and A. Malmberg, 'What is Global and What is Local in Knowledge-Generating Interaction? The Case of the Biotech Cluster in Uppsala, Sweden', *Entrepreneurship & Regional Development,* 19 (March) (2007): 137–59.
S. Winter, 'Knowledge and Competence as Strategic Assets', in D. J. Teece (ed.), *The Competitive Challenge: Strategies for Industrial Innovation and Renewal* (New York: Harper & Row, 1987): pp. 59–184.
G. S. Yip, J. Gomez-Biscarri, and J. A. Monti, 'The Role of the Internationalization Process in the Performance of New Internationalizing Firms', *Journal of International Marketing,* 8 (2000): 10–35.
H. Yli-Renko, E. Autio, and H. Sapienza, 'Social Capital, Knowledge Acquisition, and Knowledge Exploitation in Young Technology-based Firms', *Strategic Management Journal,* 22 (2001): 587–613.
H. Yli-Renko, E. Autio, and V. Tontti, 'Social Capital, Knowledge, and the International Growth of Technology-Based New Firms', *International Business Review,* 11 (2002): 279–304.
S. A. Zahra, 'The Internationalization of Entrepreneurship', *Journal of International Business Studies,* 26 (2005): 2–8.
S. A. Zahra, D. R. Ireland and M. A. Hitt, 'International Expansion by New Venture Firms: International Diversity, Mode of Market Entry, Technological Learning and Performance', *Academy of Management Journal,* 43 (2000): 925–50.

8

The Trä 50 Group: A Supplier Network to IKEA

Karolina Elmhester and Staffan Brege

Introduction

This chapter presents the case of Trä 50, a unique empirical case of a sort rarely encountered in the literature: a cooperative effort between potential competitors and their major shared customer. These companies handled demands for increased strategic competence, increased large-scale investments, increased operational effectiveness, and so on, by working together. The term 'strategic network' is sometimes used to denote the deliberate management of such cooperation (Klint and Sjöberg 2003). The case demonstrates that potential competitors can cooperate to a very positive effect and that, by cooperating, relatively small suppliers can collectively become powerful.

The empirical data cover the Trä 50 group's development from 1992 to 2000. Trä 50 was a horizontal cooperative effort involving eight Swedish furniture companies over a ten-year period. Their common denominator was that they all were large suppliers of flat-pack furniture (comprising products such as tables, counters, and cupboard doors that use board as the basis of their construction) to IKEA, on which most of them were completely dependent in terms of share of deliveries. When Trä 50 was formed, two of the participating companies were part of the IKEA group; by the end of the cooperation, three participants were IKEA owned (in the Swedwood International supplier group). At the time, all Trä 50 companies were considered important Swedish suppliers to IKEA and all were medium-sized enterprises.

Trä 50 was considered a success by its participants, and hard figures support this positive claim. This chapter analyses the success factors operative in this unique empirical case, presenting them as theoretically based propositions regarding work in cooperative supplier networks, interpreted as deliberately managed strategic networks (Klint and Sjöberg 2003).

Method

In our view, the Trä 50 case is interesting and unique – a key prerequisite when research is based on a single case (Eisenhardt 1989; Yin 2003). According to Eisenhardt (1989), the case-study methodology makes the research process interactive: a case study entails interaction between the various research steps: from theory to case, back to theory again, and so on (see also Yin 2003). Our analysis, which ends by formulating several propositions, is based on comparing empirical findings or patterns with theoretical results documented in broader empirical studies.

The empirical data were mainly collected in 2004 through personal interviews with one or two representatives from each of five cooperating companies, with the Trä 50 coordinator, and with the two Trä 50 project managers (working on a consultancy basis). A representative of their shared customer, IKEA Trading AB, was also interviewed. A total of twelve interviews were conducted.

The interviews were semi-structured to enable discussion and to prevent us from leading the interviewees. As the basis for the case, all interviews were recorded and transcribed, and some documents from the supplier network project were consulted as well. Finally, the project manager of the studied business-development project is also a co-author of this chapter.

Trä 50: a network in a network

In 1992, the Trä 50 group was initiated by the coordinator of Sydpoolen, a sort of regional strategic network (Lundberg 2008). All IKEA's suppliers in Sydpoolen were ready to join Trä 50, and additional IKEA suppliers were also invited. Finally, there were eight companies in the Trä 50 group, all of which produced flat-pack furniture. Trä 50's formation was actively supported by IKEA, which was a – in most cases *the* – dominant customer of all Trä 50 companies.

IKEA was not a member of Trä 50, but was involved in its founding, and IKEA representatives were often invited to seminars and discussions – even the CEO (chief executive officer) of the time, Anders Moberg, attended seminars. IKEA Trading (ITAB, IKEA's operational trading organization) and IKEA of Sweden (responsible for product development and strategic purchasing) were Trä 50's principal contacts.

IKEA had put pressure on its Swedish suppliers in the early 1990s, complaining largely of excessive prices and overly long delivery times. More significant, however, was IKEA's criticism of the estimation models that automatically led to these high prices. IKEA was a coveted customer because of its large purchasing quantities, but dependence on it put suppliers in a weak negotiating position. It was said that, when visiting suppliers, IKEA purchasers opened by saying 'lower your prices' before even saying 'hello'. With the formation of Trä 50, suppliers saw a chance to improve their bargaining position.

Trä 50 was project-based, so all activities were organized in project form. The cooperation involved two large projects, each running for three years.

The first project period: the lead-time project (1992–5)

This project aimed to shorten the time from order to end customer from approximately 35 days to three to seven days; however, many of the lead-time reductions involved logistics *within* IKEA and were not primarily implemented by the suppliers. The Trä 50 companies put considerable time into the project, making large investments mainly in automated and larger-scale production facilities.

In the lead-time project, the companies and the project manager devised a plan to pinpoint what areas to improve and in what order. The initial analysis indicated approximately 15 areas. Not all the companies were interested in all the agenda items, but all had their own interests covered. Some of areas considered were purchasing, estimation, organizational development, and packaging. The project was carried out between 1992 and 1995.

The Trä 50 group met at seminars four or five times a year, between which the participating companies worked on internal projects. Each company hosted at least one seminar during the lead-time project. Attendance at the seminars was always high – there was seldom anyone missing.

Before Trä 50, it was uncommon to invite competitors to see production facilities – visiting competitors had to stay in the office area, according to one Trä 50 participant. It was something completely new for competitors to visit each other, which broadened their horizons and gave them ideas for how to develop and improve their own factories. The participating companies' lead times decreased by 35–50 per cent over the course of the project, and each company kept working on lead times even after the project ended. In 1992, the year the lead-time project started, Trä 50 companies had a total turnover of approximately SEK 800 million and employed a total of approximately 830 employees. In October 1995, at the end of the project, their turnover was SEK 1,200 million and their workforce totalled 1,100. However, the companies' efforts did not end with the project, and the development and rationalization process continued for many years afterward (see Table 8.1).

In addition, the lead-time project involved the possibility of knowledge development among employees owing to, for example, changed production and wrapping processes. The new routines often meant that the employees had more responsibility, putting them into new roles they had to learn. Furthermore, both project managers (one for each project) visited all the companies to help them with current problems, contributing to knowledge development throughout the companies.

Individual Trä 50 companies might have been able implement some of the project activities by themselves, but it would likely have taken them longer, and few could have afforded a consultant to help them throughout the process (the project manager's role). One positive effect of Trä 50 was

Table 8.1 Results of the lead time project for each participating company

Company	Result of the lead-time project
Alnen AB	• Reliability of deliveries increased from 60 to 93 per cent. • Lead time reduced by 35 per cent.
Bräntorps Möbler AB	• Capacity increased from SEK 60 to SEK 200 million per year. • Lead time reduced from eight to four weeks.
Möbelknaggen AB	• Reliability increased to 100 per cent. • Lead time reduced by 35 per cent.
AB Recta	• Lead time in production area reduced by 50 per cent.
Swedform Trä AB	• Lead time in production area reduced from eight weeks to ten days.
Swedwood AB	• Turnover in the factory increased from nine to 13 times per year.
Svedplan AB	• Large lead-time reduction for new products.
Totebo AB	• Profitability increased from SEK 1.2 to SEK 11 million. Lead time reduced from 49 to 29 days.

Source: Internal documents

the high speed of project implementation, which meant that the companies noticed the effects of cooperation in just a few years. Personal competitiveness between CEOs prompted them to work hard not to fall behind – no one wanted to be the last to complete the project activities.

The second project period: the business-development project (1995–8)

The next project focused on business and marketing development. According to the project manager, the central goal was to build knowledge in the 'strategy development' area. The project was divided into two parts: establishing a closer partnership with IKEA (project partnership) and initiating exports to a shared market (project exports). The business-development project also ran for three years, 1995–8.

The outcomes of the project partnership were more formal 18–36-month partnership agreements, but IKEA placed high demands on the companies that were to become its partners and chose not to sign the same kind of partnership agreement with all Trä 50 companies. According to the project manager, however, the most important task was to maintain ongoing discussion with IKEA to establish a common arena for partnership development. IKEA's southern European suppliers were gaining ground, as were suppliers in eastern Europe, making it crucial that the Trä 50 companies increase their visibility to the IKEA organization. However, IKEA made it very clear that discussions would be held at a more principal level and that all agreements would be negotiated with IKEA on a single-supplier basis.

In strategic discussions with IKEA, the Trä 50 companies argued that they would have to double their turnover to build the financial foundation needed to automate production, reduce the share of direct labour cost, and ultimately lower their prices to IKEA. The companies wanted to become 'model factories' for other IKEA suppliers; IKEA could then transfer the knowledge gained from cooperating with the Trä 50 group to their foreign factories ('clone factories'). However, such reasoning was not fully accepted by IKEA, which claimed that some of their foreign factories were at least as efficient.

One supplier in particular dramatically changed its strategy due to Trä 50 involvement and discussions with IKEA. The company became a large supplier to IKEA, which accounted for approximately 70 per cent of its sales volume, instead of holding to its initial strategy that 'no customer share should exceed 30 per cent.' The company's total turnover increased as well.

Due to Trä 50 cooperation and discussions with IKEA, some of the companies fine-tuned their strategies to differentiate themselves and avoid head-on competition with other Trä 50 colleagues. All these companies initially had diversified production; by concentrating on fewer areas, they were able both to differentiate themselves from their competitors and specialize their production operations to increase efficiency. Of course, the suppliers competed for orders from IKEA, but they also often covered for each other and behaved towards each other in a manner that was much more complementary than competitive. Over time, as they came to know each other better, they gave each other work and helped each other out when needed. They viewed the foreign furniture suppliers as their main competitors.

For project exports, Japan was the chosen target, since a company similar to IKEA was on the rise there and the market was neutral in that none of the Trä 50 companies already had customers there. When the Japanese export initiative was almost settled as a joint marketing effort, the plans fell through: the companies felt they were simply not ready for this kind of joint effort. In any case, the companies learned a great deal about marketing from seminars and negotiations related to the initiative, and they valued this knowledge. The experience gained could be applied in reaching out to other export markets as well.

The business-development project had a less concrete outcome than did the lead-time project, according to the project manager. These projects were more about relationships and improved knowledge and awareness, which are difficult to measure. The companies' focus was on production, and marketing was not a high priority for most. The project helped the companies become more proactive when it came to market relationships and production. It was especially in their relationship to IKEA that they all learned to be more proactive, how to negotiate better, and so on.

All the Trä 50 companies remained significant IKEA suppliers. This was a main goal of the cooperation, and it was accomplished despite the considerable pressure IKEA had put on them. By cooperating, the suppliers had, among other things, improved their production processes to meet IKEA's high demands. Furthermore, the seminars and partnership discussions with IKEA made the suppliers more visible to IKEA, which might also have contributed to increased orders.

Trä 50 consisted of more than just the two projects mentioned: bonus purchasing agreements, study tours abroad for benchmarking, experience exchange meetings, and study visits to other Trä 50 companies were among the other activities. Bonus agreements were made with several suppliers, covering, for example, electricity, packaging, and chipboard/fibreboard. Agreements with producers of corrugated board packaging greatly helped the companies reduce their costs.

Furthermore, Trä 50 activities created strong personal bonds between the participating management groups of the different suppliers, especially between the CEOs. These bonds of friendship and mutual trust lent crucial support to the development of company strategies that set the Trä 50 companies apart in terms of core competence, resource base, and product range. According to participants, the management group became a sort of 'ghost board of directors' for the Trä 50 companies – a sounding board for ideas, discussion, and reflection. Broadening their horizons was one important achievement. There was also an element of positive personal competition between participating CEOs, which was another powerful driving force for new investments, especially when it came to buying new production equipment. Each CEO saw what the others were doing and thought 'if they can do it, then I can too'. There seemed to be no envy in this dynamic; instead, the competition gave them the confidence to make strategic investments. Some CEOs considered themselves primarily as 'production people' and only secondarily as 'furniture people', so investments in new machinery was important to these CEOs.

The period after the business-development project

When the business-development project had finished, the focus of Trä 50 activities shifted to benchmarking conducted via study tours. In terms of group activities, however, there has been little Trä 50 action since 2000–1. According to the coordinator, there were many reasons for this; in particular, negative industry conditions at the time meant managers had to concentrate on their own companies, and new projects were not initiated when conditions subsequently improved. 'None of the projects failed. Some of them did not achieve 100 per cent of their goals, but none of them was terminated prematurely. We kept pushing the survival time of the companies some years forward, and that's what it was all about' (The coordinator of Trä 50).

By 2000, the joint turnover of the Trä 50 companies was approximately SEK 2 billion. These suppliers had managed nearly to double their turnover, and most of this increased value and volume was accounted for by sales to IKEA. This development was attributable partly to Trä 50 cooperation but largely to the rapid growth of IKEA. One Trä 50 project manager stated that IKEA could have given its orders to other companies but, thanks to the progress in the Trä 50 companies, they were the chosen suppliers. Although the cost-benchmarking of furniture factories in eastern Europe put Swedish suppliers at a disadvantage, they managed to keep deliveries up due to highly competitive quality, logistics, and ability to ramp up production of new models. One reason for this success was the primary goal of being 'model factories', a goal that spurred the companies to work hard.

Success factors

When examining the various success factors more closely, the vital starting point is to analyse the nature of the two major projects, the lead-time project and the business-development project. The lead-time project, with its focus on shortening the lead time and reducing costs, was an ambitious and mostly internally oriented portfolio of actions to increase efficiency and productivity. It was handled by the Trä 50 companies themselves, helped by the project manager, and impinged on an area they regarded as their core competence. Compared with the lead-time project, the business-development project needed increased cooperation from IKEA, particularly in the partnership programme, and from other external parties in the export component of the project. While IKEA could fully support all dimensions of the lead-time project, the partnership project was more delicate, as IKEA did not wish to put the Trä 50 group in too favoured a position. We have identified the following success factors.

Strategic importance to suppliers and high degree of involvement

Trä 50 was *strategically important* to the participating suppliers, since improving internal efficiency and developing some form of partnership relationship with IKEA were matters of survival for most suppliers in the group. The CEOs of the Trä 50 companies felt they needed the combined strength of the group to accomplish these tasks. Furthermore, support and trust between the CEOs encouraged them to take necessary actions in their companies.

The strategic importance of Trä 50 meant that the projects were driven by a *high degree of involvement* from the participating CEOs and management team members. The coordinator and the two project managers were all impressed by high attendance at meetings, how hard attendees worked, and the enthusiasm displayed. The participants suggested activities and actively participated in all Trä 50 activities. Participant involvement and commitment are essential if cooperation is to yield positive outcomes (cf. Sahlin-Andersson 1996; Human and Provan 1997; Elmhester 2008). The people involved must believe in the projects and be willing to work to reach the project goals (Andersson 2005). Attaining positive results needs hard work from the participating companies, and involved and committed people are much more willing to do that work. It is impossible simply to join a network, sit back passively, and expect positive effects on one's company. In addition, the involvement and commitment generated a positive atmosphere in the Trä 50 group, which itself contributed to participant willingness to attend meetings and work hard.

In retrospect, one could say that involvement at deeper organizational levels of the involved companies could have been higher (Varamäki 2001). It was mostly CEOs, in some cases together with a salesperson or production manager, who represented the participating companies at Trä 50 meetings. On the other hand, the Trä 50 companies were satisfied with the project outcome, which would inevitably have been altered by higher employee involvement.

Supplier driven and supported by the biggest customer, IKEA

Another reason for the high involvement was that Trä 50 was *driven by the participating suppliers*. This meant that the suppliers themselves determined the project agendas and objectives and decided what companies to involve in the cooperation (Ager 2000). The positive atmosphere that arose from this dynamic was important to the group, as was the high degree of involvement.

At the same time, the Trä 50 cooperation was also approved of and *supported by a customer*, IKEA. IKEA was involved in founding Trä 50, and its representatives often attended Trä 50 seminars and meetings. Support from and ongoing contact with the major customer ensured that Trä 50 would focus on areas relevant to it; this reassured the companies that the projects were valuable and probably inspired them to work harder (Ager 2000; Öhrwall Rönnbäck *et al.* 2001). Close contact between IKEA and Trä 50 also let suppliers show their customers their ability to rationalize operations in production, logistics, and also product development. The result of IKEA's support and input was that Trä 50 suppliers continued to do business with IKEA, orders increased, and discussions with IKEA were on a more equal footing than when suppliers were on their own with IKEA representatives. It was both symbolically and practically important that IKEA-owned suppliers should also join the Trä 50 cooperation. These suppliers acted as 'linking-pin organizations' representing both the big customer in some way and Trä 50.

Competent coordination and stable administrative organization

When Trä 50 was formed, there was already an established administrative organization at Sydpoolen and a *competent coordinator*. This organization had been established with the help of external funding, so external financing was more crucial for the formation of Sydpoolen than for Trä 50. The coordinator initiated the Trä 50 group, applied for external funding for its projects and activities, hired project managers, and took care of most communication.

The coordinator was considered competent, based on the following abilities. First, the coordinator possessed strong entrepreneurial skill to take new initiatives and carry them to fruition. He made sure that the Trä 50 group was on a solid footing and that it included most of IKEA's largest Swedish suppliers. The coordinator also helped the participants carry out suggested Trä 50 activities.

The coordinator also possessed diplomatic skills that were important both internally in the group and externally in relations with IKEA. It was sometimes difficult to deal with eight entrepreneurs in the same room, all full of ideas they wanted to share and discuss.

The coordinator was influential in policy-making and project funding at the industry and governmental levels. In all, the Trä 50 group was coordinated by a person who was well regarded and possessed integrity and legitimacy. The fact that the coordinator handled administration let the companies concentrate on the projects and the work these entailed; this ensured project effectiveness and goal attainment (Ager 2000; Westerberg *et al.* 2002, 2003; Ager *et al.* 2004).

As mentioned, an *administrative organization* comprising a coordinator and an administrator was already in place when the Trä 50 group was formed. These two staff members ensured that the participating companies could concentrate on Trä 50 activities by taking care of all planning, communication, and paperwork and by following through on decisions. This was essential, since the CEOs and additional management team representatives who were involved in Trä 50 had companies to run and had no time for Trä 50 administration as well. The administrative organization ensured, for example, regular meetings, essential in building trust between participants and in keeping them involved (Elmhester 2008). The result was that participants were deeply involved in Trä 50 and had great confidence in each other. Elmhester (2008) discusses the importance of external project managers/coordinators for strategic network success, and Trä 50 had both an external coordinator and project managers.

Participants were competent in themselves, which made for a competent group

The suppliers participating in Trä 50 were individually *competent* in that, in both national and international terms, they were fairly large and well equipped in physical plant and competence. They were regarded as the best producers among Swedish suppliers to IKEA.

These companies had developed from small into medium-sized operations by growing organically, their CEOs regarded change positively, and their production evolved as customer demands changed. The Trä 50 companies were willing and used to making changes, but they had reached a point where external help was needed. Their experience of change facilitated the rationalizations and improvements that the Trä 50 project required.

The result was that Trä 50 amassed an impressive quantity of experience and knowledge, creating a competent group that could raise all the participants to a new level. The companies were large enough to invest in production and their CEO could spend time outside the company.

The participants were in a position to invest the time and money needed to realize the goals of the projects. This resource sufficiency also meant that the group could reach critical mass and formulate and follow a long-term strategy (Ager 2000).

Professional project management and clear objectives

Work in the Trä 50 group was mainly run on a project basis led by *professional management*. The project managers specified the objectives of the projects, supervised the CEOs, pushed the companies to work harder when needed, and so forth. Among other matters, this helped the CEOs keep focused on the right issues. The first project – lead time and cost reduction – had an ambitious scope and objectives, and each company had to choose the most important activities for its situation. The objective of 50 per cent reduction in lead time was achieved by some companies and almost achieved by the others, so the degree of goal fulfilment was high.

The objectives of the business-development project were more qualitative, so the degree of goal fulfilment was determined more subjectively by the Trä 50 companies, project manager, and coordinator. In most of the cases, the companies managed to turn their relationships with IKEA into three-year contracts – a step forward and a prerequisite for survival for at least half the Trä 50 members (especially given that survival as an IKEA supplier was the main objective when the Trä 50 group was formed). The export project must be regarded as a failure, even though all parties involved gained valuable experience.

The two Trä 50 projects had *clear objectives*. In strategic networks, especially those involving small and medium-sized enterprises, both short- and long-term goals are essential for a positive outcome (Elmhester 2008). Short-term goals lead to rapid results, which increase participant involvement and eagerness to keep cooperating in the interests of the long-term goals. Long-term goals are often the ultimate reason why companies want and need to cooperate and are usually more complex than short-term goals (Elmhester 2008).

Clear objectives are significant, because cooperation projects often have limited time and money at their disposal. To make best use of limited resources, work must be focused, and clear objectives help the cooperating parties focus on the right things. Furthermore, having clear objectives from the outset makes it easier for potential participants to know whether cooperation might interest them. Accordingly, clear objectives increase the chance of recruiting the right mix of companies for the cooperation; they also ensure that all participants share the same goals. Without this, positive results are elusive (Hamel 1991).

Flexibility in the projects

Flexibility in both the lead-time project and the business-development project was another positive feature of Trä 50 cooperation. Flexibility meant that participants did not have to do everything together at the same time or be involved in every activity: companies could choose the activities and work areas that suited them. The 15 different areas identified in the lead-time project helped companies focus on just the areas most valuable to them, or on areas perceived as problematic. If the companies had to wait for each other or spend time on issues irrelevant to them, irritation could have resulted, making people lose interest in the project. In the business-development project, each company could also choose to participate in various subprojects, which made them more committed to the work.

More generally, we can conclude that projects should be flexible enough that all members of the cooperation experience a positive answer to the question 'what's in it for me?' If project goals and activities are too inflexibly formulated, some participants may feel less involved, possibly causing lack of interest and inspiration. Every member must feel involved if the cooperation is to achieve high attendance and commitment.

Strong personal bonds among CEOs

Favouring the positive outcome and longevity of the Trä 50 group were the *strong personal bonds* that arose from the cooperation. Personal bonds are difficult to quantify or measure yet are among the most valued outcomes from strategic networks, according to participants (Elmhester 2008).

The atmosphere in the Trä 50 group was both trusting and friendly; it was also competitive, in the sense that everyone wanted to be the first to make new investments and to implement new processes. The trusting atmosphere made the dialogue more open and honest, contributing to the strong participation and hard work (Neergaard 2000; Varamäki and Vesalainen 2003). There was little disagreement or conflict between the Trä 50 suppliers, and none that posed any threat to the climate of cooperation. The CEOs' strong personalities led to many discussions, but these only seemed to have positive effects on the cooperation. The CEOs were able to discuss ideas and thoughts that otherwise lacked a forum, so the cooperation served as a sort of 'ghost board of directors' for the companies. The managers forged a network of close personal relationships that endured after Trä 50. Despite this fact, few participants cited personal contacts as a reason to cooperate, and the literature seldom mentions it as an objective (Elmhester 2008). Many of the CEOs participating in Trä 50 said that 'having someone to call' was among its most positive outcomes. The emergence of trust and friendship in cooperation is not a given but is something that needs time and patience to develop (Neergaard 2000; Elmhester 2008).

References

B. Ager, M. Bergqvist, and J. Backman, *Nätverk och kluster i Träsverige 2003,* Report 2004:062 (Dalarna: Högskolan Dalarna, 2004).

B. Ager, *Strategiska nätverk i träförädling,* Report no. 9 (Dalarna: Högskolan Dalarna, 2000).

K. Andersson, 'Suppliers in Collaboration: The Impact on the Strategies of the Individual Firm', licentiate thesis, Linköpings University, 2005.

K. Eisenhardt, 'Building Theories from Case Study Research', *Academy of Management Review,* 14 (1989): 532–50.

K. Elmhester, 'Små företag i strategiska nätverk: hur påverkas det enskilda företagets utveckling?', Doctoral dissertation, Linköpings University, 2008.

G. Hamel, 'Competition for Competence and Inter-Partner Learning within International Strategic Alliances', *Strategic Management Journal,* 12 (1991): 83–103.

S. Human and K. Provan, 'An Emergent Theory of Structure and Outcomes in Small-Firm Strategic Manufacturing Networks', *Academy of Management Journal,* 40 (1997): 368–403.

M. Klint and U. Sjöberg, 'Towards a Comprehensive SCP-Model for Analyzing Strategic Networks/Alliances', *International Journal of Physical Distribution and Logistic Management,* 33 (2003): 408–25.

H. Lundberg, 'Geographical Proximity Effects and Regional Strategic Networks', Doctoral dissertation, Uppsala University, 2008.

H. Neergaard, 'Networks as Vehicles of Internationalization: Network Relationships and the Internationalization Process of Small Furniture Manufacturers', Doctoral dissertation, Århus Handelshøjskole, 2000.

K. Sahlin-Andersson, 'I styrbarhetens utmarker', in I. Sahlin (ed.), *Projektets paradoxer* (Lund: Studentlitteratur, 1996).

E. Varamäki, 'Essays on Multilateral Cooperation between SMEs', Doctoral dissertation, University of Vaasa, 2001.

E. Varamäki and J. Vesalainen, 'Modelling Different Types of Multilateral Co-operation between SMEs', *Entrepreneurship and Regional Development,* 15 (2003): 27–47.

M. Westerberg, J. Wincent, and D. Örtqvist, *Träinnovas storprojekt trä: Utvärdering av samverkansprojekt inom träsektorn i Jämtland 2000–2002,* report (Luleå: Luleå University of Technology, 2002).

M. Westerberg, J. Wincent, and D. Örtqvist, *Ywood: Utvärdering av samverkansprojekt inom träsektorn i västernorrland 2000–2002,* report (Luleå: Luleå University of Technology, 2003).

R. Yin, *Case Study Research: Design and Methods* (Thousand Oaks, CA: Sage Publications, 2003).

A. Öhrwall Rönnbäck, S. Gullander, and S. Brege, 'Product Development in Supplier Networks: Critical Success Factors', *Proceedings IPSERA 2001,* International Purchasing and Supply Education and Research Association Conference (2001).

9

Marketing Cooperation and Public Policy in Italian Networks of Fashion Firms

Simone Guercini and Andrea Runfola

Introduction

The aim of this paper is to describe and interpret innovative forms of marketing cooperation between enterprises in specific contexts of the Italian fashion industry. The phenomena observed are linked to the changing marketing environment for companies forming part of local fashion systems (districts and other areas of production). In particular, the development of these new forms is facing two main threats. These threats are commonly described by two factors that may appear related: *increased ability of competitors from emerging countries* (the competitive ability of producers located in emerging countries [principally China] and their growing weight in the total purchases by existing and potential customers); and *increased power of direct customers,* either in terms of bargaining power or market power connected to the management of downstream phases in the chain (especially in management of brands and retail outlets). The two threats, the first 'horizontal' and international and the second 'vertical' but not necessarily international, have been widely discussed as being related to each other and linked to the more general phenomenon of globalization (Guercini and Runfola 2004).

These two threats have forced fashion firms to reconsider their marketing strategies and have led to development of innovative forms of marketing cooperation and to new behaviour. It is possible to outline the importance of driving factors such as commitment, communication, learning, shared values, and trust in the development of the new forms. At the same time, the role of public policy is crucial in initiating and supporting these new marketing activities. We describe in depth these new forms of marketing cooperation, pointing out some emerging issues.

Empirically, the chapter presents findings from a case analysis process of three Italian cases of marketing cooperation among firms operating in the fashion system, explaining the specificities in each case. The cases analysed emerged in the past decade. Longitudinal analysis is relevant in these cases, as the development of these new forms seem to follow peculiar paths. The research described in the chapter is derived from the observation of these networks arising from the cooperation between manufacturing enterprises operating within local systems of small and medium-sized Italian firms engaged in the production of fashion goods.

Integrated marketing activities in geographic-based networks

To analyse cooperation we use the concept of 'integrated marketing'. The integrated marketing theme is linked to the organizational literature on integration processes (Thompson 1967; Lawrence and Lorsch 1973). The organizational integration is seen as a response to the need for marketing activities that does not find adequate response in individual companies.

In the marketing management approach, the concept of 'integrated marketing' can be interpreted on the basis of different meanings. It is possible to distinguish concepts of integrated marketing 'within a firm' or 'outside a firm'. The former includes integration between marketing models adopted in marketing management (such as mass marketing and relationship marketing), between marketing levers understood as operational policies (distribution and communication), and between marketing and other functions (marketing and research and development (R&D), marketing and production, marketing and human resources).

The integration of marketing outside the firm in turn presents other possible cases. For example, it occurs in the interaction between buyer and seller (relationships and networks), in the forms of cooperation between competitors (for example, between firms belonging to industrial districts), and among players who have complementary resources (for example between different service firms in a tourist destination). These forms of integrated marketing, inside and outside the firm, can be explained more in detail considering the academic literature.

Integrated marketing is defined as a process of integration that involves 'the extremes of mass branding and one-to-one relationship marketing' (Iacobucci and Calder 2002: 1). This concept is clearly linked to the integration of marketing policies in terms of operational levers. We have integration of marketing levers, for example with firms operating in the high-end market in terms of coherence between retailing and communication processes (Holm 2006).

Integration between marketing and other organizational functions is partly linked. In this sense, marketing is said to be integrated when the marketing effort extends through the company in all aspects (and in all functions) rather than simply arises from the marketing department. This is another way of saying that the marketing effort has to be developed as a theme that has relevance for all functional areas. For example, the integration process can exert considerable influence on the training of operational staff that has direct contact with consumers in service, in the case of integration between marketing and human resources (Chimhanzi 2004) or on new product development in the case of integration between marketing and R&D (Souder and Sherman 1993).

Marketing can be integrated outside the boundaries of the firm. Referring to the conditions of success of small businesses exporting in international contexts, in an Italian research-oriented study, Bonaccorsi (1992: 629) showed how in industrial districts 'there are personal and friendly relationships among entrepreneurs [...] when demand is increasing, entrepreneurs feel they can give information on export markets even to their local competitors, with the expectation that it will be reciprocated in the future, when needed'. Marketing integration between competitors in local systems is not limited to the exchange of market information. In fact, marketing integration can lead to alliances for co-marketing (Gulati 1998), involving not two but a large number of actors, setting up multilateral rather than bilateral partnerships (Bucklin and Sengupta 1993).

The co-marketing alliances are defined as 'mutual recognition and understanding that the success of each firm depends in part on the other firm' (Anderson and Narus 1990: 42). These alliances are forms of 'working partnerships' undertaken by companies that want to build or amplify benefits through the implementation of a joint initiative involving coordination between the partners on one or more aspects of marketing. Unlike buyer–seller or manufacturer–distributor partnerships, co-marketing alliances are lateral relations which occur between companies at the same level in the value chain and represent forms of 'symbiotic marketing' (Adler 1966: 60).

Symbiosis is commonly defined as 'the living together in intimate association of two dissimilar organisms for mutual benefit, and it is widespread phenomenon in the natural world' (Varadarajan and Rajaratnam 1986: 7). The same concept of 'symbiotic marketing' is defined as 'an alliance of resource programs or between two or more independent organizations designed to increase the market potential of each' (Adler 1966: 60). In the field of alliances, the academic literature identifies forms of various kinds; generally it seems that 'vertical relationships' (Johnston and Lawrence 1988: 24) rather than 'lateral relationships' have received the most attention (Bucklin and Sengupta 1993: 32).

The cooperation initiatives in the field of marketing, however, seem generally connected to forms of complementarity between the resources available to the partners involved. Consequently, previous studies on relations focused on the study of the behaviour of inter-organizational exchanges, focusing in particular on the themes of functional specialization, scarcity of resources, and emergence of dependency on resources between the partners

(Pfeffer and Salancick 1978). The presence of an asymmetric distribution of resources gives rise to an asymmetric power structure (Emerson 1962) since dependence on resources determines the rising power, defined as the ability to consciously exercise a clear influence. As the perceived effectiveness of the relationship is taken as an indicator of success in organizational theory (Van De Ven 1976) to be applied in particular in the context of dyadic relations (Ruekert and Walker 1987), there is a tendency for actors to prefer exchanges with equally powerful actors because there are fewer costs attached to the exchange process (Cook 1977: 67).

This vision seems to depend on the involvement of existing resources in determining the dynamics of cooperation between existing organizations. Cooperation in the field of marketing, however, can be aimed precisely at the development of new resources, through interaction with the partner or the creation of new organizational units. The motivation for a company could be the realization of new marketing activities through the creation of new organizational units autonomous from those enterprises that will be cooperating. In this way, relevant factors such as organizational compatibility among the partners involved in the process of cooperation are of lesser importance (Achrol *et al.* 1990).

Marketing cooperation and consortium as emerging actor

Marketing can be integrated outside the organization when marketing activities not only benefit an organization but also a group of organizations. In this case, the integration of marketing activities can be made setting up one or more new organizational units, which can be autonomous and assume the nature of new actor(s). This is the organizational solution to the need for integration on which our analysis in this chapter is concentrated. In this case the emerging actor(s) assumes the role of focal player in the interaction with the environment for the network of local firms involved in the cooperative marketing initiative.

The marketing effort is undertaken mainly by this actor whose role is to engage an aggregation of organizations in a unified action. In this sense, integrated marketing may involve specific co-marketing activities, where independent players can agree to embark on a joint effort on any specific project or on a series of defined projects (Bucklin and Sengupta 1993).

When these projects call for the formation of a new organizational unit, as in the cases we propose, integrated marketing takes the form of giving a role to a particular player who directs a unified action. The new organizational unit acts as a key player for the interaction with the market, established by driving factors such as trust and shared values and facilitating the possibility of support for the cooperative initiative by public policy-makers.

Different situations can emerge when the integrated marketing initiative creates this new organization. The integrated marketing in this context refers to a process that connects with the market, set in motion by an actor who takes a system of roles with reference to a group of companies and organizational concerns operating in a certain context. The form of marketing here is integrated in the sense that it refers to an aggregation of operators. It integrates the strategic and operational needs of these players and their effort to establish suitable links with the market. These operators can be 'localized' in a specific area or alternatively share a specific context or specific needs.

This new actor emerging from the integrated marketing initiative of a firm network can assume the legal form of a consortium. The concept of consortium is defined as an association of businesses, institutions, or investors, for the purpose of engaging in a joint venture. Following this definition, a consortium is a cooperative arrangement among firms, groups, or institutions to pursue a set of shared goals. This is an organizational form which is traditionally diffused in Italy, especially in the contest of marketing cooperation in local systems of small and medium-sized firms, where consortia manage the integration of marketing activities over a number of enterprises, as occurs for example in the organization of trade fairs and the management of geographically characterized brands. Consortium is not especially innovative under this perspective.

We identify in the consortium the answer to the need for an actor which achieves the shared aims of the organizational network of local firms. The consortium is an organizational tool of cooperation between firms. The phenomenon of cooperation we observe is justified by the firms and often communicated outside, as an emerging response. In particular, the forms of cooperation observed seem to present the following characteristics, summarized through a series of parameters listed below:

- They involve small and medium-sized manufacturers in the fashion industry.
- They aggregate together companies on a territorial basis, nationally in the cases proposed here (made in Italy).
- They include complex marketing activities such as opening of retail outlets and creation of brands.
- They benefit from the role of leader entrepreneurs which create consensus on the initiatives.
- They enjoy support from public policy-makers (regional institutions) either in the creation of the new forms or in the development of activities.

Cases of innovation in geographic-based networks of fashion firms

In this paragraph we are going to illustrate some cases which show interesting evidence in terms of innovation in marketing cooperation.

Table 9.1 A summary of the cases analysed

Case (new actor set-up)	Sector	Firms' localization	No. of companies	Motives behind integration	First store opening	Main customers of the firms belonging to the new forms
Classico Italia Retail (consortium and limited company)	Luxury menwear	Mainly regional base (Tuscany, Campania, Lombardy, Veneto, Emilia Romagna and Piedmont)	22	• defence of 'Made in Italy' brand • production • shift of events from Florence to Milan • brand awareness	2005	Fashion brands Retail chains Independent stores
Centopercento Italiano (consortium)	High-end leather market	Regional base (Tuscany)	64	• loss of creative contribution to customer • defence of 'Made in Italy' brand and decision not to delocalize production in emerging market	2007	Fashion brands
I Love Italian Shoes (project groups and limited company)	Footwear	National base (Italy)	100	• Loss of awareness in the final market • Anti-counterfeit	2007	Shoe manufacturers Retail chains

Table 9.2 Main institutional actors supporting the integration of marketing activities in the case analysed

Actor	Public policy and main features	Cases
ICE	• It is a public body responsible for developing, facilitating, and promoting economic and trade relations with Italians firms abroad, with particular attention to the needs of small and medium enterprises, their consortia and associations. • ICE, operates in close collaboration with the Italian Ministry of Economic Development, developing the programme of promotional activities. • ICE has its headquarters in Rome and has a network of 16 offices in Italy and 115 offices in 84 countries worldwide.	Support to the retail project in the I Love Italian Shoes case Support to the branding policies in the Classico Italia case
Regions	• Regions are devoted to the government of specific portions of the Italian territory. • Among different tasks, regions, along with the state, are devoted to the promotion of the territory abroad and to the support of the internationalization of enterprises.	Support to the formation and to the development of Centopercento Italiano Support to the retail project in the I Love Italian Shoes case.
Ministry of Economic Development	• The ministry is devoted to the planning, coordination, and support of the project on a territorial or sectorial basis. • It has a specific section devoted to the development of internationalization of Italian enterprises.	Support to the retail project in the I Love Italian Shoes case.
Other institutions	• This category covers a wide number of institutions (either public or private and public) in the local area, including: chambers of commerce, municipalities, provinces, and associations.	Support to create consensus over the initiatives in all of the three cases with different degrees of participation.

The cases Classico Italia, Centopercento Italiano, and I Love Italian Shoes differ from each other at least in the sector of the fashion industry involved, the number of firms linked to the projects, and the peculiarities in terms of different levels of integration between business-to-business (BTB) and business-to-consumer (BTC) competencies. Moreover, all the cases are founded within a specific region (Table 9.1). However, all cases show a general trend in integrating branding and retailing activities as an emerging response to

Table 9.3 Research methodology for data collection and analysis

Methodology	Aims	Sources	Cases
Secondary research	• Selection of cases of aggregation of firms in the Italian fashion system • Search for secondary data • Developing case studies	• Published articles • Firm's reports • Firm's Internet Websites • Fashion magazines • Academic Journals on fashion topics	• Centopercento Italiano • Classico Italia • I Love Italian Shoes
Preliminary Contacts	• Preliminary analysis of the case	• Phone contacts with firm's representatives • Preliminary contacts with managers	• Centopercento Italiano • Classico Italia
Case analysis	• Focus on specific issues regarding the new actor • Search for primary data • Developing case studies	• Face-to-face in-depth interviews with managers (managing and marketing directors) through ad-hoc questionnaire	• Centopercento Italiano • Classico Italia

threats perceived in the marketing environment and benefit from the role of a leader entrepreneur and from institutional support (Table 9.2).

From a methodological point of view, while Classico Italia and Centopercento Italiano are built following entirely the path listed in Table 9.3, the case of I Love Italian Shoes is mainly the result of an in-depth analysis on secondary data.

Classico Italia

The Classico Italia case is a relevant example regarding the integration of marketing activities for its most recent evolution from a consortium that exclusively represents members in BTB markets to a consortium that supports activities with reference to BTC relationships. Classico Italia is a consortium that represents 22 companies, including those that operate in the high-end fashion menswear market located predominantly in Tuscany, Campania, Lombardy, Veneto, Emilia Romagna, and Piedmont. Classico Italia was set up as a means to defend the *Made in Italy*.

The development of the associative form has seen the implementation of BTC practices, along with BTB practices. The outset, in the 1980s, is linked to common sensitivities of associates to a competitive threat found in the difficulties of protecting the 'Made in Italy' production in the competitive landscape of men's fashion. Another threat over the years was a gradual shift of events from Florence to Milan, at least for women's fashion, and the resulting willingness of a series of entrepreneurs (not just Tuscan) to maintain the city as the reference for male fashion.

Consequently, the consortium was founded, to confront common problems faced by competing companies belonging to the same level of the supply chain. The consortium was set up for joint participation to one of the most significant men's fashion events worldwide, Pitti Uomo. In this sense, from the beginning (the foundation dates back to 1986), Classico Italia has exhibited the collection of companies participating in the consortium in a dedicated pavilion. The management interviewed stresses the role of interpersonal relationships between entrepreneurs in the formation of the consortium and the focal role of some of them in promoting the initiative. In fact, Classico Italia was set up thanks to a series of informal personal contacts, prompted by an entrepreneur (who acted as a leader). The manager interviewed stresses the leading role of one of them who represented the leadership of the association, allowing the collaborative phase.

Since its foundation, the consortium operate in BTB marketing. In particular, it represents a way to improve the effectiveness of the relationships between associate firms and business customers. The activities of the consortium, in the twenty years since its founding, have been enhanced with other content, which are not in themselves novelties in the consortia scenario. Classico Italia manages participation in Pitti Uomo, organizes events, and develops reports on foreign selling markets. In 1996, the consortium launched the magazine *Classico*, which is not a house magazine dedicated only to companies in the consortium but a means of sharing fashion trends and building, maintaining, and strengthening a strong awareness of the brand name Classico Italia. More recently, the consortium has integrated BTC marketing activities, along with traditional activities in BTB markets. Again, the stimulus for enlargement of the integration of marketing activities comes from environmental changes and the perception of a state of tension on regarding the effectiveness of initiatives directed only to industrial customers. In 2005, some of the firms associated with the consortium created an autonomous reality, Classico Italia Retail Spa, in order to manage the opening of outlets 'Classico Italia' in international markets. This is in line with the most recent trends of increasing relevance of the strategies of integration between industrial and commercial functions and the growing commitment on the part of many companies in the fashion industry to vertically integrate retailing with the opening of outlets.

The retailing initiative starts from the results of previous research commissioned by the members of the consortium to a consulting firm, which aimed to identify the reputation of the brand Classico Italia with different stakeholders, such as industrial customers and retailers as well as end consumers and opinion leaders. A strong knowledge of the consortium for business customers and a lack of awareness of the consortium by the end market were highlighted. This was not a surprise considering the previous initiatives of the consortium which were oriented exclusively to BTB markets. (No Classico Italia labels were then or are now put on the products.) The same research aimed to find new strategies and new possible markets for the activities of the consortium.

The decision to integrate the opening of outlets within the consortium has as its goal the effective positioning of Classico Italia in final markets through joint management by the consortium or in partnership with foreign operators of shops with the brand name 'Classico Italia'. The initiative has already started with the opening of a store in Almaty (Kazakhstan). The store displays a selection of member firms' products in an area of approximately 300 square meters. The retail project includes only a sample of the associates (13 firms) who can get access to space in the store. There are already projects for future expansion through outlets in Russia and China, which are particularly sensitive to 'Made in Italy' products.

The integration of retail marketing skills within the consortium reveals interesting evidence at least with regard to the following issues:

1. the relations with traditional customers;
2. the coexistence of BTB marketing policies with BTC marketing policies;
3. the relations between members in the consortium.

With reference to the first, it should be noted that relationships with customers mainly concern three types of customer:

1. industrial buyers, represented by large manufacturing luxury firms (for example Hermès);
2. distribution chains with high-end positioning (for example Neiman Marcus);
3. independent shops (heritage shops, boutique).

Regarding the former, some of the members manufacture for major brands of fashion. These products are presented in the stores either with both brands (the brand of the supplier and the brand of the customer) or solely with the brand of the customer. The management interviewed points out that there are no particular conflicts between the retailing initiative done by the consortium and the maintenance of these relationships. Rather, the strengthening of the brand Classico Italia in the final market represents an element that can enhance the relationships with traditional industrial customers. Equal considerations can be highlighted with regard to retail customers (retail chains and independent stores), where the initiative seems to be considered positively. In some cases, however, the management interviewed underlines that the relational dimension is also a burden in developing the initiative. Previous relationships (licence or exclusive contracts) with distributors located in certain foreign markets may limit the participation of some members in the retail project.

With reference to the second aspect, it is appropriate to point out that the opening of the first store was a managerial experiment, which will, in the opinion of managers, lead to an increase in the number of sales outlets (at least another two or three openings in the coming years). Apart from these, the retail initiative, in the intention of the management, is not meant to replace relations in industrial markets. In this sense, BTB skills remain central in the consortium's future. This is also due to the fact that a huge and growing number of outlets is not considered consistent with the craft nature of the Made in Italy production of the consortium. Rather, the integration of BTC activities is seen as a means of learning for the members taking part in this initiative and a way to create brand awareness in the final market.

With reference to the third aspect, one can highlight a different degree of participation in the retail initiative among the companies. Some companies associated with Classico Italia have already developed autonomous retailing strategies. This downstream vertical integration actually restricts participation in the Classico Italia retail project. Other firms, which have no access to the end market, have joined the initiative. And it is presumed by the management interviewed that in these terms the development of Classico Italia Retail could include other companies not currently participating in the consortium Classico Italia but which may have an interest in gaining access to the market. This could represent an extension of the assortment with categories useful in a total look offer. Consequently different paths could be shown to cooperation among firms in Classico Italia and cooperation among firms in Classico Italia Retail Spa, which represent at the same time a challenge for the survival of both associative forms.

Centopercento Italiano

The Italian Centopercento Italiano consortium was set up in December 1997 on the initiative of a group of Tuscan leather entrepreneurs who were aiming to create a tool that would support their decision not to delocalize their manufacturing activities but instead to maintain them within the original local area of their own entrepreneurial experience. At present, roughly a decade on, the number of members of the consortium has increased to over 60.

The consortium's activity is underpinned by the relation between leather firms operating in a local system and the marketing abilities acquired by entrepreneurs and managers present within the local system. This background enables the consortium managers to have an in-depth view of the different aspects of the local area and the changing situation as it has affected manufacturing firms belonging to the consortium. This integration among the actors who share the context – which leads to the above-described integrated marketing – is embodied in the idea expressed by the marketing manager of Centopercento Italiano that 'lines of action that start out from awareness that we are experiencing the same range of problems [...] this implies that we can grow together [...] or die together.'

Thus it has been noted that in recent years the manufacturing firms belonging to the consortium have suffered a certain loss of creative contribution to their customers, tending instead to accentuate the typical characters of an operator who sells only executive ability or only working with and processing time. 'The idea we have been trying to uphold', the consortium management stresses,

> marketing manager initiatives which will allow the firms to revive their position on the market as a result of their creativity and not just on the basis of their processing ability. The first objective of our action has been to ensure that we do not lose a genetic heritage of creative ability which is still present.

The case of Centopercento Italiano shows distinctive features as regards to its retailing and branding policies. The role of these distinctive features is acquiring increasing importance in the type of aggregate marketing represented by the consortium producers who participate in this specific initiative.

What becomes clear from this overview is that the retailing and branding operations have a strategic nature and represent a response to a structural change in the market. In the past there was a prolonged period during which placing their products did not represent an extremely arduous task for the leather manufacturers who now belong to the consortium. As pointed out by the top management of the consortium, 'are not accustomed to selling: they are used to being sought out by the purchasers [...] when world production shifted to a different area and there was a dramatic drop in orders, our producers often proved quite unable to sell.' Today, the traditional manufacturing abilities are no longer felt to be sufficient, although they have by no means been lost and indeed are still strongly present. But it is necessary to foster a less 'passive' manner of relating to the market among small leather producers, given the new structure of the international market.

The consortium management highlights the importance for the consortium's activities of relations, including personal relations that have been built up with their members, with the local system policy-makers and with the great fashion system groups. In the management's vision, such relations also have an important human dimension and are not based exclusively on economic considerations.

As far as relations with stakeholders in the local area are concerned, substantial importance is awarded to the interface with associations in the leather sector and above all with local authorities, in particular as regards support for training. In addition, the situation in which the consortium's activity takes place is strongly linked to some of the celebrated fashion brands, which represent the most significant sources of orders for the firms belonging to the consortium. These brands include some of the more famous names in the world of international luxury (Chanel, Dior, Roberto Cavalli, Valentino, Bulgari, Aigner, Hermès, Louis Vuitton, Fendi, Dolce & Gabbana, etc.), and some of them, such as Gucci, Prada, Céline and Ferragamo, have production activities of their own in the same local area as the majority of the consortium enterprises (Central Tuscany). In developing its activity, the consortium has sought to avoid entering into conflict with these famous names and their production activities but has aimed instead at setting up a relation of cooperation for mutual support of the interests involved. The management of Centopercento Italiano believes that at least a part of the management of these luxury groups share the view that the enhancement of relations between leather-goods suppliers and the market is also in the interest of the great brands. The relationship with these brands (the 'griffes' in the terminology utilized by the Consortium management) played a role in the positioning of the project to open the sales outlet according to the formula described earlier. The interest shown by great luxury-brand purchasers in Centopercento Italiano's activities can be summarized by at least the following two points:

1. keeping alive and stimulating the capacity for independent research shown by manufacturing suppliers of leather goods involved in the project;
2. supporting the product image so that pricing policies adopted remain coherent with the typical characters of products belonging at least to a medium-high band.

The first point is particularly consitent with luxury brand purchasers' interests in maintaining an array of local suppliers that have creative energy and inspiration. With regard to the second point, this has been taken into account by Centopercento Italiano in the sense of adopting a non-aggressive approach to pricing for the products sold via the direct channel arising from the 'I-place' format. As the Chair of the Consortium points out:

> our relation with the large customers of the individual enterprises is good [...] the large clients could have adopted a hostile attitude but actually

> this did not prove to be the case; in the eyes of these enterprises our presence has been associated with something that is also useful for their policy of local sourcing [...] by generating dynamic forces capable of preserving creativity and the independent contribution of their reference suppliers [...] in some cases we received concrete support from them [...] the main referents showed a desire to demonstrate cooperation and good neighbourly relations.

The particularly good relations with certain customers is underlined by the request stemming from some of the latter to have the consortium certification on their products, and this has prompted other suppliers of these customers to join Centopercento Italiano. The Consortium Chair underlines that their action 'seeks to refocus attention on the product, on its material dimension but also on the associated immaterial dimensions [...] in the stance adopted by some brands the value given to the product risks being minimal as compared to the brand image [...] for our best customers the product remains an important element of their strategy' and the policy espoused 'has been that of placing emphasis on the sale of products and of value, not just of a status symbol' Moreover, the consortium has opened a distributive format under the name of I-place. In particular, the prefix 'I', which evokes the idea of Italy while at the same time also calling attention to the first person singular – 'I myself' – in English, is increasingly being used in consortium member projects. The I-place concept can thus be expressed in various different forms: for instance, after the first sales outlet opened in December 2006 and the second one in January 2007, there are plans for possible further openings and also events and promotional measures in other European markets. According to the Chair of the Consortium, 'the idea of I-place is that of a meeting place, a venue where today one finds the possibility of working in a business-to-consumer framework but with an approach that is non-antagonistic, an approach that is not necessarily viewed as a substitution for business-to-business activities.' On the contrary, the firms are prompted to interact directly with the worldwide consumer, one of the reasons being that this helps them to be more successful in offering their own specificity in response to the demand arising from the great industrial customers in relations with these buyers.

Suggestions have also been put forward to integrate the first permanent I-place outlet in the Florentine area (Scandicci) with other activities of significance for the consortium. Such activities include the Service Centre, for prototyping, computerized cutting and tailor-made formulas. In the words of the consortium's top management, 'this is a co-presence that is fully in harmony with the role of I-place as a meeting point for contacts with the industrial customers, as well as its role as a point of sale for retail consumption.' However, the nature of the main danger stemming from relations with the great international luxury-brand groups is clear to Centopercento Italiano. The consortium's leaders note that this local system

> has become fundamental for their purchasing activities, because it is qualitatively significant, but it is in some sense also a 'fief' of the great players [...] with small but even medium-sized businesses increasingly oriented toward the 'sale of minutes' of working capacity [...] in our view, competing on production efficiency is unlikely to lead to a positive outcome for the manufacturing experience of this area [...] if that is the route adopted, then within the space of ten years this whole area could be de-industrialized.

The mission of the consortium and the first goal of its projects are precisely to avoid this kind of evolution, and this is a goal with which it is fully in tune with the approach adopted by the main regional industrial policy-makers and the other local authorities of this area.

I Love Italian Shoes

I Love Italian Shoes was set up by ANCI, the National Association of Italian Footwear Manufacturers, which groups together approximately 1,000 Italian footwear manufacturers. The turnover produced by the member companies represents approximately 70 per cent of the overall Italian footwear production. ANCI has represented the Italian shoe industry since 1945. The purpose of ANCI is 'to examine, support and promote projects (of an economical, technical and scientific nature) and to represent the same on all institutional levels ANCI Servizi Srl is the association's own services company through which it manages the communication mix of the association and it organizes the MICAM Shoevent, a leading worldwide footwear exhibition'.

In this context, the 'I Love Italian Shoes' initiative was set up. It was designed and managed directly by ANCI. Even in this case, the stimulus for the integration of marketing activities is related to the state of tension generated by new trends in the international arena. Considering the latter point, the National Association of Italian Footwear Manufacturers in 2003 created an initiative to sustain the authenticity and value of Italian footwear production through the development of the logo and the brand 'I Love Italian Shoes'. The main aim of the initiative is to make consumers more aware when buying footwear, of the origin of the product and, in particular, of the characteristics of a product made in Italy, as well as protecting Italian products from risks of counterfeiting.

This initiative, which is managed by project groups inside ANCI, has seen over the years gradual integration of marketing activities, which have joined, from time to time, only part of the associates. It is possible, on the basis of activities carried out, to highlight an evolutionary path that has followed the following steps:

- launch of the brand 'I Love Italian Shoes' and development of communication campaigns;
- inclusion of labels 'I Love Italian Shoes' on footwear products of firms belonging to the association, which are produced wholly in Italy;
- retail-development project, with the opening of 'I Love Italian Shoes' outlets.

The association has initially concentrated its efforts on developing brand awareness on the logo of the initiative, by building a strong brand name. We can consider separately the brand components as the prefix 'I', the figurative elements which are used to represent the verb 'love' and the verbal component 'shoes'. The prefix 'I' evokes the idea of Italy and at the same time also calling attention to the first person singular – 'I myself' – in English. The figurative component concerns the word 'love', which was developed through a figurative sign formed by two red shoes put together to outline a heart. The brand includes the term shoes, which obviously represent the products of the associated firms. For the launch of the brand, the initiative provided a strong communication campaign through mass media (releases in newspapers, magazines, and so on) and through merchandising in specialized footwear outlets. The integration of marketing activities, in the first stages regarding the initiative then covered the creation and dissemination of brand awareness in order to sensitize the market to the characteristics of Italian production and to some elements of superiority compared to foreign productions.

With the growing awareness of the brand, especially in the domestic market, the association has promoted the use of 'I Love Italian Shoes' labels; to date nearly 12 million copies have been stamped on footwear produced by the firms associated to ANCI, whose production is fully Italian. There are about 100 associates of ANCI, proposing their product with two labels: the firm's label and the 'I Love Italian Shoes' brand. In this sense there is a virtue circle which enforces the awareness of the brand to the public and which gradually can effectively achieve the goal of fighting against counterfeiting and protect the genuine Italian production.

More recently, the 'I Love Italian Shoes' initiative has taken a further step, with the launching of the retail project in March 2007. The association, supported by regional and national public institutions, is now focusing its efforts on opening stores under the name 'I Love Italian Shoes' in foreign countries. This is an initiative of vertical integration in the management of outlets, which enriches the arrangements for liaison with the market for companies involved in the project.

The retail project initiative can be analysed, taking into account two events. First, the project was presented MICAM event. On that occasion, a prototype store called 'I Love Italian Shoes' was set up in the Fiera Milano. Many contacts were initiated by ANCI with foreign entrepreneurs, former owners of shoe shops in their countries of origin, who had shown interest in opening outlets of 'I Love Italian Shoes'. Applications were received from many international actors: 22 from different Russian cities, with others from Hungary, Brazil, Canada, the USA, Turkey, and South Africa. It was then followed by the opening of a store in Russia. The first 'I Love Italian Shoes' outlet was opened on 3 March 2007 in Omsk in Russia. This store displays a qualified selection of footwear production made in Italy over an area of 350 square metres. The retail initiative has involved 20 national brands from Tuscany, Puglia, and Marche (all ANCI associates), with the financial assistance of the three regions and a contribution from the Ministry of Economic Development. The investment was €1.2 million and has been shared by a private partner, which already operates in Russia and which has coordinated the initiative. The success of the initiative has attracted interest from potential customer in other markets (India, South Africa, China, and some European countries) which will be the focus of future initiatives. With this in mind, a working group has been formed to manage such projects in order to guarantee the partners of the real origin of the 'Made in Italy' products. In the coming months, six to eight outlets are scheduled to be opened.

Considering this case in terms of relationships with traditional customers, the strategy of response to environmental changes adopted by ANCI can be seen as a fact or element that accentuates the closure of buyer–supplier relationships in the industrial markets (for a greater connotation of consumer marketing) or feeds with new items relations between companies located territorially and traditional industrial customers (greater powers of branding and marketing outlets can promote the relationship, they speak the same language). At this stage, the later seems to be the most likely to occur.

Emerging issues in new cooperative marketing forms

The cases considered in the chapter are a limited number (three) but involve a large number of small and medium enterprises (in total about 200). The three cases are similar in several aspects, starting from the context in which they have been developed, which is the fashion system (leather goods, clothing, and footwear). The cases analysed present some forms of cooperation between enterprises in the field of marketing that are 'innovative' in the sense that marketing initiatives were not carried out by single companies. These marketing initiatives affect the field of consumer marketing, in particular retail strategies and branding policies, and are added to the traditional marketing activities in the field of BTB marketing. In all the three cases, the support by public policy-makers (mainly at a regional level) is a key factor in explaining the success of these new experiences of marketing cooperation and integration.

The evaluation of the success of the three consortia can be done in terms of performance parameters of each consortium as a specific organization (turnover, profits, and competitive capabilities). But this is not the only, nor is it the main, way for evaluating their success. The new actor created is successful if it achieves the goals of cooperation which are the reason why it has been started. In other words, the consortium is successful if it is the tool by which the associated firms pursue their aims (pre-competitive learning about branding and retailing, sharing marketing investments, etc.). The support from public policy-makers is both financial and relational, helping the formation of an atmosphere favourable to the cooperative marketing activities.

We must say that the cases presented in the previous paragraph do not support the assertion that there is an increase in the size of the unit devoted to specific marketing initiatives. The cooperative initiative seems to be naturally associated with a widespread thinking that these companies 'together' can do things that are not possible to be done individually. These initiatives include marketing activities which are new for district firms, such as branding and retailing. The basic idea can be summed up with the famous words 'unity is strength'. In fact, these initiatives present some strengths and weaknesses that we try to summarize in the following terms.

The strengths include:

- The access to experiences of BTC or BTB without important investment for individual members;
- The new autonomous actor (made up by cooperative marketing strategies) is able to do things that individual companies are not able to do.
- In addition to these forces, there are weaknesses such as:
- The new actor is often a new 'small' actor, which is in addition to existing individual companies.
- The new actor's action could result in competition with that of existing individual companies. This can happen after the outset of the new player.

From the case analysis emerges a first question, which we might define as follows:

> Q1: What kind of integrated marketing is set up through the processes of cooperation between the observed companies?

At this point, we can only stress that the cases presented reflect the creation of new organizational units (consortium) and the creation of forms of integration among the marketing activities carried out by these and the marketing activities carried out by individual companies. The integration of existing resources generally appears difficult and, in fact, quite limited. Using the words of a member of one of the cases analysed above: 'The sum of many compact cars is not a sports car' (Managing Director of Centopercento Italiano).

The development of the new players is associated with innovative marketing policies for the firms of the fashion system involved. These policies are translated in the development of branding and retailing processes which directly affect the relationship with the final market. These initiatives, however, do not seem to make, at least in some cases, a relevant impact on the turnover of the companies involved. For example, as regards the policies related to the opening of new stores, these cases of aggregation lead to a still-limited number of outlets, and also the scheduled openings do not seem to absorb a large proportion of the total turnover of the companies involved. For firms oriented to a slight investment (Bonaccorsi 1992: 631), this form of cooperation is a way to avoid investing heavily in learning processes regarding branding and retailing. This explanation is important, but the question seems worthy of further study. A second question then follows from the analysis of cases. We might define it as follows:

> Q2: What are the reasons that encourage companies to establish these innovative forms of marketing cooperation?

The reasons do not seem linked, given the existence of these consortia for years, to the searching either for a replacement of direct customers with the final market or for the substitution of old business customers with the acquisition of new business customers. The phenomena analysed seem quite connected with the activation of learning processes by companies involved in integrated marketing initiatives. This is not a new way, which has already been observed in earlier forms of marketing cooperation between small and medium firms in Italy. The collective nature of the learning processes has been found in the literature (Becattini 1987). These companies, or at least a leader among them, feel the need to learn from BTC in order to improve their BTB relationships. This path can be assessed as a way to develop the 'service' attribute as a factor which small and medium companies in fashion can use in their existing relationships. Italian exporting companies have been successful not because of their marketing excellence but for the characteristics of the products and services they offer (Bonaccorsi 1992: 626). The cases we analyse can be read as attempts to develop learning processes in term of marketing abilities and/or as integration of marketing resources from the outside, sharing costs with others. These learning processes are not limited to the relationship with final consumer, to whom the marketing initiatives are directly oriented but also to business customers, both the new and existing ones (Håkansson and Snehota 1995).

> Q3: Does the consortium, with which the company is involved, change the relationship with the direct customer?

We wonder how and if, within the network, relationships between firms involved in these new forms of cooperation and their direct customers could change. The buyer–seller relationship is within a network context, in which the actor generated by the marketing cooperation is fully a part. This change could have, for example, a negative impact if this initiative could be perceived as threatening by the direct customer and therefore could lead to a negative reaction against companies involved in the cooperative form.

The cases, however, reveal that the direct customer has a positive attitude towards these integrated marketing initiatives, since the extension and the approach to the final consumption do not appear to represent a real threat. Rather, one can find benefits for direct customers, resulting from the learning processes and the improvement of the image of their suppliers.

The phenomena of marketing cooperation observed are significant even in a logic related to the territorial context. It seems clear that in the cases analysed the phenomenon of innovation in marketing cooperation is made possible by a widespread perception of threats which must be faced and the perception of the limits of individual firms in dealing with these threats. The aggregation, however, would not have been possible in absence of leader entrepreneurs. In particular, the territorial context assumes a central role in the cases examined. This leads us to formulate a fourth and final question:

> Q4: Does the territorial context represent an effective base for the integration of the organizations involved? And what is the role of public institutions in supporting the initiative?

Companies in the cases analysed in the previous paragraph are put together on a territorial basis to exploit the origin of the product (country-of-origin effect). However, the integration processes observed are pre-existing and take characters of typical social and cultural realities of their district (Dei Ottati 1995) or at least the local systems business (Podolny 1994). It seems that innovative forms of marketing cooperation appear as the result of continuity with the legacy of the territory, even with the limits they have. Unlike typical district firms, however, the new actor created covers a function which could be not covered within the district. Moreover, the new actors are the result of cooperation between firms, encouraged by leader entrepreneurs who decided not to found them autonomously.

Final remarks

This chapter has explored new cases of marketing cooperation to evaluate the specificities of these innovative forms, their points of strength and weakness. The phenomenon to which we refer regards the emergence of cases of aggregation of companies that set up new forms aimed at the implementation of marketing initiatives. These forms are associated with the development of BTC practices, related to the creation and the management of a brand and/or the opening of retail outlets. Participating companies describe these initiatives as relevant innovations in their activity. Such forms of cooperation have features which differ from traditional cooperative strategies in systems of local firms, such as the formation of consortia that organize exhibitions.

In conclusion, it is possible to summarize the main features of the new integrated marketing forms investigated in the chapter. These features can be related to three main aspects:

1. *The nature of the marketing activities which have been integrated.* In all the cases we observed, branding and retailing have been considered relevant activities in order to face the changing environment. This integration seems in line with the general tendency proposed by large-scale players which are more and more vertically integrated in the downstream phases of the supply chain.
2. *The integration between marketing management practices and industrial practices through the creation of a new actor,* which is a new player in the network. However, this integration between BTB and BTC functions seems to be unbalanced, as the industrial marketing competencies remain dominant within the companies involved in the cooperative marketing initiatives. Furthermore, the core business of the cooperative actor remains, at this stage, the development and the maintenance of business relationships in BTB networks.
3. *The integration of marketing activities by marketing cooperation and the formation of the new actor* are made possible by the role of a leader entrepreneur, which could act in virtue of trust and commitment by other entrepreneurs, and by support by public institutions.

Future research should consider the effectiveness of these innovative forms in terms of performances, either for individual companies or for the cooperative actor, which assumes the form of a consortium in the cases analysed. Another theme to be further addressed regards the sustainability of the new actor in the long term, especially if we consider that many of the activities planned and communicated to the market seem to face problems related to difficulties in managing several new dualities (BTB vs. BTC, cooperative retailing vs. company retailing, company branding vs. cooperative branding, aided development vs. autonomous development).

These challenges represent elements which can lead to the failure or success of the innovative marketing forms.

References

R. S. Achrol, L. K. Scheer, and L. W. Stern, *Designing Successful Transorganizational Marketing Alliances* (Cambridge, Mass.: Marketing Science Institute, 1990).

L. Adler, 'Symbiotic Marketing', *Harvard Business Review,* 44 (1966): 59–71.

J. C. Anderson and J. A. Narus, 'A Model of Distributor Firm and Manufacturer Firm Working Partnership', *Journal of Marketing,* 54 (1990): 42–58.

G. Becattini, *Mercato e forze locali: il distretto industriale* (Bologna: Il Mulino, 1987).

A. Bonaccorsi, 'On the Relationship between Firm Size and Export Intensity', *Journal of International Business Studies,* 23 (1992): 605–35.

L. P. Bucklin and S. Sengupta, 'Organizing Successful Co-marketing Alliances', *Journal of Marketing,* 57 (1993): 32–46.

J. Chimhanzi, 'The Impact of Marketing/HR Interactions on Marketing Strategy Implementation', *European Journal of Marketing,* 38 (2004): 73–98.

K. S. Cook, 'Exchange and Power in Networks of Interorganizational Relationship', *Sociological Quarterly,* 18 (1977): 62–82.

G. Dei Ottati, *Tra mercato e comunità: aspetti concettuali e ricerche empiriche sul distretto industriale* (Milan: Franco Angeli, 1995).

R. M. Emerson, 'Power–Dependence Relations', *American Sociological Review,* 27 (1962): 31–48.

S. Guercini and A. Runfola, 'Sourcing Strategies in Clothing Retail Firms: Product Complexity versus Overseas Supply Chain', *Journal of Customer Behaviour,* 3 (2004): 305–34.

R. Gulati, 'Alliances and Networks', *Strategic Management Journal,* 19 (1998): 293–317.

H. Håkansson and I. Snehota, *Developing Relationship in Business Networks* (London: Routledge, 1995).

O. Holm, 'Integrated Marketing Communication: From Tactics to Strategy', *Corporate Communications,* 11 (2006): 23–33.

D. Iacobucci and D. Calder (eds), *Kellogg on Integrated Marketing* (New York: John Wiley & Sons, 2002).

R. Johnston and P. R. Lawrence, 'Beyond Vertical Integration: The Rise of the Value-Adding Partnership', *Harvard Business Review,* 66 (1988): 94–101.

P. R. Lawrence and J. W. Lorsch, *Diagnosi dello sviluppo delle organizzazioni: schemi di azione* (Milan: ETAS Kompass, 1973).

J. Pfeffer and G. R. Salancick, *The External Control of Organization: A Resource Dependence Theory* (New York: Harper & Row, 1978).

J. M. Podolny, 'Market Uncertainty and the Social Character of Economic Exchange', *Administrative Science Quarterly,* 39 (1994): 458–83.

R. W. Ruekert and O. C. Walker, 'Marketing's Interaction with Other Functional Units: A Conceptual Framework and Empirical Evidence', *Journal of Marketing,* 51 (1987): 1–19.

W. E. Souder and J. D. Sherman, *Managing New Technology Development* (New York: McGraw-Hill, 1993).

J. D. Thompson, *Organizations in Action* (London: McGraw-Hill, 1967).

A. Van de Ven, 'On the Nature, Formation, and Maintenance of Relations among Organizations', *Administrative Science Quarterly,* 21 (1976): 679–703.

P. R. Varadarajan and D. Rajaratnam, 'Symbiotic Marketing Revisited', *Journal of Marketing,* 50 (1986): 7–17.

10

Strategy Selection in Business-Angel Networks: Venture-capital strategy and Entrepreneurial Business-Angel Strategy

Lars Silver, Nicolaus Lundahl and Björn Berggren

Introduction

Access to capital is an area of greatest concern for the survival and development of most firms. Although entrepreneurs provide almost two-thirds of the seed and start-up capital for their new ventures (Bygrave and Hunt 2005), individual resources only last so long; by the time a firm is ready for expansion, the need for additional capital is often relatively large. There is a particular need for equity capital (Aernoudt *et al.* 2007), and research has demonstrated that early-stage equity capital is the scarcest resource for emerging enterprises (Tucker and Lean 2003). Business angels and venture capital have become the institutionalized forms of equity capital available for early stage financing. In general, business angels invest in earlier phases than do venture capitalists, but both sets of actors have developed investing models, the venture capital one being more formalized and standardized, although the basic principles remain common to both. Furthermore, business angels may have additional motives apart from profit-maximizing for investing, such as altruism (Maula *et al.* 2005). In recent years, business angels have become somewhat more formalized through the increased use of syndication and business-angel networks. Although there is growing research in the fields of both venture capital and business angels, there is relatively little research into business-angel networks (exceptions include Aernoudt and Erikson 2002; San José *et al.* 2005; Sörheim 2005). In addition, there is an overall scarcity of studies of business angels focusing on the investing process, so-called second-generation studies (Freear *et al.* 2002).

The present study enlarges the body of knowledge concerning business-angel networks and the investing process by examining strategy selection, using a case-study methodology. By following the development of a business-angel network, the study presents a number of issues connected with the overall choice between what is referred to as a venture-capital strategy and an entrepreneurial business-angel strategy. The differences identified in the study reflect an overall dilemma for business angels, namely, the choice of underlying model for angel activity and investments. The choice is essentially between adopting a formalized portfolio-based investment strategy based on a proven venture-capital model or using the knowledge of self-made entrepreneurs in slowly moulding a select number of portfolio firms over time. In addition to emphasizing the differences between the above two approaches, the study also highlights the consequences of being unable to select one strategy. The overall purpose of the study is therefore to provide a framework for understanding business-angel network strategies and to identify some implications for practitioners. The study formulates five hypotheses for further research based on an actual business-angel network case study.

Venture capital and business angels compared

Equity financing in early-stage enterprises has traditionally been made by investors in close geographic proximity to investees. Harrison and Mason (1992) and Sörheim (2005) emphasize the importance of business angels in local economic development, due to their preference for investments located close to home. By investing locally, business angels can reduce gaps in funding and assistance experienced by many small and medium-sized enterprises (SMEs) due to, among other factors, the tendency of traditional venture-capital firms to focus on major cities. Several explanations can be found for the region-specific preferences of business angels. According to Freear *et al.* (1994), the preference for investments close to home can be explained by the fact that adopting this strategy facilitates the provision of non-financial support and the monitoring and control of venture performance.

Over the past decade, the investment process has generally shifted. There is a widening gap between business angels and venture capital, to the extent that venture capital is increasingly being invested in later phases. This process of distancing between business angels and venture capital has increased since the advent of the internet era, as venture capital has abandoned the seed and early financing phases to an even greater degree (Mason 2006). Syndication, that is, several investors sharing an investment, is common among venture capitalists and is on the increase among business angels, especially among experienced business angels (Kelly and Hay 2000). The syndication process, together with more formalized deal flow, due diligence, and monitoring activities, has helped make some business angels, in particular, business-angel networks, more similar to venture-capital firms in terms of their modus operandi (EBAN 2008, interview with Colin Mason).

The European Commission has estimated that business angels invest €10–20 million annually in early phases, while venture-capital firms contribute €3 million to the same phases (Aernoudt and Erikson 2002). In the USA, business angels are claimed to invest in 50,000 firms annually, whereas venture capital invests in only 3,000 enterprises (Sohl 2003). Other investigations find that business angels invest five (Reynolds *et al.* 2002), 10 (Wetzel 1987), or 13 (Gaston 1989) times the amount invested by venture-capital firms. In comparison, it can be concluded that business angels invest far more capital in the phases for which external financing is scarce and are therefore of enhanced importance from a governmental perspective (Lindström and Olofsson 2001; Mason 2006). In addition, studies report great untapped potential in form of 'virgin angels' who have yet to invest but who are willing to do so (Sohl 1999). It can be argued that there are in fact two major sources of early-stage equity financing, one being formal venture capital and the other the business-angel network.

Venture-capital firms and their strategies

Venture capital is a form of financing available primarily for entrepreneurial activities aiming at fast growth and in situations in which the firm's cash-flow distribution is highly risky and positively skewed, with low probability of success, low liquidation value, and high returns if successful (Winton and Yerramilli 2008). Research into venture capital includes studies of venture-capital monitoring and advising (Sapienza *et al.* 2005), venture-capital portfolio size (Jääskeläinen *et al.* 2006), the impact of new regulation on venture capital (Wonglimpiyarat 2009), liquidity issues (Lerner and Schoar 2004), venture-capital exits (Neus and Walz 2005), venture-capital syndication (Wright and Lockett 2003), professionalization of portfolio firms (Hellmann and Puri 2002), and decision-making in venture-capital firms (Zacharakis and Shepherd 2005).

Venture-capital firms make extensive use of covenants, contracts, and close monitoring to handle moral hazard and adverse selection (Gompers and Lerner 1999). The ability to attract a deal flow, screen, and subsequently monitor investments is at the core of venture-capital activity (Kirilenko 2001). One particular effect of the structure of the venture-capital industry is the need to accommodate outside investors, as venture-capital firms do not generally invest their own capital, instead using investment funds as capital (Cumming *et al.* 2008). This results in venture-capital managers being forced to economize their actions by adding more portfolio firms to each manager, which in turn results in venture-capital managers needing to chose carefully when and where to invest their time (Bernile *et al.* 2007). Larger portfolios per manager result in less governance and advice to investees, so manager portfolio size is a crucial parameter for venture-capital success. In general, seed and early financing funds have more portfolio firms per manager, whereas buyout funds have fewer (Cumming 2006). This has implications for how venture-capital managers perceive their investments, seed and early financing entailing a larger proportion of failed ideas left without long-term supervision. Comparative studies have demonstrated that the most prominent characteristic of venture-capital firms is an absolute focus on providing short-term monetary incentives for venture capitalists and entrepreneurs in terms of high return in risky situations (Hellmann 2006).

The exit strategy is central to venture-capital-firm operations, and invariably the liquidity of national stock exchanges has been a strong predictor of venture-capital success (Jeng and Wells 2000). Although other alternatives are available, the ability to reach the stage of listing a portfolio firm on the stock exchange has been regarded as a vital target for venture capital (Barnes *et al.* 2003). In particular, the strategy used for new ventures is geared towards demands for high rates of return – the risk premium (Bodie *et al.* 2005).

A venture-capital strategy for handling investments in new entrepreneurial firms is based on several principles. These principles are not necessarily identical for every venture-capital firm, and their relative importance may also vary among venture-capital firms; however, they do constitute an appropriate set of principles for the purposes of comparing a venture-capital strategy with a business-angel strategy. These principles are as follows:

- The investment process is handled by professional investment managers.
- There are specific internal rate of return (IRR) requirements.
- Ownership is perceived to be a relatively short-term commitment.
- Portfolio theory is used to find the few winners in a portfolio.
- The investor uses hands-off management to handle a large portfolio.

Business angels and their strategies

Internationally, a relatively large number of studies of business angels and informal investors has been conducted over the years (see, for example, Hindle and Rushworth 1999; Månsson and Landström 2005), and the importance of these investors as resource providers has been highlighted in several reports (OECD 2002; Bygrave and Hunt 2005). Business angels are defined as individuals who invest in equity in small, unlisted enterprises and thereby contribute both capital and knowledge to SME development in the seed and early finance phases (Aldrich 1999). Business-angel research has been divided into first-generation studies that primarily focus on measuring the available quantity of business angels and their characteristics and second-generation studies that focus on the investment process itself (Mason 2006). It is claimed that there is a general lack of second-generation studies (Freear *et al.* 2002). Current business-angel research focuses on business-angel motivation (Stedler and Peters 2003), business-angel categorization (Avdeitchikova 2005), the investing process (Haines *et al.* 2003), influence of business networks on decision-making (Atkin and Esiri 1993), reliance on intuition in the decision-making process (Haines *et al.* 2003; Mason and Stark 2004), rejection rates (Mason and Harrison 1996), the success ratio of investments (Bygrave and Hunt 2005), reliance on the entrepreneur (Landström 1998), syndication between business angels (May 2002; San José *et al.* 2005), and business angels as serial entrepreneurs (Mason and Harrison 1995; Sörheim 2005).

As investors, business angels are much more fragmented and heterogeneous than are venture capitalists. Business angels invest more often in early-stage ventures than do venture capitalists because they tend to have longer investment horizons and accept lower rates of return (Harrison and Mason 1992). They also primarily invest in fields in which they have prior experience (Mason and Stark 2004). Lindström and Olofsson (2002) argue that business angels have access to wider networks than do other actors and that the involvement of angels with entrepreneurial experience adds credibility and legitimacy to a venture (see also Sörheim 2005). In theory, business angels and venture-capital firms constitute a ladder of investment for SMEs, as venture capital has the ability to take over more mature investments as the demand for capital increases.

In fact, the relationship between business angels and venture-capital firms is stressed as their different investment motives, investment durations, degree of formalization (venture-capital firms being more formalized), and levels of financial strength contribute to an uneasy relationship (Harrison and Mason 2000). In situations involving altruistic motives, that is, in which business angels are willing to sacrifice resources such as time, energy, and money, thereby transferring benefits from one individual to others (Jensen 1994; Fehr and Fischbacher 2003), the relationship between venture-capital firms and business angels is especially problematic. The added motive of having fun (Lindström and Olofsson 2002) has also been highlighted as important for business-angel investments. However, according to Hindle and Wenban (1999), the possibility of having fun was the least important motivation uncovered in their study of Australian business angels.

A business-angel strategy (hereafter referred to as 'entrepreneurial business-angel strategy') for handling investments in new firms is based on several principles. These principles are not necessarily identical for every business angel, and their relative importance could vary among business angels; however, they do constitute an appropriate set of principles for the purposes of comparing an entrepreneurial business-angel strategy with a venture-capital strategy. These principles are as follows:

- The investment process is handled by self-made entrepreneurs.
- There are no specific IRR criteria.
- Ownership is perceived as a long-term commitment.

- Winners are created by entrepreneurial development.
- The investor uses hands-on management to develop enterprises.

Business-angel network strategies

Business-angel networks enable larger investments (Carriere 2006) and constitute an alternative mode of operation for business angels who perceive independent business-angel activity as too time consuming (Mason and Harrison 1997). Although earlier research indicates that business angels have been around for a long time, the emergence of formal angel networks is much more recent (Aernoudt and Erikson 2002). Among the more salient benefits of such networks is the reduction of search costs for both business angels and entrepreneurs (Aernoudt *et al.* 2007), as business-angel networks are far more visible and accessible than are individual angels (Aernoudt and Erikson 2002). Accordingly, San José *et al.* (2005) describe angel networks as important tools for raising awareness of the existence of the market for entrepreneurs and potential angels alike.

The mere fact that the number of business-angel networks in Europe has grown from around 50 in the early 1990s (EBAN 2007) to close to 300 today (Aernoudt *et al.* 2007) is a clear indication of the prevailing opinion regarding the positive effects of business-angel networks. Taking part in syndicated investments, like those occurring in a business-angel network, has been described as among the best ways to learn the 'tricks of the trade' for inexperienced or passive business angels (Aernoudt and Erikson 2002; San José *et al.* 2005; Carriere 2006). Apart from risk sharing, Johnston *et al.* (2003) emphasize the possibility of sharing opinions, receiving inputs from peers, and gaining access to a potentially larger deal flow as important reasons for participation in an angel network.

In particular, Freear *et al.* (2002) stress the need to understand the formation and evolution of business-angel groups. The pooling of individuals implies that different types of informal investors can be active in the same business-angel network, some passively and others very actively. This suggests that business-angel networks could be of a variety of shapes and sizes. Mason and Harrison (1997) present four fundamental types of business-angel networks. The authors conclude that privately funded business-angel networks tend to invest in larger deals in later stages of the portfolio firms' life cycles. In not-for-profit business-angel networks, a larger portion of the investments is focused on small investments in portfolio firms in the seed and start-up phases.

The present study addresses the limited understanding of the process and evolution of business-angel networks highlighted in earlier research (Freear *et al.* 2002). The study posits that business-angel networks can apply various investment strategies that fundamentally influence how the network operates. Based on the model developed by Avdeitchikova (2005), it can be posited that business-angel networks operate according to either a trader or a business-angel perspective. The trader perspective originates in the venture-capital industry, which in recent decades has been increasingly engaged in short-term stock investments rather than long-term efforts (see Bygrave and Timmons 1992). In business-angel networks, the trader perspective is akin to an investment network in which the overall objective is profitability and there is little room for philanthropy. According to the trader perspective, it is important to focus on portfolio theory, as some investments will inevitably fail. Portfolio theory combined with a short-term profitability objective reduces the overall time available for the hands-on management of each portfolio firm. A business-angel network using a trader perspective instead opts for a professional, standardized approach similar to that of venture-capital firms (Aernoudt and Erikson 2002).

The original business-angel strategy is to focus on a combination of capital and in-depth knowledge. According to this strategy, the main reason for success is the long-term involvement of business angels with extensive experience of entrepreneurial activity. This strategy differs from the venture-capital strategy in that it is less formalized in both the requirements placed on the portfolio firm and the development of the relationship with the portfolio firm. Business-angel strategy focuses on the long-term entrepreneurial development of portfolio firm management. Established entrepreneurs who perceive business-angel investments as part philanthropy and part business are typical of a business-angel strategy orientation (Carriere 2006). This approach stresses that business-angel investors are able to maintain investments over time and therefore have access to considerable capital to begin with (Mason and Harrison 1995).

In the Swedish case, business angels often emerge in contexts in which successful entrepreneurs invest in local start-ups, leading to the development of informal business-angel networks (Lindström and Olofsson 2001). One problem with a business-angel strategy is that the work conducted in business-angel networks using this strategy is voluntary (Mason and Harrison 1997). The business-angel strategy works well for business angels preferring to rely on intuition rather than fixed venture-capital models (Aldrich 1999) and on personal relationships with the SME entrepreneur (Mason and Stark 2004).

Table 10.1 Main strategies of business-angel networks

Venture-capital strategy	**Entrepreneurial business-angel strategy**
Professional investment managers	Self-made entrepreneurs
Specific IRR requirements	Flexible targets
Short-term ownership	Long-term ownership
Portfolio theory	Entrepreneurial development
Hands-off management	Hands-on management

In accordance with the preceding discussion, we argue that business-angel networks have two main strategies: the venture-capital strategy and the entrepreneurial business-angel strategy. Table 10.1 summarizes the main characteristics of these strategies.

Methodology

Any attempt to gain increased knowledge that is representative of an entire population requires knowledge of the size and characteristics of the population. When reflecting on the definition of business angel, the obstacles in terms of clearly delimiting the population and identifying these individuals become apparent. The difficulties researchers face when studying business angels have frequently been highlighted. Early on in research in the field, Wetzel (1987) stated that the informal venture-capital market was 'virtually invisible' and characterized by many unanswered questions. Wetzel highlighted the fact that highly diverse individuals comprise the business-angel population and that there are no public records of their investments or any directories of individual investors.

Furthermore, individual business angels arguably prefer to remain anonymous (Haar *et al.* 1988) to avoid being flooded with investment proposals. Accordingly, Harrison and Mason (1992) argue that the size and characteristics of the population are unknowable, rendering it impossible to conduct a survey based on a representative sample of investors. Consequently, most studies of the topic have adopted one, or in some cases a combination, of the three main approaches reviewed by Harrison and Mason (1992). According to these authors, the most common approach has been to send surveys to a large number of individuals who could be investors based on their income levels.

The second approach has been to contact business angels through the firms in which they have invested. Third, researchers have also been known to use snowball sampling in which the identification of one respondent typically leads to the identification of others, since investors tend to be linked to each other by friendship and business networks. The material and discussion presented in the following parts of this chapter are based on interviews with ten of the eleven founders of the studied local business-angel network. The study's findings emerged from an embedded, explanatory case study (Yin 1994; Corley 2004).

In this study, we follow a business-angel network from its inception. The business-angel network was established in December 2003 in an effort to support local investments in a small town; the studied network comprises the 11 original founders and 51 shareholders. This study is part of a larger research project investigating the relationship between local context, mainly in terms of the variety of supporting actors available in the local environment, and SME creation and development. Within the project framework, originally initiated in the autumn of 2002 in a Swedish community with approximately 50,000 inhabitants, over 100 interviews and two postal surveys targeting Swedish SMEs have been carried out so far. To identify respondents for the larger study, snowball sampling, as described by Harrison and Mason (1992), was used.

The interviews, conducted with SMEs, local banks, government officials, auditors, and business angels, yielded detailed knowledge of the local community, entrepreneurial networks, and formal and informal financial infrastructure. Since the business-angel study is part of a larger project encompassing many interviews, local seminars, and the compilation of material, the present study incorporates a strong element of triangulation in its material (Yin 1994; Hawke and Heffernan 2006). This enabled interviewers to compare the results of interviews with material from other sources. The interviews and the snowball sampling technique used in the overall project provided access to key figures in the emerging business-angel network, which in turn enabled the researchers to obtain the full list of the network's founding members. The interviews, which were taped and later transcribed, generally lasted 1.5–2 hours. By adopting this technique, the risks of distorting what was actually said in interview and of forgetting significant points when the material was compiled decrease significantly. Although the respondents were allowed to tell their stories quite freely, the interviewers had a questionnaire as an aid to ensure that issues of special interest were addressed in each interview.

A brief history of the case

After the closure of the local army base in 2003, a local recommendation was made to organize locally available venture capital to attract firms in the very early stages of their development, firms that usually encounter severe difficulties in seeking financing. The recommendation appealed to Sven Olofsson, who was CEO (chief executive officer) of the local campus, characterized by a mix of educational institutions, enterprises, and student housing, and a discussion group was formed to find individuals regarded as suitable cofounders of the business-angel network. The search process, which involved a variety of sources, eventually resulted in fifteen names, and a preliminary meeting was held at which an external partner, Tomas Johansson, presented his proposal regarding appropriate ways of setting up and managing the network.

The structural model advocated by Johansson was similar to those used by traditional venture-capital firms. The proposed strategy involved using a formalized model focusing on evaluating each proposed investment according to five factors: technology, competition, market, financing, and entrepreneurship. The modus operandi of the network would be as follows. Initial screening would be carried out by an object committee, which, if it found a sufficiently interesting object, would pass it on to an executive committee.

If the object was still regarded as interesting, the final investment decision would be approved by the board of directors of the network. In seeking suitable investment alternatives, priority would, in accordance with the evaluation carried out by Tomas Johansson, be given to ventures in the electronics sector, preferably ones prepared to set up their activities at the campus.

Although the idea appealed to most meeting attendees, some doubts were also expressed. Some individuals felt that the proposed financing amounts were far too low, while others were concerned about engaging in something of which they had no prior experience, namely, the difficult process of finding suitable investment options. Finally, there was some hesitancy regarding the business model and whether it would actually work. As a way of handling the lack of experience in the field, one individual said that he would become a cofounder on the condition that Tomas Johansson, who had prior experience of setting up business-angel networks, became a cofounder as well. According to Hans Strömberg, the former CEO of a large local electronics firm, finding suitable investment options would not be a problem, and he was confident that some objects could be found in the stream that approached his former company in the search for financing. This process eventually led to the final group of 11 individuals, including Tomas Johansson, which formed the network in December 2003.

The first crisis that occurred stemmed from lack of capital. The inceptor of the network, Tomas Johansson, was disappointed by the resistance displayed by the network founders to putting up significant capital. One explanation for this behaviour turned out to be lack of trust in Johansson, who was virtually unknown locally. Tomas Johansson had an academic background and had obtained many of his investment ideas from the US venture-capital industry, which made many local business owners reluctant to provide backing. The first crisis was eventually sorted out, as one of the locals guaranteed the network's ethics, and another guaranteed, through his local standing, the technological competence of the group, particularly in electronics.

A new crisis emerged as the group around Tomas Johansson, due to increasing reliance on a fixed model of how to organize the business-angel network, rejected a proposal due to the share price at time of entry. The local businessmen who had gathered around the project thought otherwise and formed a sub-group that we refer to as 'the entrepreneurial strategy advocates', due to their backgrounds as self-made businessmen. Some of the other businessmen reacted by forming an alternate network, referred to as the 'business-investment network', that was prepared to invest in the proposed investment. This alternate network was smaller than the original network in number of participants but quickly outgrew the original in terms of capital.

One of the most active members of the original network, Hans Strömberg, with a background as a successful entrepreneur in the electronics industry, took the initiative to form the alternate network. The main reason he stated was a perceived lack of respect on part of the original network's inceptor for alternative views on how to evaluate investment alternatives. Despite having developed huge success locally, he felt that the preconceived ideas of Tomas Johansson failed to leave any room for local input. Johansson had elected to appoint a semi-retired military officer to run the network, and the appointment was conducted according to the formalistic principles he introduced.

An analysis of an investing business-angel network in practice

Thematically, the interviews were organized into theoretical substructures based on the findings. Participant motivations (Stedler and Peters 2003), perspective on syndication (May 2002), remuneration (Bygrave and Hunt 2005), the importance of locality (Lindström and Olofsson 2002; Sörheim 2005), and the investment process in terms of both deal flow and due diligence (Haines *et al.* 2003) were determined to be five crucial issues under discussion in the business-angel network. In short, the business-angel network had to strike a balance between a venture-capital strategy and an entrepreneurial business-angel strategy, in effect hampering further progress as the participants debated the merits of each approach.

Participant motivations

The network was started with different motivations on the part of the participants. The supporters of the venture-capital strategy in the network consisted mainly of civil servants and were led by Tomas Johansson, who had significant experience of the venture-capital industry. Since most of them lacked entrepreneurial experience, they based their assumptions on published knowledge of how businesses function. Their source of inspiration was the American venture-capital industry, where fixed models have replaced a lack of direct experience. The knowledge that guided their decision-making was theoretical in nature, based on written materials and formal models, generated by others and by themselves, that were generally agreed upon in advance. The venture-capital strategists specifically targeted rapidly growing high-technology businesses on the assumption that such businesses were radically different from other types, especially in terms of product development and marketing needs.

> We should have known more about how to organize the process. One may wonder how ten men of a reasonable age could fail to know how to organize, form a company, and run it. It was sheer luck that we found someone who knew how to do this, who knew more about the capital requirements and how to select investment objects.
>
> (Lars Garpsten, CEO of the business-angel network, former army colonel)

The advocates of the entrepreneurial business-angel strategy in the network consisted of self-made men who made their own fortunes in diverse lines of business, typically not in high technology. They used their own experience of business in trying to reach decisions regarding investments and portfolio firms. They acquired their own knowledge and experience of various types of businesses and were convinced that business acumen is generic knowledge that can be applied in a range of industries. According to them, there is no great difference between the ability needed to run a high-technology firm, a real-estate business, or a manufacturing firm.

> What I did not notice in the original concept for the network was that many of the founders had 'administrated their way to success'. But I have certainly not 'administered' my way to success as a businessman. I simply cannot deal with all those rules and paragraphs they set up for the network.
>
> (Hans Strömberg, self-made entrepreneur)

> Hypothesis 1. The more profit-maximizing a business angel's motivation to participate in a business-angel network, the more likely it is that a venture-capital strategy will be used.

The remuneration process

An important dimension of the venture-capital strategy is that portfolio managers should be compensated by the hour for their work on the investments, as the venture is seen as a professional effort. This solves any problems of having free riders unwilling to participate in the investment process. In the portfolio firm, there was also to be management compensation for staff work, based on market rates. This is perceived to be the only way to find the best managers available. The investments are made based on principles of profitability, and there is no room for philanthropy in investment decisions made by the network.

> Thomas has always had knowledge of the process, and several entrepreneurs have wondered about what they were supposed to do, and how their knowledge was supposed to contribute, but you have to find ways to get there. Some said from the start that you have to erect a barrier, to make it a little difficult to get in so as to exclude free riders, and even to bar those who just want to do things their own way. We have tried all kinds of trial-and-error processes to make it work, but it is not simply a case of selling a good tool.
>
> (Sven Olofsson, CEO local campus)

Return on invested capital as compensation is the rule for advocates of the entrepreneurial business-angel strategy. They prefer not to withdraw resources from the invested capital to compensate for the efforts of those who deal with the portfolio firms. To a certain extent, entrepreneurial business-angel strategists do not need to be compensated in order to survive. Furthermore, they demand that the management of the firms in which they invest also invest their own equity, and management is expected to forfeit any luxurious perquisites before the portfolio firms generate sufficient revenue. Management should share the risks and be prepared to make short-term sacrifices. The investment decisions of entrepreneurial business-angel strategists are partly based on philanthropic arguments, as they do not actually need the investment for their wealth generation. Part of their motivation is to see whether they can do it again and to help a younger generation to start businesses.

> The aim of my core business is to gain a substantial return on investment, and I do use distinct models for key ratios. But in the case of the business-angel network, I do not use that model. In terms of income, engagement in the business-angel network is less important. It is more for the sake of having made a local investment and because I understand the importance of this to others. The locality is important, and I would not have made this investment in another community.
>
> (Fred Andersson, self-made entrepreneur)

Hypothesis 2. The more remuneration is perceived to be short-term in nature, the more likely it is that a venture-capital strategy will be used.

Perspectives on syndication

Share ownership, according to supporters of the venture-capital strategy, should be short-term, for as long as the price is fair. Again, profitability is at the core of decision-making, and since the portfolio firms are supposed to grow rapidly, it is often in the best interests of both parties to find more capital elsewhere. Venture-capital strategists have no problems whatsoever incorporating new owners to bolster the capital of the portfolio firm, nor do they perceive relinquishing control to that external owner as a problem. The whole issue of control is unimportant according to this strategy, as the network is not supposed to make a large investment in terms of knowledge.

> I am in a phase in which I want to have more order. And I do feel somewhat guilty about that, because I have not been firm enough. But it has been too sensitive a topic to raise – regarding the syndication of capital and competence – and since I am the prime source of competence, I am forced to be at the centre of the discussion. But the first chairman resigned due to differences regarding option schemes in the network.
>
> (Tomas Johansson, external expert on venture capital, member of the business-angel network)

The entrepreneurial business-angel strategists are prepared, if necessary, to take on long-term ownership in the firms in which they invest. The idea is to aid firm development by exerting all the positive influence they can, which entails working closely with the firms for as long as necessary. The entrepreneurs are reluctant to include new owners, as they may threaten the interaction between the investors and the portfolio firm. If new owners should be brought aboard who refuse to adopt the entrepreneurs' approach, the opinion is that it would be better not to retain the investment. Control is an issue, as the entrepreneurs are trying to guide the portfolio firm in the right direction. Ownership is therefore also important.

> In one firm in which my organization invested, the others in the network believed that the shares were inappropriately valued – they were deemed too expensive. But if no one had done anything, the enterprise would have died, so I threw in enough money for it to survive a while longer. According to all the formalized models, it was too expensive, but it was this price or not having the chance at all.
>
> (Self-made entrepreneur Hans Strömberg)

Hypothesis 3. The more open a network is to syndicating with outside investors, the more likely it is that a venture-capital strategy will be used.

The importance of locality

The locality of the network was less important to those participants who advocated a venture-capital strategy. This was primarily because, given the large deal flow necessary to find the right investments, they were unlikely to find a suitable enterprise that could be relocated in the small town where the network was based. They were even more unlikely to find an enterprise locally that met their requirements. Since the overall goal was to find the best investment available, the search was conducted at almost a national level.

> I have told them that I want to discuss how to act in the future, because I want us to raise more capital until we have USD 10–20 million to invest. We need to bring in professional investors who will look at the entire chain from initial investment to IPO, and we have already attracted a former CEO of an insurance company. I do not want to have a fight over this, but I want to use the occasion to make sure that everyone agrees. We are not building a small local operation but an actor that needs to move in a larger market.
>
> (Tomas Johansson, external expert on venture capital, member of the business-angel network)

From the outset, the local investors intended to relocate promising ventures at the local campus, a goal advocated to build local support for the network. However, as discussions progressed, several participants felt that this goal might not be realistic. The advocates of the entrepreneurial business-angel strategy had a different idea. Their goal was to locate enterprises locally, not primarily to create second-order effects for the local business community but to enable closer monitoring and control over operations. As their idea was to develop the firms through infusing their entrepreneurial knowledge, it was convenient to demand that the firms be located near the entrepreneurs.

> We have built this small venture-capital firm as an alternative to the business-angel network to be able to focus on innovation processes. We operate in the same area as the network but have a different setup. We want to have our own staff situated in this town, whereas the network cannot afford to hire staff but instead uses idealists. We want our alternative to have shorter and faster decision-making processes, so there are only the three of us who make the decisions, and we have daily interactions with the CEOs of the companies we fund.
>
> (Arvid Fernholm, self-made entrepreneur)

Hypothesis 4. The more flexible a network is in accepting geographically distant enterprises, the more likely it is that a venture-capital strategy will be used.

The investment process

Proposals are evaluated according to specific principles. This is also true in how the network makes decisions and in how the venture-capital strategists work with the portfolio firm. The venture-capital strategists only target investments based on profitability, firm location not being an issue. The relationship between the business-angel network and the portfolio firm should, according to the venture-capital approach, consist of hands-off management, especially since the idea is that a portfolio needs at least ten portfolio firms to ensure success, based on American venture-capital ideas. With a portfolio of this size, there would be little time for hands-on management of the investments.

> When Hans [a self-made entrepreneur] and others do not put their minds into this or do not want to take it in and instead believe that they are instantly able to cherry-pick the ventures that will go all the way as long as you put a lot of effort into it they have not really understood the trade as I see it and Hans will be successful just because he has energy and he combines that with access to a loyal group of people who develop companies for him.
>
> (Tomas Johansson, external expert on venture capital, member of the business-angel network)

Since the entrepreneurial business-angel strategists come from a business background, they typically use informal methods to make business decisions. Models can exert an influence, but in the end it is gut feeling based on years of business experience that determines whether to accept a business proposal. The entrepreneurs have great confidence in their own ability to succeed in business. They like to maintain close proximity between themselves and the firms in which they invest, to facilitate transferring their knowledge and experience to them; therefore, they argue for the importance of location. The governance of the portfolio firm is extremely hands-on, as they essentially follow their investments from day to day and even participate in events and meetings. This hands-on management of the portfolio firm ensures, according to the entrepreneurial business-angel strategists, that the management teams in their portfolio firms will replicate the success they have experienced themselves.

> In our alternative organization, we run a very informal operation where we take more of an entrepreneurial perspective. We do have board meetings and we do write protocols, but those are not central tasks in themselves. The main task is actually to work with these entrepreneurs.
>
> (Hans Strömberg, self-made entrepreneur)

Hypothesis 5. The more hands-off management is in the investment process, the more likely it is that a venture-capital strategy will be used.

Conclusions

Over time, many differences have emerged between the two groups in the business-angel network, and most of them remain unresolved. The primary contributions to the few firms in which the network has invested have been improving internal administrative routines, developing contractual agreements and financing strategies, and, finally, angel presence on the board of directors. The entrepreneurial business-angel strategists, some of whom defected to the alternate network, demand much greater control over their investments. In the business-investment network formed by the entrepreneurial business-angel strategists, the relationship between investors and the firms in which they invest is very close. They even reside in the same area, as the business-angel strategies have forced the firms' CEOs to move to the small town of the investors. Two altogether separate strategies have emerged in the network.

This study has highlighted five issues likely to be crucial for the functioning and organization of most business-angel networks. The study also demonstrates that these issues stand out as a potential breeding ground for conflict arising from differing opinions among the angels regarding the quite different methods of the formal venture-capital industry and more informal business-angel financing. Business-angel networks function as an intermediate form of governance, between that of a venture-capital firm and the solo business angel capable of making decisions on the spot. Many business-angel networks defuse this conflict by maintaining that they are only engaged in deal-flow activities and therefore do not handle the investment itself (Macarty and Payne 2002).

In business-angel networks that also engage in the actual investment process, there is a distinct need for open discussion of the points of departure. One failing of the case network presented here has been its inability to agree on the modus operandi. Of the five major differences of opinion, it is clear that participant motivation (Stedler and Peters 2003) and remuneration (Bygrave and Hunt 2005) depend on whether the investors perceive business-angel activity primarily as an opportunity to generate wealth or whether philanthropic ideals or other motivational factors also come into play. This is partly dependent on the prior wealth of the participants.

The other major issue is the perception of entrepreneurial development. The study provides evidence that the self-made entrepreneurs, who advocated the entrepreneurial business-angel strategy, believed that their prior knowledge would be instrumental in coaching the supported enterprises to succeed, whereas the venture-capital strategy relied more on finding the right enterprise than on coaching ability per se. Thus, perspectives on syndication with outside investors (May 2002), the importance of locality (Lindström and Olofsson 2002; Sörheim 2005), and the investment process (Haines *et al.* 2003) differed significantly between the two approaches. The entrepreneurial business-angel strategists preferred not to syndicate with outsiders, keeping the supported enterprises in geographical proximity to themselves; during the investment and subsequent management processes, they focused on hands-on management to guide the enterprises in the right direction. The venture-capital strategists, on the other hand, relied on a portfolio approach that is common in the venture-capital industry: a number of investments are made, and only those displaying a reasonable degree of success will be followed through. Syndication with others and flexibility in location is in line with a hands-off management style.

This study's contribution to research into business-angel networks is to provide a second-generation study that addresses questions rarely discussed before. The study provides evidence as to why there are problems formalizing investment processes for business-angel networks. By focusing on the issues and outcomes associated with strategy choice, the study provides a framework and five hypotheses usable in future studies of business-angel networks. This case provides an example of inexperienced business angels searching for business models and selecting a matching process applicable to the network (Mason and Harrison 1999). Earlier research has determined that the matching problem is particularly important to inexperienced business angels, who could benefit from a business-angel academy setting where business angels are trained to understand the particulars of business-angel investments (Aernoudt and Erikson 2002; Lange *et al.* 2002). A business-angel network with inadequately developed investment routines runs the risk of adverse selection in the investment process (Knyphausen-Aufsess and Westphal 2008). This is exacerbated by a desire to maintain a local investment policy (Landström 1998). In the end, most business-angel networks that – apart from providing information about possible investment opportunities – actually invest as part of their strategy, are run by hired managers but are led by experienced business angels (Preston 2004).

Managerial implications

The study advocates business-angel academies and promoting interaction among business-angel networks to facilitate the discussion of business-angel network strategies. The studied case shows how the investing process is slowed by an undercurrent of discussions regarding influence over decision-making processes. We have isolated motivation and remuneration as indicators of the balance between profit-maximizing and other reasons for participating in a business-angel network. These background variables should be discussed when first planning a business-angel network. In addition, syndication, locality, and investment process issues were discussed as indicators of which management style the business-angel network uses: the choice of hands-on management of a select few firms or of a hands-off portfolio strategy significantly affects how a network operates. The main managerial implications of this study are therefore to emphasize the importance of discussing motivation, remuneration, syndication, locality, and investment process, already from the outset in order to facilitate the creation and development of an aligned business-angel network.

For policy-makers, it would be useful to identify the decisions, associated with strategy choice, that a business-angel network involved in actual investments must make in order to succeed. The European Business Angel Network (EBAN) association has produced a white paper (EBAN 2007) discussing how business-angel networks can be used to increase the availability of business-angel financing. It should be remembered, however, that organizing business angels could entail a cost as well. The renowned researcher Colin Mason explains that there is a risk that overly formalizing business-angel networks may in fact lead to a situation in which business angels lose their most distinguishing feature: the ability to operate informally in a way in which venture capitalists and banks cannot because of their business models (EBAN 2008, interview with Colin Mason). This study reinforces this assessment to the degree that a fully fledged venture-capital strategy may lead business-angel networks to act more like venture-capital firms and even choose to go up the investment ladder and leave the early-stage financing phase altogether. In the end, the strategy choice is up to the members of a business-angel network, and a network that cannot choose may need to split up according to investment strategy or restructure as an informational business-angel network.

Limitations

As argued by Shaw (1999), studies are constrained by the researchers' choice of methods. It is our opinion that the main limitations of the present study concern the difficulty of generalizing the results to a wider population of business-angel networks. However, one of the authors of this paper has participated in a government study of over 20 Swedish business-angel networks (Silver 2008). Based on his experience, it can be ascertained that the business-angel network studied here resembles other networks in Sweden. In this study, we have investigated the founders of a single business-angel network located in a community with a context-specific industrial structure and approximately 50,000 inhabitants, which, taken together, might have affected the process of seeking suitable network founders. Accordingly, some of the difficulties highlighted and the differences of opinion regarding strategy choice may be traced to the founders' backgrounds. Furthermore, the respondents' recollections of the process and their reactions may have been at least partly altered by the time lag between the events and the interviews. Despite these considerations, the study should be viewed as a step towards filling the gap in research into strategy selection and resultant issues in business-angel networks.

References

R. Aernoudt, A. San José, and J. Roure, 'Executive Forum: Public Support for the Business Angel Market in Europe: A Critical Review', *Venture Capital: An International Journal of Entrepreneurial Finance,* 9 (1) (2007): 71–84.

R. Aernoudt and T. Erikson, 'Business-Angel Networks: A European Perspective', *Journal of Enterprising Culture,* 10 (3) (2002): 177–87.

H. Aldrich, *Organizations Evolving* (New York: Sage Publications, 1999).

R. Atkin and M. Esiri, 'Informal Investment: Investor and Investee Relationships', Paper presented to the 16th National Small Firms Policy and Research Conference, Nottingham, 17–19 November 1993.

S. Avdeitchikova, 'Typologies of Informal Venture Capital Investors in Sweden', Paper presented at the 50th World Conference of the International Council for Small Business, 2005, Washington, DC, USA.

E. Barnes, E. Cahill, and Y. McCarthy, 'Grandstanding in the UK Venture Capital Industry', *Journal of Alternative Investments,* 6 (3) (2003): 60–80.

G. Bernile, D. Cumming, and E. Lyandres, 'The Structure of Venture Capital and Private Equity Fund Portfolios', *Journal of Corporate Finance,* 13 (4) (2007): 564–90.

Z. Bodie, A. Kane, and A. Marcus, *Investments* (Boston, MA: McGraw-Hill Irwin, 2005).

W. D. Bygrave and S. A. Hunt, *GEM 2004 Financing Report* (London: Babson College and London Business School, 2005).

W. D. Bygrave and J. Timmons, *Venture Capital at the Crossroads* (Boston, MA: Harvard Business School Press, 1992).

S. R. Carriere, *Best Practices in Angel Groups and Angel Syndication* (London: British Business Angels Association, 2006).

K. G. Corley, 'Defined by Our Strategy or Our Culture? Hierarchical Differences in Perceptions of Organisational Identity and Change', *Human Relations,* 57 (9) (2004): 1145–77.

D. J. Cumming, 'The Determinants of Venture Capital Portfolio Size: Empirical Evidence', *Journal of Business,* 79 (2006): 1083–126.

D. Cumming, G. Fleming, and A. Schwienbacher, 'Financial Intermediaries, Ownership Structure and the Provision of Venture Capital to SMEs: Evidence from Japan', *Small Business Economics,* 31 (2008): 59–92.

European Business Angel Network (EBAN), *White Paper: Stimulating the European Informal Venture Capital Market* (Ixelles: EBAN, 2007).

EBAN, 'Interview with Colin Mason', *Conference Proceedings* (EBAN Congress 2008 Arnhem, Netherlands).

E. Fehr and U. Fischbacher, 'The Nature of Human Altruism', *Nature,* 425 (23) (2003): 785–91.

J. Freear, J. E. Sohl, and W. E. Jr Wetzel, 'Angels on Angels: Financing Technology-Based Ventures – A Historical Perspective', *Venture Capital: An International Journal of Entrepreneurial Finance,* 4 (4) (2002): 275–87.

J. Freear, J. E. Sohl, and W. E. Wetzel Jr., 'Angels and Non-Angels: Are There Differences?', *Journal of Business Venturing,* 9 (2) (1994): 109–23.

R. J. Gaston, *Finding Private Venture Capital for Your Firm: The Complete Guide* (New York: Wiley, 1989).

P. A. Gompers and J. Lerner, *The Venture Capital Cycle* (Cambridge, MA: MIT Press, 1999).

N. E. Haar, J. Starr, and I. C. Macmillan, 'Informal Risk Capital Investors: Investment Patterns on the East Coast of the USA', *Journal of Business Venturing,* 3 (1988): 11–29.

G. H. Haines Jr., J. J. Madill, and A. L. Riding, 'Informal Investment in Canada: Financing Small Business Growth', *Journal of Small Business and Entrepreneurship,* 16 (3–4) (2003): 13–40.

R. T. Harrison and C. M. Mason, 'International Perspectives on the Supply of Informal Venture Capital', *Journal of Business Venturing,* 7 (1992): 459–75.

R. T. Harrison and C. M. Mason, 'Venture Capital Market Complementarities: The Links between Business Angels and Venture Capital Funds in the UK', *Venture Capital: An International Journal of Entrepreneurial Finance,* 2 (2000): 223–42.

A. Hawke and T. Heffernan, 'Interpersonal Liking in Lender–Customer Relationships in the Australian Banking Sector', *International Journal of Bank Marketing,* 24 (3) (2006): 140–57.

T. Hellmann, 'IPOs, Acquisitions, and the Use of Convertible Securities in Venture Capital', *Journal of Financial Economics,* 81 (2006): 649–79.

T. Hellmann and M. Puri, 'Venture Capital and the Professionalization of Start-up Firms: Empirical Evidence', *Journal of Finance,* 57 (1) (2002): 169–97.

K. Hindle and S. Rushworth, 'The Demography of Investor Heaven: A Synthesis of International Research on the Characteristics, Attitudes, and Investment Behaviour of Business Angels', Paper presented at the conference: Financing the Future: Small Medium Enterprise Finance, Corporate Governance and the Legal System, Sydney, 1999.

K. Hindle and R. Wenban, 'Australia's Informal Venture Capitalists: An Exploratory Profile', *Venture Capital: An International Journal of Entrepreneurial Finance,* 1 (2) (1999): 169–86.

L. Jeng and P. Wells, 'The Determinants of Venture Capital Funding: Evidence across Countries', *Journal of Corporate Finance,* 6 (2000): 241–89.

M. Jensen, 'Self-Interest, Altruism, Incentives, and Agency Theory', *Journal of Applied Corporate Finance,* 7 (2) (1994): 40–45.

J. Johnston, S. Paul, and G. Whittam, 'The Operation of the Informal Venture Capital Market in Scotland', *Venture Capital: An International Journal of Entrepreneurial Finance,* 5 (4) (2003): 313–35.

M. Jääskeläinen, M. Maula, and T. Seppä, 'Allocation of Attention to Portfolio Companies and the Performance of Venture-capital firms', *Entrepreneurship Theory and Practice,* 30 (2006): 185–206.

P. Kelly and M. Hay, '"Deal Makers": A Reputation that Attracts Quality', *Venture Capital: An International Journal of Entrepreneurial Finance,* 2 (2000): 183–202.

A. A. Kirilenko, 'Valuation and Control in Venture Finance', *Journal of Finance,* 56 (2001): 565–87.

D. Knyphausen-Aufsess and R. Westphal, 'Do Business-Angel Networks Deliver Value to Business Angels?', *Venture Capital: An International Journal of Entrepreneurial Finance,* 10 (2) (2008): 149–69.

H. Landström, 'Informal Investors as Entrepreneurs', *Technovation,* 18 (1998): 321–33.

J. Lange, B. Leleux, and B. Surlemont, 'Angel Networks for the 21st Century: An Examination of Practices of Leading Networks in Europe and the USA', in D. Cetindamar (ed.), *The Growth of Venture Capital: A Cross-Cultural Comparison* (Westport, Conn.: Quorum Books, 2002).

J. Lerner and A. Schoar, 'The Illiquidity Puzzle: Theory and Evidence from Private Equity', *Journal of Financial Economics,* 72 (1) (2004): 3–40.

G. Lindström and C. Olofsson, 'Early Stage Financing of NTBFs: An Analysis of Contributions from Support Actors', *Venture Capital: An International Journal of Entrepreneurial Finance,* 3 (2) (2001): 151–68.

G. Lindström and C. Olofsson, *Affärsänglar och teknikbaserade tillväxtföretag* (Stockholm: SNS Förlag, 2002).

M. Macarty and W. Payne, 'The Anatomy of an Angel Investing Network: Tech Coast Angels', *Venture Capital: An International Journal of Entrepreneurial Finance,* 4 (4) (2002): 331–6.

C. M. Mason, 'Informal Sources of Venture Finance', in S. Parker (ed.), *The Life Cycle of Entrepreneurial Ventures* (*International Handbook Series on Entrepreneurship,* vol. III) (Springer: USA, 2006).

C. M. Mason and R. T. Harrison, 'Closing the Regional Equity Gap: The Role of Informal Venture Capital', *Small Business Economics,* 7 (2) (1995): 153–72.

C. M. Mason and R. T. Harrison, 'Why "Business Angels" Say No: A Case Study of Opportunities Rejected by an Informal Investor Syndicate', *International Small Business Journal,* 14 (1996): 35–51.

C. M. Mason and R. T. Harrison, 'Business-Angel Networks and the Development of the Informal Venture Capital Market in the UK: Is There Still a Role for the Public Sector?', *Small Business Economics,* 9 (1997): 111–23.

C. M. Mason and R. T. Harrison, 'Public Policy and the Development of the Informal Venture Capital Market: UK Experience and Lessons for Europe', in K. Cowling (ed.), *Industrial Policy in Europe* (London: Routledge, 1999).

C. M. Mason and M. Stark, 'What Do Business Investors Look for in a Business Plan? A Comparison of the Investment Criteria of Bankers, Venture Capitalists and Business Angels', *International Small Business Journal,* 22 (3) (2004): 227–48.

M. Maula, E. Autio, and P. Arenius, 'What Drives Micro-Angel Investments?', *Small Business Economics,* 25 (5) (2005): 459–75.

J. May, 'Structured Angel Groups in the USA: The Dinner Club Experience', *Venture Capital: An International Journal of Entrepreneurial Finance,* 4 (2002): 337–42.

N. Månsson and H. Landström, 'Business Angels in a Changing Economy: The Economy May Be Changing but What Happens with the Business Angels?', Paper presented at the EDGE Conference, Singapore, 11–13 July 2005.

W. Neus and U. Walz, 'Exit Timing of Venture Capitalists in the Course of an Initial Public Offering', *Journal of Financial Intermediation,* 14 (2005): 253–77.

OECD, *OECD Small and Medium Enterprise Outlook* (Paris: OECD Publications Service, 2002).

S. L. Preston, *Angel Investment Groups, Networks and Funds: A Guidebook to Developing the Right Angel Organisation for Your Community* (Kansas City, MO: Ewing Marion Kauffman Foundation, 2004).

P. D. Reynolds, W. D. Bygrave, E. Autio, and L. W. Cox, *2002 Executive Report: Babson College* (Babson Park, MA, Kansas City, MO, and London: Babson College, Ewing Marion Kauffman Foundation Centre, and London Business School, 2002).

A. San José, J. Roure, and R. Aernoudt, 'Business Angel Academies: Unleashing the Potential for Business Angel Investment', *Venture Capital: An International Journal of Entrepreneurial Finance,* 7 (2) (2005): 149–65.

H. J. Sapienza, D. De Clercq, and W. R. Sandberg, 'Antecedents of International and Domestic Learning Effort', *Journal of Business Venturing,* 20 (4) (2005): 437–57.

E. Shaw, 'A Guide to the Qualitative Research Process: Evidence from a Small Firm Study', *Qualitative Market Research: An International Journal,* 2 (2) (1999): 59–70.

L. Silver, *Utvärdering av Nuteks stöd för affärsänglanätverk och affärsänglar* (Stockholm: Verket för näringslivsutveckling – NUTEK, 2008).

J. E. Sohl, 'The Early Stage Equity Market in the United States', *Venture Capital: An International Journal of Entrepreneurial Finance,* 1 (1999): 101–20.

J. E. Sohl, 'The Private Equity Market in the USA: Lessons from Volatility', *Venture Capital: An International Journal of Entrepreneurial Finance,* 5 (2003): 29–46.

H. Stedler and H. H. Peters, 'Business Angels in Germany: An Empirical Study', *Venture Capital: An International Journal of Entrepreneurial Finance,* 5 (3) (2003): 269–76.

R. Sörheim, 'Business Angels as Facilitators for Further Finance: An Exploratory Study', *Journal of Small Business and Enterprise Development,* 12 (2) (2005): 178–91.

J. Tucker and J. Lean, 'Small Firm Finance and Public Policy', *Journal of Small Business and Enterprise Development,* 10 (1) (2003): 50–61.

W. E. Wetzel Jr., 'The Informal Venture Capital Market: Aspects of Scale and Market Efficiency', *Journal of Business Venturing,* 2 (1987): 299–313.

A. Winton and V. Yerramilli, 'Entrepreneurial Finance: Banks versus Venture Capital', *Journal of Financial Economics,* 88 (2008): 51–79.

J. Wonglimpiyarat, 'The Influence of Capital Market Laws and Initial Public Offering (IPO) Process on Venture Capital', *European Journal of Operational Research,* 12 (2009): 293–301.

M. Wright and A. Lockett, 'The Structure and Management of Alliances: Syndication in the Venture Capital Industry', *Journal of Management Studies,* 40 (2003): 2073–104.

R. K. Yin, *Case Study Research Design and Methods,* 2nd edn (London: Sage, 1994).

A. L. Zacharakis and, D. A. Shepherd, 'A Non-Additive Decision-Aid for Venture Capitalists' Investment Decisions', *European Journal of Operational Research,* 162 (3) (2005): 673–89.

11

Increased Internationalization for Small and Medium-Sized Enterprises through Joint Export Networks

Hans Jansson and Petter Boye

Introduction

The increased globalization and restructuring of geopolitical markets, exemplified by a growing European Union (EU) that is incorporating new members from the formerly Communist states of eastern Europe, has caused a shift in the European business world, creating both business opportunities and threats for the firms there. Increased competition from low-cost countries has forced many European firms to increase their efficiency, specialization, and international trade to remain competitive. New opportunities and threats have emerged out of the transition processes in East European, Asian, and other emerging markets. Vast sums are flowing into investments and regional development efforts in these areas to lift them to a higher international level, for example, by improving infrastructure and reducing environmental pollution. These investments have created business opportunities for European companies, leading, for example, to increased international activity among Swedish small and medium-sized enterprises (SMEs) (Boye *et al.* 2004; Jansson and Sandberg 2008; Hilmersson and Sandberg 2007).

A main question is how firm competitiveness has been influenced by this change in international business conditions. Compared with large companies, SMEs are usually at a disadvantage in international trade because they are traditionally home-market oriented and therefore characterized by a low degree of internationalization. However, this could be compensated for by forming cooperative networks to develop joint competitive advantage. By sharing resources, synergies similar to those enjoyed by large firms can be achieved. This change not only opens up new business opportunities but also creates new threats; for example, new international trade across the Baltic Sea is rendered difficult by the great differences in business environment between the transitional economies of the area and their western European trading partners.

Research issues and main purpose

The main issue discussed here is how SMEs cooperate in order to access export markets. Their limited individual resource bases are assumed to be the main factor prompting joint actions such as these. We know from earlier theories of industrial districts and entrepreneurial milieus that SMEs that develop in a local or domestic market tend to make use of complementary external resources via cooperation with partners in close geographical proximity. Such cooperation often occurs in the form of networks. This study focuses on such local networks to see how they function as a vehicle for SME export development.

Specifically, this chapter considers how SMEs establish joint network organizations to use local resources and capabilities to gain competitive advantage in international markets. We first examine a theoretical framework developed for describing and analysing such SME export cooperation; thereafter, this framework is illustrated using empirical examples from a study. The methodology used is described, and some conclusions are presented.

The strategic approach to export cooperation

Porter (2000: 16) defines a cluster of companies as: 'a geographically proximate group of interconnected companies and associated institutions in a particular field, linked by commonalities and complementarities'. The competitiveness of such a cluster or local network is largely determined by its internal characteristics; however, it is also determined by its external environment, in this case the geographical setting and environments beyond the particular cluster. Such internal and external factors underlying the competitive advantage of regional networks in international markets are explored here.

Economic explanations dominate the literature on internal factors. A common explanation of the spatial closeness of Marshall's (1923) self-contained networks in traditional industries is the efficiency of clusters, for example, in fostering and accessing supply chains, labour markets, and subcontractors. Another economic explanation relates to why shared regional knowledge is developed through rapid formal and informal communication between firms, employees, and the community – namely, that it is a non-tradable, regional public good for which there is no market mechanism. Such a mix of economic and social explanations is a common research perspective, one also adopted here. According to Piore and Sabel (1984), for example, industrial districts consist of relationship-based firms that obtain institutional support in a close community in which social factors provide the context for economic success. The industrial district is a socio-geographic entity in which economic factors are socially embedded. This shared regional knowledge base is the main factor underlying the competitive advantage of regional networks, being seen as non-transferable knowledge that creates a dedicated and specific geographically bound capability.

The growing importance of clusters in industrial development has made them popular industrial policy instruments. The establishment and operation of such networks are increasingly supported by external public agencies. Such network initiatives manifest themselves as cooperative projects in networks consisting of firms, government bodies, and the research/education community. In 2003, the Global Network Initiative Survey identified 509 initiatives to build-up such clusters worldwide (Lindqvist 2004). The present study researches the importance of such network initiatives in fostering the clusters involved in international business. Whether or not public bodies are included in the network depends on how the initiative is organized; if their task is limited to initiating or serving a specific network, they are normally left outside the cluster/network.

Based on the literature, three major perspectives on the competitiveness of a regional network are distinguished:

1. The network has no strategic intention of its own. Why some groups of firms are more successful than others is explained by favourable economic and social factors, for example, a positive environment supporting the network.
2. The network is seen as an actor with its own intentions, for example, expressed through a deliberate strategy based on network-specific capabilities.
3. The network is seen from the perspective of the individual member firm. The focus is on firm-specific competitive advantages and how these can be improved through membership in a regional grouping, which benefits from network-specific capabilities.

This chapter combines the second and third perspectives, focusing on initiatives endogenous to the network, normally treating public network initiatives as exogenous. However, if such initiatives result in the participation of public units in the intended network operations, they are regarded as included in the network.

The theoretical framework

An overview of the theoretical model developed for describing and analysing how SMEs develop international competitiveness through cooperation is shown in Figure 11.1 and discussed in detail in this section. The joint

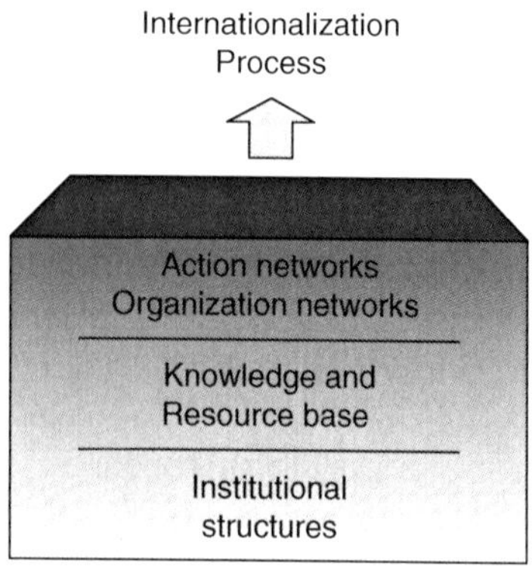

Figure 11.1 The joint export network framework

export network functions as a vehicle for SME internationalization and helps individual SMEs with limited resources to access international markets. The internationalizing joint network consists of action and organization networks. The competitiveness of this regional network organization is based on a shared knowledge and resource platform, which is embedded in a deeper, underlying institutional structure.

The joint export network framework illustrated in Figure 11.1 concerns a collaborative inter-organizational network, which differs from an intra-organizational network (within a firm) or inter-organizational industrial marketing network as it works in another way. The joint export network consists of hierarchies and operates as an 'actor' in one or several market networks. The structure of the joint export network is determined by the characteristics of the firms involved and of the market network in which it operates. This type of collaborative network is defined as a regional joint network organization.

The basis of the competitive advantage of the network in foreign markets concerns how resources and capabilities are integrated through the network into network-specific capabilities. The ability of the joint export network to drive internationalization is determined by how it is organized in terms of the following significant factors: network organization, resource/competence base, and institutional structures. These factors are dependent on the network's geographical setting.

Joint Export Network

According to Figure 11.1, the competitiveness of the joint export network is determined by three layers of interrelated factors situated in a specific geographical setting or region.

Action and organization networks

The first layer consists of nodes connected by relationships or linkages, forming action and organization networks. The organization network is a larger and more permanent social structure from which members are drawn for participation in temporary action networks. The action network is a temporary set of units formed of various organization network units for a specific task. When the task is completed, the action network is dissolved and the units remain in the organization network, awaiting the formation of future action networks.

An export network consisting of these two major types of networks has a dualistic quality, serving the interests of individual organizations while being part of a larger collective with the right to carry out work on behalf of the whole network. A network member therefore serves its own interests simultaneously with the joint interests of the other network organizations. This trade-off needs to suit each member for the network to persist for any extended period. This means that networks describe and explain entire social structures and comprehend particular elements of these structures. Three aspects of a firm's network structure are important: the number of direct and indirect links it possesses, together with their connectivity, that is, the *degree* to which partners are linked to each other (Ahuja 2000). According to the latter dimension, a distinction is made between open and closed networks. An open network, for example, is one in which the firm has direct contacts with all its partners, which do not, however, have any direct contacts with each other. The existence of many 'structural holes' means that the network consists of a few redundant contacts and that it is information-rich, since people on either side of a hole have access to different information flows (Burt 1992). The structure of an open network is suitable when the cooperation concerns market information and maximizing the number of contacts. The opposite is the closed network, in which all partners have direct and strong ties with each other. This network is centred on social capital, which is built through trust and shared norms and behaviour (Coleman 1988). This type of network is suitable when the partners' objective is to collaborate in action, for example, via collective marketing actions. This latter type of network itself comprises two major types of networks: organization networks and action networks (Aldrich and Whetten 1981; Jansson *et al.* 1995; Jansson 2007b).

Size, defined as the number of strong ties, seems to matter, since it affects performance – in our case, competitiveness (Uzzi 1996). The trade-off between open and closed networks in the internationalization process, or the evolving closure of the network, is therefore vital to analyse. According to Soda *et al.* (2004), there seems to be a U-shaped relationship between network closure and performance. According to their study of projects in the Italian TV industry, the best-performing projects were those with a high degree of past closure and a high number of current structural holes. Network closure has a strong long-term effect. The effects of bridge ties are temporary, meaning that they decay and are unstable, which could be expected from weak ties. These have important implications for building open networks; for example, the cost of creating and maintaining bridge ties must be evaluated in the context of their short-term advantages. Transferred to the context of joint export network organizations, this means that networks should be based on both past working relationships among members and simultaneous links with other firms/people for best performance.

Network leader

The key role of the joint export network is defined as the network leader, a role assumed by an organization in the inter-organizational network or a person in the social network. In the former case, the role is formal and in the latter case it is informal. How these organizational and social aspects are combined in the network leader role varies between networks. The leader's main tasks are to lead and organize the export network. The network leader thus plays a major role in forming the identity of the network, which is related to the name of the joint export network, or to its vision, image, and brand. Its identity makes the joint export network a separate organization, forming the network's world view (see, for example, the discussion of imaginary organizations (IOs) and IO leaders in Hedberg *et al.* 2002). The network identity provides a collective basis for the joint strategy of the network, uniting it as one unit. The network leader's influence on the network's identity provides a way of indirectly leading a group of voluntarily cooperating actors (member firms) in the absence of the power to control their activities directly. In this way, the leader represents, symbolizes, and forms the joint export network.

Knowledge and resource base

The second layer consists of the knowledge and resource base, which plays a pivotal role in the strategic process of the network, which is in this sense a regional competence platform (Boye 1999). In this there are several similarities to the resource-based theory of strategic formulation (Wernerfelt 1984; Barney 1991; Grant 1991; Jansson 2007a) in which strategy aims to enable the optimal exploitation and upgrading of the organization's resources and capabilities. However, the strategy process in a network is not in the hands of a single manager or firm; rather, it is a collective strategy formed through the network. As for the local industrial knowledge base, it is possible to view the network as a 'distributed' knowledge system (Tsoukas 1996).

In highly integrated networks, the knowledge/resource structure is combined through the network into distinctive network-specific capabilities or core capabilities, which create synergies for the units involved in the competence network. Such resource-sharing through combining knowledge, skills, and physical assets occurs most efficiently within a closed network, since it involves significant conversion of tacit knowledge, which normally requires repeated and regular meetings, a focus on specified objectives, close and trusting cooperation, and mutual dependency. When access to new information is the primary goal, on the other hand, open networks are the most suitable (Ahuja 2000).

Internationalization of the export network occurs when competitive advantage is achieved in foreign markets by actors creating joint core competencies based on complementary resources (Boye 1999). These network-specific capabilities are based on the individual firm-specific resources and capabilities of the partners, which form the competence base of the network. This collective capability to use teams of resources in purposeful ways creates synergies for the firms involved. These synergies are the outcome of knowledge integration through the networking and trust-building activities of local actors. These social activities are easier to carry out in a local community, where spatial proximity enables interaction between individuals. Some of the joint resources and capabilities are tangible and articulated, making them easier to identify, while others are intangible or tacit, making them more difficult to discover and trade. According to the resource-based strategy theory, two major conditions must be fulfilled if these capabilities are to make the international business of the joint export network competitive. First, these capabilities must create customer value by improving product effectiveness or quality. Second, they must be unique or rare compared with the competitors' capabilities. Once established, competitive edge can become sustainable because the interconnectedness of various knowledge and resource structures creates a socially complex capability, which is often difficult to understand, codify, or imitate for competitors (Jansson 2007a).

Two types of network-specific capabilities can be distinguished based on Tallman *et al.* (2004). *Component knowledge* is found in individual network firms. It is simple, tangible, explicit, and transferable, including, for example, blueprints, product patents, and step-by-step operation instructions. *Architectural knowledge*, in contrast, is developed jointly by the network firms, which together create understandings through application. This knowledge is embedded in social networks and represents a kind of social capital of the network. Architectural knowledge is non-transferable or non-tradable and is thus bound to the joint export network organization.

Institutional structure

Institutional structure is the third major strategic basis of the regional network. Here, regional actors, seeking economies of scale and scope, take initiatives to reduce barriers between countries and to harmonize systems. Firms' and other organizations' perceptions and interpretations of their environment are filtered through both individual and shared cognitive frames, including industrial recipes (Hellgren and Melin 1992) and definitions of local region and competitive context. Values, norms, and regulative mechanisms significantly influence how organizations act in relation to their environment.

As in the discussion of regional industrial concepts in Boye (1999), some of the beliefs and ideas that form the export networks are shared by others in society, and the more institutionalized these beliefs and ideas are, the more integrated and sustainable the network concept. The network concept serves as a frame of reference for interaction and negotiation between the actors and their intentions and activities. It provides a way of seeing, thinking, and sense-making that ultimately triggers action. Over time, a strong concept becomes institutionalized and taken for granted, becoming convincing enough that it constitutes a common outlook throughout the network.

Institutional structures, such as values and norms prevailing within and outside the network, also influence the identity of the joint export network. In turn, an identity shared by network members also supports the formation of resource teams and the development of shared knowledge in the network.

Internationalization process

Joint export networks are involved in internationalization processes, which are assumed to follow patterns typical of firms in general (Johanson and Wiedersheim-Paul 1975; Johanson and Vahlne 1977), including SMEs (Hohenthal 2001). However, 'new international ventures' tend to follow another pattern (Oviatt and McDougall 1994; Madsen and Servais 1997). According to the network approach to internationalization (Jansson 2007b; Timlon and Hilmersson 2009), the more relationships a firm has in a foreign country, the more established and experienced it becomes and the higher its degree of internationalization. Relationships are integrated into Cavusgil's (1980) internationalization process model as suggested in Jansson and Sandberg (2008). Relationships at the core of the process follow a pattern similar to that of the internationalization process as a whole, showing how the gradual build-up of internationalization knowledge takes place through increased experiential knowledge in the network. The node used to plug into the local market network is defined as the entry node. Relationships with customers may be either direct, for example, through a wholly owned sales subsidiary, or indirect, for example, through an intermediary. The mode of entry of the entry node varies (Jansson 2007b). The more a firm's relationships in a foreign country are developed, the more established and internationally experienced the firm becomes and the higher its degree of internationalization. In addition, the more countries with which the firm has established relationships, the more internationally experienced it is. By establishing more relationships abroad, the firm moves further along the internationalization process, starting in the experimental export stage.

The larger the number of relationships established, the more of the firm's resources and capabilities are dedicated to international business, which means, among other things, that they are increasingly located abroad.

During the pre-relationship stage, the firm's experience with the customers/suppliers is lacking, uncertainty is high, distances are great, and commitment and adaptation are absent. For an SME with a domestic market focus, that is only starting to internationalize its relationships with a foreign country, the pre-relationship stage corresponds to the pre-export stage for the first foreign market. Relationship development in foreign markets starts early on, when commitments and experience are on the increase. According to Cavusgil's (1980) five-step model, this is similar to the experimental export stage of an internationally inexperienced firm. Relationship establishment in a foreign country market is a mutual learning process in which the involved parties learn more about each other. The first few adaptations are made when uncertainty is still considerable and great distance remains between the parties. This early stage is followed by the development stage, during which business between the customer and the supplier starts to grow and resources are increasingly shared. In this stage, the buyer/seller relationship develops further, signified by delivery build-up and the signing of contracts. Intensive mutual learning results in increased experience on both sides and in reduced uncertainty and distance. Trust and commitment increase, signified by both formal and informal adaptations as well as cost savings. Relationships change in nature and become entirely focused on the dyad, becoming deeper and broader. Next, after several major purchases or deliveries, the relationship settles into a stable long-term stage marked by continuous business between the parties. The exporter and importer have now learned to know and trust each other: experience is considerable and the uncertainty is perceived as low, distances are small and commitment high, and adaptations are extensive and cost savings considerable. The main aim of relationship-building is to reach the long-term stage, that is, to establish an ongoing long-term relationship. If this is not accomplished, the relationship may revert to an earlier stage, even to the pre-relationship stage. In the latter case, relationship-building may well commence anew, perhaps this time with a new buyer/supplier. By the final stage, the relationship has become extensively institutionalized and habitual with commitment being taken for granted. The downside is that the relationship might be stalled, becoming unadaptable in the face of ongoing environmental change. The high trust, short distances, and lack of uncertainty might also lead the parties to become complacent. Despite the high degree of institutionalization, this makes the relationship susceptible to environmental changes and to competitor attack.

The organizational acquisition of experiential knowledge underlies the stepwise nature of internationalization models. According to Sharma and Blomstermo (2003), such organizational learning is discontinuous, as if accompanied by changes in the learning platform. New stages of internationalization are established, with the firm extending its business from one major type of market to another or from one type of foreign environment to another. These foreign market environments or contexts are defined as institutional settings based on the institutional network approach (Jansson 2007a). Like the interplay between network relationships and institutional structure within the joint export network, there is interplay between this network and the external institutional structure on the export market. This is an external rule system faced by the joint export network, including 'macro rules' such as judicial and penal systems.

Methodology

The methodological strategy underlying this research is mainly an abductive approach, that is, a mix of deduction and induction, to developing theory based on case studies (Alvesson and Sköldberg 1994; Boye 1999; Dubois and Gadde 2002; Jansson 1994; Jansson *et al.* 1995). The combined process starts from a preliminary frame of reference, using the case-study approach (Merriam 1998; Yin 1994). This theoretical framework is continuously refined via an iterative shifting of perspectives between the deductive and inductive approaches. The aim is to create a solid theoretical and empirical foundation while strengthening the practical validity of the research, making the results relevant to organizations and society. The research process underlying this chapter started deductively by assembling a preliminary theoretical framework based on previous research (Boye 1999; Hedberg *et al.* 2002; Jansson 2007a, 2007b). This framework was in turn tested against reality via case studies of export cooperation networks in Sweden.

The chapter builds on a survey of companies in Kalmar County engaged in trade with eastern Baltic customers, as reported in Boye *et al.* (2004) and Jansson and Sandberg (2008). In this survey and in other studies, Kalmar County was scanned for export cooperation networks. Initial attempts to initiate such cooperation were found in a few cases. However, these networks were mainly formed for other reasons and have yet to start on international business (Boye 2000). One such export network with approximately 35 members was found in the environmental industry and involves cooperation in industrial marketing activities. A short account of this environmental technology regional (ETR) joint network will be presented later in the chapter. To learn more about how such regional joint network organizations form and develop, another joint network organization was studied, Woodhouse Aurora Borealis (WAB), which has approximately 40 active members in northern Sweden. Despite the great importance of the wood-products industry in Kalmar County, only a few examples of export collaboration in this industry, involving three to six companies in their early stages, could be found there, making it useful to study more developed cooperation elsewhere in Sweden. Another region was selected, where there was an industry cluster similar to the one in Kalmar County and a regional joint export network selling to a similar type of market, that is, a market very different from the Swedish market. Japan is comparable in this regard to the emerging markets of the Baltic region. Based on these studies, the preliminary theoretical framework has been developed into a more refined framework, presented here.

Empirical examples

Some major characteristics of the start-up of two joint export networks to build network-specific competitive advantages are summarized in this section. The first case is that of an export-marketing network in the environmental technology industry in southern Sweden, which was founded early in the 21st century and has now started to accept orders. The second case concerns the formation of an export-marketing network in the wood-products industry in northern Sweden. An overview of the compared cases is given in Table 11.1 in the end of this chapter.

Action and organization networks

Network purpose

The purpose of the joint export networks studied is to market product and service offerings to specific target markets. This concerns the offerings of individual firms as well as more systemic offerings involving resources and competencies of more than one network firm.

The main task of the network leader, Sustainable Sweden Southeast (SSSE), is to market the products and services of the network's member firms by forming action networks. The purpose of SSSE is to increase the network's customer base by marketing the products and competencies of network members. Specific target markets are Poland, Lithuania, Kaliningrad, and Kina, whose growing economies increasingly demand environmental technology.

SSSE (see www.sustainable-sweden.se) argues that its role is to:

1. offer 'one-stop shopping' for the region's total supply of environmental technology;
2. create business concepts;
3. transfer experience and knowledge;
4. support business relationships between Swedish industry and international partners;
5. support financial solutions.

The main purpose of WAB is to establish long-term cooperation between firms in its region and in Japan, mainly to promote exports but also to attract Japanese investment to the region (Jacobsson and Strömberg 2004).

The plan is also to include the Chinese and Korean markets. WAB builds on previous attempts by the Swedish Export Council to initiate export cooperation in the region's wood-products industry and on experience gained during the brief existence of a previous sub-supplier network.

The organization of these networks is characterized by:

1. their member entities;
2. how they are managed and coordinated;
3. their activities;
4. their resources and competencies.

Network actors

The joint export network consists of several members in the form of companies and public organizations.

The ETR joint network is an organization network that fits the description of a regional joint export network. Its broad partner base comprises 21 firms, 10 municipalities, two universities, two county councils, and an energy agency.

The WAB joint export network is larger than the ETR. Of approximately 260 firms in the two northernmost Swedish counties, 50 are members, of which 35–40 are active. The member firms each employ 5–500 personnel. The firms cover the whole value-added chain of building material and house components, including all inputs except raw material for wooden houses. The largest company in the industry in the region, Norra Skogsägarna, is a passive member of the network, mainly contributing its marketing experience to the project. Collaboration partners are local governments, a few central government units, and some organizations in Tokyo.

A house-building network of 25 firms has been established as part of the larger joint export network. WAB also cooperates with two other similar projects in northern Sweden: Building Wood and Arctic lumber group.

Network activities

The activities carried out within and by the network have developed over time as the network has confronted new business deals. This potential of this work is considered in detail by examining how the marketing of a few promising business deals is organized. One concerns a water and sewage project in Panevezys, Lithuania, and another concerns smaller environmental projects in Kaliningrad, Russia. Two major opportunities have been found for such projects, representing two offerings in which either the whole project is supplied or only parts of it. In the first case, the action network will be a main contractor involving many different network competencies; in the second, only one or a few firms are involved as subcontractors.

A main activity of WAB is matchmaking, that is, identifying suitable suppliers in Sweden and customers in Japan and bringing them together.

Another activity is providing market information through documentation and visits by Swedish firms to Japan and vice versa. These visits are important to the third activity, which is contact creation. The project is primarily meant to create contacts, give advice, and follow up on network activities.

Network leader

The networks are managed and coordinated by relatively small organizational entities. The ETR has a formal network leader in the form of an enterprise that handles the strategic management of the network, for example, by developing marketing strategies and defining core competencies. This network leader also strongly influences the development of the network identity. In this case the organization's, that is, the network leader's name – Sustainable Sweden Southeast – implies the network's core competence.

WAB is held together by informal contracts based more on trust than on formal mechanisms; other unifying factors are synergy, clear vision, and a working business concept. IT also plays an important facilitative role. In this, the role of WAB's network leader differs from that of the ETR, in that his role is more informal and personal. WAB's network leader is a man who serves as a bridge between the internal and external networks while primarily coordinating the internal network and inspiring actions within it. He is a broker who is also engaged in contact building and maintenance both inside the WAB network and outside, in relation to the Japanese market customer network. He focuses more on this task than on making, closing, and following up on deals, which is the task of the ETR network leader. The WAB leader also has extensive experience of doing business in Japan. Because of these abilities, he has been accepted as a leader by the network members. In the initial stages, it is also valuable that he is able to create new business concepts for the SMEs.

Knowledge and resource base for internationalization

In the ETR case, the network firms, with their substantial production competencies but inadequate marketing competence, are supplemented by international marketing competence (see Figure 11.2 below). This latter competence, mainly embodied in one full-time manager, forms a kind of 'marketing department' for the inter-organizational network, heading its marketing activities. As the main representative of SSSE, this woman is also the network leader, both formally and informally.

To market industrial products and services on specific emerging markets, the network firms need broad and detailed knowledge of these markets and the broader market environment. They must understand the institutional structures and societies of the countries with which they wish to trade, for example, gaining the cultural knowledge needed to interpret markets and understand how to build network relationships. Knowledge is required about the formal and informal rules and the institutions that drive the target

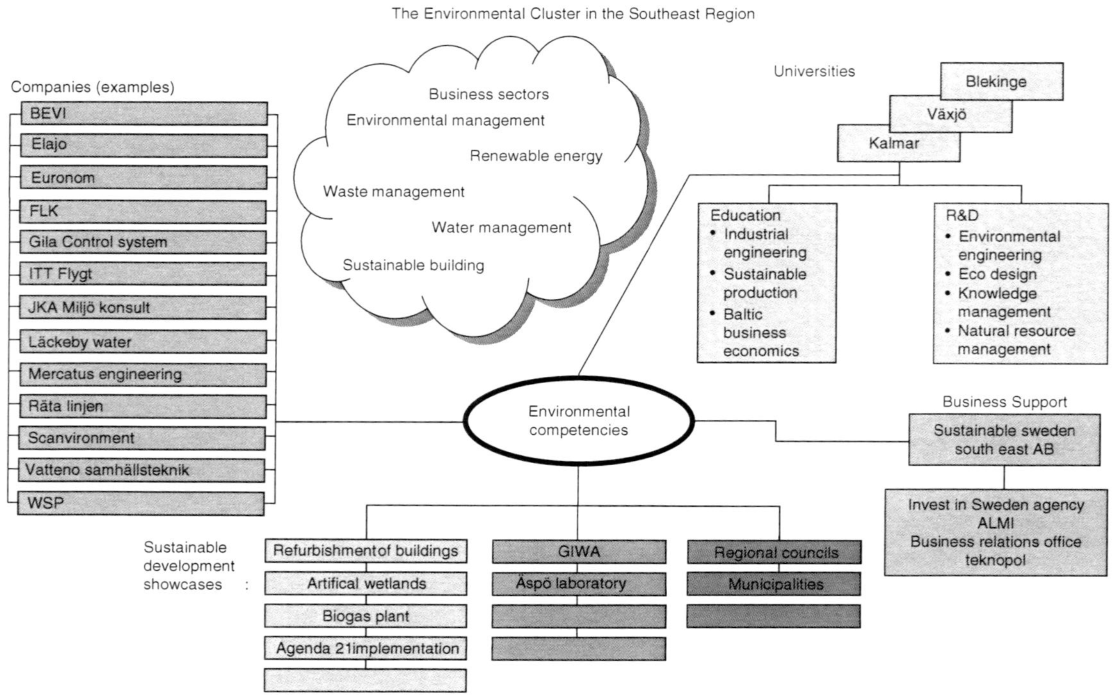

Figure 11.2 The ETR joint network

foreign markets and about how to act on these markets, for example, how business marketing takes place through local networks in these countries. A smaller organization, such as SSSE and its network, normally has difficulty acquiring such know-how. For certain markets and customers in the eastern Baltic area, this market knowledge is mainly possessed by the network leader and, to some extent, by other managers in the network firms. The network leader has long experience of marketing projects on emerging markets and knows that networking is a key marketing activity.

If successful, SSSE will establish an export platform by creating profitable export business through its marketing activities. SSSE is already formally established but is still in the process of creating trust among the members of the ETR by demonstrating that, among other outputs, it works as a marketing organization producing orders for its members. So far, the customer base is too small for this joint export network organization to have reached a long-term stage, so the network is still in the development stage. If the marketing of ongoing offers results in orders, the organization will come closer to this 'firmly established' and stable long-term stage.

WAB's basic resources are the high-quality timber growing in the region, long experience of making high-quality products throughout the value chain, high-class production facilities, and an effective transport system. It has amassed good knowledge of the Japanese market and how to do business there. The network possesses much of the required know-how concerning how to establish business in foreign markets. By combining the resources of highly niched SMEs, the network can offer a broad range of products. The marketing routines thus learned are shared within the network as success stories or best practices. The name of the network functions as a brand, giving the joint export network a regional identity in Sweden and a common brand name for its international business in Japan.

The WAB project is financed by its local partners and the EU; the fee for active members is SEK 20,000 and for passive members SEK 10,000. The project's good finances have eliminated one of the main difficulties confronting SMEs that want to start exporting: lack of financial resources for marketing.

There are definite limits on the project side to joint export networks consisting of small firms. Although forming a larger organization and competence base, a joint network is still too small to compete with large corporations for most projects. It lacks the resources and competencies required to offer and construct larger projects, for example, engineering skills, marketing know-how, and principal contractor capacities such as project administration skills and other organizational capabilities. In addition, the shorter-term business outlook of small firms, which require more immediate results, is a considerable drawback in this kind of long-term business. The situation is aggravated when exporting to the foreign emerging markets of the eastern Baltic rim.

Internationalization process

The international marketing capacity of the network is limited, since international marketing is mainly carried by one person: the network leader. It is not enough simply to establish a customer base large enough to satisfy ETR members. Outside marketing assistance is required, for example, to monitor the rapid transformation of the target markets and to help with certain networking activities. SSSE is in the process of recruiting agents and possibly also distributors. This represents a further extension of the external network by adding more marketing competencies, for example, to help with market research and customer and government contacts. This development is in line with internationalization process theory, which indicates that internationalization is gradual and slow, particularly in emerging markets. For example, more marketing initially occurs through indirect than direct entry nodes, and smaller organizations tend to use entry modes such as agents, distributors, and other intermediaries, even more so in emerging markets. However, for organizations such as SSSE, which possess high technical competence and to which knowledge linkage is critical, it is more a question of combining direct and indirect customer relationships.

WAB activities are concentrated in the first stages of the internationalization process. The emphasis is on helping resource-poor SMEs help each other start exporting to Japan: to leave behind the domestic market focus, pass through the pre-export stage, and enter the experimental export stage. Its activities are primarily concentrated in the pre-relationship stage, through matchmaking and information, and in the early stage, through help with contact making.

Conclusions

WAB is classified as a semi-open joint export network. During the pre-relationship stage, it functions as an open network, in which opportunity exposure and information collection dominate. Later, when marketing starts through contact building, direct links between a smaller numbers of firms become necessary. The export network starts to become closed through the formation of smaller and more integrated networks. The separate and smaller house-building network seems to be a good example of a more closed network, similar in some ways to the action networks within the ETR. In the former case, there are more direct, interconnected, and mutual relationships and more shared meanings, trust, and routines. Other smaller networks have also been formed within WAB.

The size of the ETR seems to favour the establishment of a semi-closed network for shared marketing activities, through direct and mutual ties between members, while keeping it semi-open to foster an efficient information-dissemination network. However, the joint network organization is still far from this state, since it is still in the experimental internationalization stage and in the early stage of building relationships to expand its customer base, particularly the customer base shared by the ETR. Moreover, the two exporting regional joint network organizations differ in size, and smaller networks have emerged within WAB.

The network structure of WAB as it has evolved in the internationalization process has some interesting characteristics in terms of the trade-off between open and closed networks. A flexible form of organization has been found to be useful in export networks that are unstable due to rapid change and in which uncertainty is high. In addition, the strength and performance of the network leader are vital when the network is becoming closed. There could also be drawbacks to a high degree of network closure. An excessively strong identity built on shared meanings and language, and strengthened by social norms such as trust, might make the network too inflexible, for example, by making too many members too mutually connected. This also means that information-dissemination networks should be kept flexible where exposure is critical in accessing new bridges between markets and different cultures.

Regarding the evolving competitiveness of the exporting joint networks, WAB is in the early stages of the internationalization process and seems to have developed a good competitive position for its products and projects on the Japanese market. In the case of the ETR, this has been impossible for large and medium-sized projects, since the valuable and unique resources and capabilities needed to deliver such projects are beyond the network's reach. However, small projects are feasible, since suitable competence and resource structures found within this joint export network are being developed and integrated into valuable ETR capabilities. These capabilities are classified as consisting of component knowledge. So far, this joint export network only seems to have reached a position in which it is competitive in the case of certain individual products and services sold through the network. However, this does not mean that the cooperation has been useless to the individual network firms. On the contrary, individual network firms could improve their competitive advantage by making even more use of the network; for example, the network-specific capability embodied by the joint network organization could be exploited as a product distribution channel. This seems to be the case in both the studied export networks.

WAB seems to be involved in the development stage of the house-building sub-network, where it is trying to build competitive advantage by developing more advanced network-specific component knowledge. For ETR, this stage lies within reach for smaller projects, because it possesses specific knowledge and joint resources adaptable to specific customer needs and is therefore difficult for competitors to imitate, at least in the short term. There might also be the possibility of achieving some temporary

Table 11.1 Comparison of the networks

Concept	ETR network	WAB network
Action and organization networks	Purpose: to market the offerings (products and services) of individual members and 'systemic' offerings of groups of members to specific target markets (mainly the Baltic countries and Poland). Actors/Members: 21 SMEs, 10 municipalities, two universities, two county councils, and an energy agency, all from south-east Sweden and all working on different environmental technology solutions. Several smaller networks have been established within the larger network, for example, a five-firm sub-network concerning offerings to hospitals. Activities: • *Identify potential customers* in target markets; • *arrange technical visits* for potential customers from target markets to sites in south-east Sweden; • *provide one-stop shopping;* • *identify opportunities for financial support* of various marketing activities. Leader: An enterprise called Sustainable Sweden Southeast (SSSE) with two to three employees. The leader makes, closes, and follows up specific business deals. SSSE is partly financed by member fees. The smaller networks within the ETR are held together via informal contracts based on trust more than by formal means. Other unifying factors are synergies, clear vision, and a working business concept. IT also plays an important facilitative role.	Purpose: to establish long-term cooperation between the home region and Japanese firms (subsequently, Chinese and Korean firms as well) regarding exports and foreign direct investment in the home region. Actors/Members: 50 members from the two northernmost Swedish counties, 35–40 of which are active. The firms each have 5–500 employees and cover the whole value-added chain of building materials and components for wooden houses. A house-building sub-network of 25 firms has been established within the larger joint export network. Activities: • *Matchmaking* between Swedish suppliers and Japanese customers; • *provide market information* through documentation and by arranging visits between Swedish and Japanese firms; • *initiate contacts* and support the establishment of Swedish–Japanese business relations. Leader: A project organization acts as a broker of contacts between WAB network members and customer networks in Japan. The project leader provides knowledge of the Japanese market and inspires action in the internal network. The leader also supports the creation of new business concepts for SMEs in the network.

Knowledge and resource base	The members have the complementary resources and competencies needed for systemic offerings. The leader has the knowledge and resources for marketing environmental technology to the Baltic countries and Poland. The network name is a resource in itself, functioning as a legitimacy-conferring brand and enabling one-stop shopping. The network has also developed the ability to mobilize financial resources needed for export activities.	The members have complementary resources and competencies covering the entire value chain. The leader has knowledge of the Japanese market and of how to do business there. The network name is a resource in itself, functioning as legitimacy-conferring brand and enabling one-stop shopping. The network has also developed the ability to mobilize financial resources needed for export activities.
Institutional structure	Trust has grown over the years as the members have experienced successful cooperation in their joint export activities. The firms have gone from being competitors in the home market, through being partners in export markets, and from there becoming partners in the home market as well. They have also developed routines for doing business together.	Trust has grown over the years as the members have worked together in value chains in their home region. This trust can then be used for joint export activities.
Internationalization process	The leader helps network members with market research and networking activities concerning, for example, customer and government contacts. SSSE is also in the process of recruiting agents and possibly distributors as well. Internationalization is a gradual process, particularly in emerging markets. Marketing initially takes place through indirect rather than direct entry nodes. Small firms, in particular, use entry modes such as agents, distributors, and other intermediaries. For SSSE, where the knowledge linkage is critical, it is a question of combining direct and indirect customer relationships.	WAB's activities are concentrated in the first stages of the internationalization process: helping resource-poor SMEs help each other start exporting to Japan, leaving behind the domestic market focus, passing through the pre-export stage, and entering the experimental stage. In addition, the activities are primarily concentrated in the pre-relationship stage through matchmaking and information dissemination and in the early stage through helping with the contact-making.

competitive advantage in the case of certain products and services offered by this joint export network.

The joint export networks studied have not yet reached a stable competitive position, which requires the establishment of more network-specific knowledge and further network closing. For the ETR, this would entail developing network-specific marketing knowledge (such as project marketing routines and principal contractor organizational skills) beyond the reach of this joint network organization at this early development stage. For WAB, such knowledge could be achievable in the case of the smaller house-building sub-network.

Although we have found some examples of more preliminary joint network organizations, such export cooperation seems uncommon among Swedish SMEs in general, likely because the total export volume is too low and the firms are too small. An industry structure dominated by small firms becomes fragmented, consisting mainly of stand-alone firms operating in isolation in the market: there are too few leading firms to serve as role models or that can initiate cooperation efforts.

References

G. Ahuja, 'Collaboration Networks, Structural Holes, and Innovation: A Longitudinal Study', *Administrative Science Quarterly,* 45 (3) (2000): 425–55.

H. Aldrich and D. A. Whetten, 'Organization-Sets, Action-Sets, and Networks: Making the Most of Simplicity', in P. Nyström and W. H. Starbuck (eds), *Handbook of Organizational Design* (Oxford and New York: Oxford University Press, 1981).

M. Alvesson and K. Sköldberg, *Tolkning och Reflektion* (Lund: Studentlitteratur, 1994).

J. Barney, 'Firm Resources and Sustained Competitive Advantage', *Journal of Management* 17 (1) (1991): 99–120.

P. Boye, *Developing Transnational Industrial Platforms: The Strategic Conception of the Öresund Region* (Lund and Copenhagen: School of Economics and Management, Lund University and Scandinavian Academy of Management Studies, 1999).

P. Boye, *Place for Growth: Core Competencies and Network Environments in the Kalmar Region* (Kalmar: Regionförbundet i Kalmar Län, 2000).

P. Boye, H. Jansson, and S. Sandberg, *Transnationell Affärssamverkan i Östersjöregionen* (Kalmar: BBRI Rapport, 2004).

R. S. Burt, *Structural Holes: The Social Structure of Competition* (Harvard University Press, 1992).

S. T. Cavusgil, 'On the Internationalization Process of Firms', *European Research,* 8 (6) (1980): 273–81.

J. S. Coleman, 'Social Capital in the Creation of Human Capital', *American Journal of Sociology,* 94 (1988): 95–120.

A. Dubois and L.-E. Gadde, 'Systematic Combining: An Abductive Approach to Case Research', *Journal of Business Research,* 55 (2002): 553–60.

R. Grant, 'The Resource-Based Theory of Competitive Advantage: Implications for Strategy Formulation', *California Management Review,* (Spring) (1991): 114–35.

B. Hedberg, P. Baumard, and A. Yakhlef (eds), *Managing Imaginary Organizations: A New Perspective on Business* (Amsterdam: Pergamon, 2002).

B. Hellgren and L. Melin, 'Business Systems, Industrial Wisdom and Corporate Strategies', in R. Whitley (ed.), *European Business Systems: Firms and Markets in Their National Contexts* (London: Sage, 1992).

M. Hilmersson and S. Sandberg, 'EU-Enlargement Effects on International Trade in the Baltic Sea Region: The Case of Exporting/Importing SMEs from Southern Sweden', Paper presented at the International Business Conference in Vasa, Finland, 19–21 August 2007.

J. Hohenthal, *The Creation of International Business Relationships: Experience and Performance in the Internationalization Process of SMEs* (Uppsala: Department of Business Studies, Uppsala University, 2001).

L. Jacobsson and M. Strömberg, 'Exportnätverk: en Lösning på Regionens Industrikris?', Masters thesis, Baltic Business School, University of Kalmar, 2004.

H. Jansson, *Industrial Products: A Guide to the International Marketing Economics Model* (New York: International Business Press [Haworth Press], 1994).

H. Jansson, *International Business Strategy in Emerging Country Markets: The Institutional Network Approach* (Cheltenham: Edward Elgar, 2007a).

H. Jansson, *International Business Marketing Strategy in Emerging Country Markets: The Third Wave of Internationalization of Firms* (Cheltenham: Edward Elgar, 2007b).

H. Jansson, M. Saqib, and D. D. Sharma, *The State and Transnational Corporations: A Network Approach to Industrial Policy in India* (Cheltenham: Edward Elgar, 1995).

H. Jansson and S. Sandberg, 'The Internationalization of Swedish Small and Medium-Sized Companies to the East Baltic Sea Region', *Journal of International Management,* 14 January (2008): 65–77.

J. Johanson and J.-E. Vahlne, 'The Internationalization Process of the Firm: A Model of Knowledge Development and Increasing Foreign Market Commitments', *Journal of International Business Studies,* 8 (1) (1977): 23–32.

J. Johanson and P. F. Wiedersheim, 'The Internationalization of the Firm: Four Swedish Cases', *Journal of Management Studies,* 12 (3) (1975): 305–22.

G. Lindqvist, 'Network Initiatives in Practice: Choosing Objectives', Unpublished article, 2004.

T. Madsen and P. Servais, 'The Internationalization of Born Globals: An Evolutionary Process', *International Business Review,* 6 (6) (1997): 1–14.

A. Marshall, *Industry and Trade,* 3rd edn (London: Macmillan, 1923)

S. B. Merriam, *Qualitative Research and Case Study Applications in Education* (San Francisco, Calif.: Jossey-Bass, 1998).

B. M. Oviatt and P. P. McDougal, 'Toward a Theory of International New Ventures', *Journal of International Business Studies,* 25 (1) (1994): 45–64.

M. Piore and C. Sabel, *The Second Industrial Divide* (New York: Basic Books, 1984).

M. E. Porter, 'Location, Competition and Economic Development: Local Networks in a Global Economy', *Economic Development Quarterly,* 14 (1) (2000): 15–34.

G. Soda, A. Usai, and A. Zaheer, 'Network Memory: The Influence of Past and Current Networks on Performance', *Academy of Management Journal,* 47 (6) (2004): 893–906.

D. D. Sharma and A. Blomstermo, 'The Internationalization Process of Born Globals: A Network View', *International Business Review,* 12 (2003): 739–53.

S. Tallman, M. Jenkins, N. Henry, and S. Pinch, 'Knowledge, Networks, and Competitive Advantage', *Academy of Management Review,* 29 (2) (2004): 258–71.

J. Timlon and M. Hilmersson, 'Balancing Intermediated Relationships in Emerging Country Markets', *International Journal of Trade and Global Markets,* 2 (2009): 3–4.

H. Tsoukas, 'The Firm as Distributed Knowledge System: A Constructionist Approach', *Strategic Management Journal,* 17 (winter, special issue) (1996): 11–25.

B. Uzzi, 'The Sources and Consequences of Embeddedness for the Economic Performance of Organizations', *American Sociological Review,* 61 (1996): 674–98.

B. Wernerfelt, 'The Resource Based View of the Firm', *Strategic Management Journal,* 5 (1984): 171–80.

R. K. Yin, *Case Study Research: Design and Methods,* 2nd edn (Thousand Oaks, CA: Sage, 1994).

12
Challenges, Complexities and Advantages of Regional Strategic Networks

Heléne Lundberg

Interaction between companies cannot be taken for granted even when cluster conditions seem to be at hand as exemplified by Claus Steinle, Holger Schiele and Kai Mietzner in Chapter 4. In response to such interaction deficits, networking is frequently used by national and regional policymakers as a way to 'engineer' regional development. This book presents relevant cases from around the world, the similarities of which are pronounced. These attempts to promote networking meet with difficulties, while presenting various potential advantages for companies that choose to participate actively in them. The chapters provide examples of various outcomes in terms of marketing cooperation, production cooperation, knowledge transfer, and knowledge development, all of which likely support regional development.

Major challenges in publicly backed network initiatives

However, even if such 'engineered' networks prove beneficial, there is always a risk that public funding may crowd out private investment. In other words, publicly funded network initiatives may consume time and resources that otherwise would have been devoted to even more beneficial work designed, undertaken, and financed by the companies involved in the networks. It is undeniable that 'no business is an island' (Håkansson and Snehota 1989), as all firms must have relationships in order to exist on the market. However, it cannot be assumed that additional or stronger relationships with firms that happen to be located in the same region will necessarily be of prime importance for the focal company's business development in an increasingly global market. Neither can it be assumed that relationships giving rise to economic value and regional development will necessarily develop in the group. The reported outcomes of networking initiatives are inconsistent, and the utility of such initiatives has been questioned (Huggins 2000). Nevertheless, the engineering of regional networks to foster regional relationship development and cooperation is a frequent policy response, so it is in the interest of all taxpayers that best use be made of them.

Though firms may have most of their key relationships with firms located outside their immediate surroundings (e.g., Markgren 2001; Malmberg 2002; Kingsley and Malecki 2004), they may still benefit from support initiatives that extend their network horizon (Snehota 2004) and provide more opportunities for relationship development, knowledge transfer, and knowledge development. However, the development of relationships and fellowship among network participants could conceivably benefit individual organizations without benefiting the region. It might even be detrimental to regional development if the firm, in response to new knowledge and relationships, decides to relocate all or part of its business to other areas.

Engineered regional networks often lack clarity as to what is to be achieved and how to achieve it. Business people may accordingly find it hard to motivate themselves and others to participate in activities that may initially have vague goals and means. They may join the network as a goodwill gesture but then remain passive with a low rate of attendance at network activities. Managers lack resources, and lack of time is probably the most frequently used argument against participating in networking activities. The network coordinator, the hub (which may be an individual or an organization), is thus initially a key actor that must provide enthusiasm, motivation, and visions of a brighter future arising from cooperation until the rewards of network participation become visible in practice. The central role of the hub and of a guiding concept that provides meaning and motivation for networking was illustrated by the case presented by Håkan Pihl in Chapter 3. Recruiting an individual or individuals to assume the role of hub is a pivotal event in network initiation and is crucial to the future success of the network. However, the hub's role and the business involvement achieved also depend on the role of the owner/buyer of the network initiative. In Chapter 2, Peter Parker and Christer Ekelund argue for increasing the empowerment of regional governments so they can become more active and assume more responsibility for network management. They further advocate less bureaucratic control in exchange for clarifying and simplifying the roles involved in the initiative and an increased focus on tangible functional achievements.

The complexity of evaluating network initiatives

The true extent of the benefits produced by regional strategic network initiatives has been questioned, but a thorough discussion of the value of such measures is hampered by the fact that the outcomes of such initiatives are very hard to evaluate. These initiatives are often evaluated at the end of the period of state aid, usually after three or four years of subsidized operation. However, as relationship development may pass through several stages (Ford

2002), some of the intended outcomes may take more time to develop and important results may not appear for many years.

Evaluations are further complicated by the very complex goal structure of these networks, as various goals are simultaneously present at several levels, goals that may change over the course of the evaluated period. There are goals on behalf of financers, coordinators, organizations, and participants at and for each of these levels; there may be goals pertaining to regional, firm, and personal development. These various dimensions have different characteristic outcomes, and the choice of what outcomes to evaluate will greatly influence the results of an evaluation.

Furthermore, as these network initiatives complement a region's business transactions, it is very hard to identify direct cause-and-effect relationships between measures and outcomes. The financial crises of recent years, for example, most likely hampered such network initiatives, as such severe crises tend to make managers and firms concentrate on their core business and look for short-term ways of cutting costs.

Moreover, while some outcomes are directly measurable in economic terms, other outcomes are intangible and thus hard to capture in figures and surveys. The logic underlying the regional development policies and measures applied in many countries builds on voluntary learning processes, based on informal networks. Such a logic stands in sharp contrast to the logic of formal evaluation obligations imposed by the European Union Cohesion Policy. Both cooperation and trust are needed to produce a climate conducive to successful learning characterized by a willingness to address both successes and failures. Informal networks based on voluntary participation may be well suited to providing such conditions, especially when a shared external threat or opportunity motivates the managers to undertake change. Awareness of upcoming evaluations might also function as an external input that sparks motivation. However, effective processes and outcomes can never be forced by administrative demands and regulations.

In addition, finding new business opportunities concerns not only information access but is also a question of timing, as the window of opportunity may be quite limited. In that respect, relationships can generate advantages in terms of information access, timing, and references (Burt 1992). Extensive relationship networks increase the probability of information access as such and of *early* information access, allowing for first-mover advantages. Extensive networks further increase the probability that a company will be referred to by others in the marketplace – a form of marketing that is the most credible and therefore the most efficient. Finally, the existence of an extensive network is a marketing advantage, as it makes a member company more attractive as a business partner (Johanson and Mattsson 2002). New relationships may prove an important outcome in the long run, even if no immediate economic benefits are evident. Although relationships per se cannot guarantee successful business development, network initiatives may nevertheless make a contribution. Studies have demonstrated that the ability to achieve positive outcomes in cooperative relationships increases with experience of such contexts, at least up to a certain level (Draulans *et al.* 2003).

Some view network survival as a general indicator of network success, arguing that if a network continues operating after state support ends it has proved successful. This view is, of course, rather simplistic. Survival and longevity are undoubtedly signs of success, but such networks are very complex and cannot be expected to persist unaltered indefinitely in a changing world. However, it is often found that network interaction continues in subgroups that developed over the lifetime of the network initiative.

Advantages identified in regional network initiatives

The outcomes achieved in the presented cases resulted mainly from the development of trust in the network vision and in fellow participants. This increased trust enabled the sharing of information and production capacity as well as joint marketing initiatives that otherwise would not have taken place. By increasing trust among regional firms, regional conditions were developed so as to bring out the characteristics of successful clusters described by Gordon and McCann (2000: 520), which reflect 'not simply economic responses to patterns of available opportunities and complementarities, but also unusual levels of embeddedness and social integration'. Trust has also been emphasized as a key characteristic of Italian industrial districts by Becattini (1991), who describes the interplay between production and daily life activities that engenders a governance mechanism characterized by mutual trust underpinned by an underlying threat of social sanctions in the community. Embeddedness in a local community implies that any behaviour will quickly become known to many actors. Both positive action and misconduct will be exposed, strengthening or damaging the actor's reputation. The development of social relationships may be valuable from a regional development perspective, even if not followed by the development of business exchange, as embeddedness is expected to deter wrongdoing and foster trust. However, trusting social relationships have also been identified as an important first step towards business exchange (Larson and Starr 1993).

Production cooperation

The Swedish case presented in Chapter 8 by Karolina Elmhester and Staffan Brege exemplifies successful network cooperation. This case provides interesting examples of competitors recognizing networking advantages and choosing to share production information for the benefit of all, leading to increased specialization – a development often attributed to successful cluster regions. For example, Saxenian (1994: 2) describes the Silicon Valley cluster as 'a regional network-based industrial system that promotes collective learning and flexible adjustment among specialist producers of a complex of related technologies'. Ongoing competition among suppliers in a cluster is expected to reduce their prices and transaction costs. However, competition is caused not only by pressure from local business competitors; Staber (1996) also emphasizes the importance of the greater potential for interpersonal competition arising from the effects of embeddedness and the striving for status and position in the local community.

Marketing cooperation

Marketing cooperation was exemplified in the Italian case presented by Simone Guercini and Andrea Runfola. They demonstrated how large numbers of Italian manufacturers, by joining forces in designed networks, developed new ways of marketing their goods by creating joint marketing organizations and strong shared brands. In addition, by developing these organizations, they developed new competencies by specializing in marketing tasks, thereby reaping economies of scale and scope. Such outcomes would have been unlikely without the network initiatives, which we can presume provided the intended support for regional development.

Knowledge transfer and knowledge development

Knowledge spillovers have been defined as 'a prototypical externality by which one or a few agents investing in research or technology development will end up facilitating other agents' innovation efforts (either unintentionally [...] or intentionally)' (Breschi and Lissoni 2001: 975). The Swedish case presented by Katarina Elmhester and Staffan Brege also gave evidence of knowledge spillover, as the companies involved managed to reduce their lead times markedly through knowledge transfer, knowledge development, ongoing comparison, positive personal rivalry, and joint problem-solving.

The existence and value of ongoing comparison has previously been observed and discussed by Porter (1990), who concluded that ongoing comparison and rivalry foster innovation. Following this line of reasoning, Maskell (2001), referring to Marshall (1891), argues that the possibility of observing and comparing parallel experimentation is a major advantage of clusters and that the range of resources and capabilities found in a cluster would be very difficult to replicate in a single firm. As competitors' behaviour and methods can easily be observed and compared by co-localized firms, promising opportunities are available to co-localized observers. Firms would be able to imitate the best practices of others and, in so doing, add their own ideas and considerations. Maskell even argues that 'as long as the firms share a common language and certain codes that ease their interpretation of local events, no trust is required', as they are able to monitor each other 'constantly, closely and almost without effort or cost' (2001: 930). The issues of knowledge acquisition and access under cluster conditions were addressed in Chapter 7 by Sylvie Chetty and Snejina Michailova, who gave further evidence of the claim that cluster membership indeed provides such advantages. They further argue that these circumstances in turn proved beneficial for the cluster members' internationalization. This is a pivotal topic, as the threat of lock-in effects in clusters has been identified as a potential threat to the sustainability of cluster advantages (Grabher 2004). Several Italian researchers (Lazerson and Lorenzoni 1999) have also highlighted the importance for an industrial district's well-being of companies having relationships with counterparts outside their region, fostering the inflow of information about changes in markets and technologies. If cluster conditions facilitate internationalization, they will facilitate information access and counteract lock-in effects.

Boari *et al.* (2003) distinguishes competition from rivalry, defining *competition* as occurring among firms that depend on the same resources and that may remain largely unknown to one another, and *rivalry* as mutual recognition entailing more of a struggle for supremacy on the part of each firm by means of observation and comparison. The rival firms thus constitute a sub-group among the competitors. Boari *et al.* studied exporting firms with fewer than 50 employees in an Italian cluster and concluded that ease of identifying and comparing with rivals in a cluster could explain the tendency of these firms to engage in non-price competition and that 'the competitive advantage of clusters and individual firms inside the clusters could perhaps be ascribed more to a different way of competing than to more intensive competition' (2003: 486). In the case presented by Karolina Elmhester and Staffan Brege, the managers describe their experience of rivalry in this manner. Learning more about, and comparing, each others' ways of working gave them the impetus to undertake investments and changes that they otherwise would not likely have done. The network thus served as an arena for individual and collective reflection that facilitated learning and knowledge development. This mutual trust and confidence permitted 'old truths' to be challenged and new perspectives on products and processes to develop.

Regional strategic networks are likely to be of particular value to small and medium-sized enterprises (SMEs), as such firms possess limited managerial resources. In SMEs, owner/manager influence is often extensive, and the manager's personal characteristics not only directly affect his or her ability to learn but also the organization's ability to learn. For knowledge development, smaller firms often depend on knowledge inputs from external sources, mainly customers and suppliers. The impact of external stimuli, however, depends on the owner/manager's ability and willingness to adopt modern management techniques and technologies. The survival of his or her firm thus hinges on the owner/manager's willingness and ability to identify and exploit new knowledge. Reviewing research linking the networking behaviour of firms with their innovative capacity, Pittaway *et al.* (2004: 137) concluded that 'those firms which do not co-operate and which do not formally or informally exchange knowledge limit their knowledge base on a long-term basis and ultimately reduce their ability to enter into exchange relationships'. They find it surprising that the published research into institutional mechanisms for facilitating networking is still very limited and emphasize that, given the important policy implications of this area, this lack requires urgent attention. In Chapter 5, in their study of outcomes in Brazilian small-firm networks, Jorge Verschoore and Alsones Balestrin address this lack. Their study demonstrates that promoting cooperation through small-firm networks is a promising way to develop local economies. They identified five outcome categories of importance to the participants: access to solutions, scale and market power, learning and innovation, social relationships, and cost and risk reduction. In addition, the case study presented by Petter Boye and Hans Jansson in Chapter 11 examines how a group of SMEs were able to increase their internationalization by establishing joint export networks. Using local resources and competencies, they improved their ability to exploit international markets.

Managerial implications for initiators and facilitators

The networks presented in the chapters of this book have not included prospective entrepreneurs. However, small firms and, in particular, start-ups will likely suffer from the liabilities of newness and smallness. Access to networks for prospective entrepreneurs will be crucial, as a network of relationships implies potential access to resources and to both emotional and business support. Baum *et al.* (2000) found that start-ups that had already been able to establish networks at the time of funding were able to access social, technical, and commercial competitive resources that otherwise would presumably have taken years of operating experience to accumulate. These resources functioned as a buffer against the hazards typically facing new firms. They accordingly found that variation in start-up network composition resulted in significant differences in performance. Policy-makers pondering the initiation of measures to support start-ups should seriously consider networking alternatives.

The cases illustrate the importance of social relationships for the development of trust, knowledge transfer, cooperation, and knowledge development among network participants. In fact, most of the regional strategic networks presented in the book were not networks to begin with, as a lack of relationships among regional companies is the reason for network initiation. To start with, these groupings merely represented *visions* of networking, and relationships had to develop among the participants for an actual network structure to grow. The network coordinator and facilitator, that is, the hub, must therefore start by arranging arenas and occasions that facilitate such a development. The case presented by Edith Andresen, Anette Bergman, and Lars Hallén in Chapter 6 illustrates the importance of choosing an appropriate communication strategy to reach the network members as intended and to the desired extent.

In their seminal paper, Morgan and Hunt (1994) propose shared values, communication, and non-opportunistic behaviour as factors influencing the trust that can lead to committed relationships. These factors likely form the basis of commitment in regional strategic networks as well. It is vital for the hub to address issues of goals, values, and ethics to stimulate discussion and interaction that increase the overlapping of opinions and expectations. It is then vital to keep in mind that network participants are not motivated solely by economic self-interest. Important social and emotional benefits can also be sought from networking. Managers, for example, might wish to support the local community or share experiences with others in the same position to feel more secure in their role.

Finally, a major challenge in regional strategic networks concerns the role of the network hub in relation to its degree of involvement in network activities. The hub should initially take a leading role, but its ultimate goal should be to make the role of facilitator and coordinator unnecessary, as the intention of the network initiators is that network relationships will become ongoing based on their own inherent value. However, if the hub fears losing his or her job, there is a risk that the hub will try to hold on to the network by initiating and emphasizing new activities that require hub participation. In other words, by creating and supporting activities that genuinely aim to bring the participants together, the hub may ultimately make itself less useful to participants and end up unemployed – unless, of course, a new network is initiated in which such skills are sought.

Limitations

Undoubtedly, network initiators and hubs would prefer to present success stories. Success stories may be overrepresented, not only in this book but in circulation in society as well. Nevertheless, such stories are instructive as they may highlight the characteristics of some of the many paths to successful regional development measures.

There is definitely a benefit to be gained from interregional comparisons of regional development strategies and measures. However, conclusions from interregional benchmarking must be made with caution due to contextual differences, such as the different institutional settings of the regions being compared. Such conclusions should therefore mainly concern how to facilitate better understanding of one's own policy, as part of a mutual learning process.

Further research

Since the functioning and outcomes of regional strategic networks are still largely neglected, numerous aspects of such initiatives need further research attention. Accordingly, we would like to identify some topics for further research that we find particularly interesting. First, though this book presents a number of case studies, there is a need for additional quantitative studies, and in Chapter 2, Claus Steinle, Holger Schiele, and Kai Mietner present a promising methodological advance for further quantitative studies of localized clusters. Such approaches can provide useful inputs for policy-makers wishing to support clusters.

Second, in Chapter 2, Peter Parker and Christer Ekelund argue that governments should take a more agile approach to business network development, premised on empowering regional governments to purchase and review regional resource development. That new role would, according to Parker and Ekelund, imply a limit on the number of network participants, preferably, to no more than six to eight people. In this vein, it would be valuable to examine how the varying roles of local government and structural dimensions, such as network size, both affect network outcomes.

Third, the business-angel network examined in Chapter 10 by Björn Berggren, Nicolaus Lundahl, and Lars Silver suggests that network initiatives to promote regional development need not be directed towards established companies only. They may also serve to support other actors important for regional development. Further studies of less common kinds of networks could provide valuable contributions to policy-makers' toolboxes. For example, some network initiatives take a 'triple helix' (Etzkowitz and Leydesdorff 2000) approach by including not only companies but also universities and local government representatives.

References

J. A. C. Baum, T. Calabrese, and B. S. Silverman, 'Don't Go It Alone: Alliance Network Composition and Startups' Performance in Canadian Biotechnology', *Strategic Management Journal,* 21 (2000): 267–94.

G. Becattini, 'Italian Industrial Districts: Problems and Perspectives', *International Journal of Management and Organization,* 21 (1991): 83–90.

C. Boari, V. Odorici, and M. Zamarian, 'Clusters and Rivalry: Does Localization Really Matter?' *Scandinavian Journal of Management,* 19 (2003): 467–89.

S. Breschi and F. Lissoni, 'Knowledge Spillovers and Local Innovation Systems: A Critical Survey', *Industrial and Corporate Change,* 10 (2001): 975–1005.

R. S. Burt, *Structural Holes: The Social Structure of Competition* (Cambridge, MA: Harvard University Press, 1992).

J. Draulans, A.-P. deMan, and H. W. Volberda, 'Building Alliance Capability: Management Techniques for Superior Alliance Performance', *Long Range Planning,* 36 (2003): 151–66.

H. Etzkowitz and L. Leydesdorff, 'The Dynamics of Innovation: From National Systems and "Mode 2" to a Triple Helix of University-Industry-Government Relations', *Research Policy,* 29 (2000): 109–23.

D. Ford, 'The Development of Buyer–Seller Relationships in Industrial Markets', in D. Ford (ed.), *Understanding Business Marketing and Purchasing* (London: Thomson Learning, 2002).

I. R. Gordon and P. McCann, 'Industrial Clusters: Complexes, Agglomeration and/or Social Networks?' *Urban Studies,* 37 (2000): 513–32.

G. Grabher, 'The Weakness of Strong Ties: The Lock-in of Regional Development in the Ruhr Area', in G. Grabler and W. W. Powell (eds), *Networks* (Cheltenham: Elgar Edward, 2004).

R. Huggins, 'The Success and Failure of Policy-Implanted Inter-Firm Network Initiatives: Motivations, Processes and Structure', *Entrepreneurship and Regional Development,* 12 (2000): 111–35.

H. Håkansson and I. Snehota, 'No Business Is an Island: The Network Concept of Business Strategy', in D. Ford (ed.), *Understanding Business Markets* (London: The Dryden Press, 1989).

J. Johanson and L.-G. Mattsson, 'Network Positions and Strategic Action: An Analytical Framework', in D. Ford (ed.), *Understanding Business Marketing and Purchasing* (London: Thomson Learning, 2002).

G. Kingsley and E. J. Malecki, 'Networking for Competitiveness', *Small Business Economics,* 23 (2004): 71–84.

A. Larson and J. A. Starr, 'A Network Model of Organization Formation', *Entrepreneurship: Theory and Practice,* 18 (1993): 5–15.

M. H. Lazerson and G. Lorenzoni, 'The Firms that Feed Industrial Districts: A Return to the Italian Source', *Industrial and Corporate Change,* 8 (1999): 235–65.

A. Malmberg, *Klusterdynamik och regional näringslivsutveckling: begreppsdiskussion och forskningsöversikt* I. f. t. studier, ed. (Östersund, 2002).

B. Markgren, *ÄR NÄRHET EN GEOGRAFISK FRÅGA? Företags affärsverksamhet och geografi: en studie av beroenden mellan företag och lokaliseringens betydelse* (Uppsala: Företagsekonomiska Institutionen, Uppsala Universitet, 2001).

A. Marshall, *Principles of Economics* (London: Macmillan, 1891).

P. Maskell, 'Towards a Knowledge-Based Theory of the Geographical Cluster', *Industrial and Corporate Change,* 10 (2001): 921–43.

R. M. Morgan and S. B. Hunt, 'The Commitment-Trust Theory of Relationship Marketing', *Journal of Marketing,* 58 (1994): 20–38.

L. Pittaway, M. Robertson, K. Munir, D. Denyer, and A. Neely, 'Networking and Innovation: A Systematic Review of the Evidence', *International Journal of Management Reviews,* 5/6 (2004): 137–68.

M. Porter, *The Competitive Advantage of Nations* (London: Macmillan, 1990).

A. Saxenian, *Regional Advantage: Culture and Competition in Silicon Valley and Route 128* (Cambridge, MA: Harvard University Press, 1994).

I. Snehota, 'Perspectives and Theories of Market', in H. Håkansson, D. Harrison, and A. Waluszewski (eds), *Rethinking Marketing: Developing a New Understanding of Markets* (Chichester: John Wiley, 2004).

U. Staber, 'Networks and Regional Development: Perspectives and Unresolved Issues', in U. Staber, N. Schaefer and B. Sharma (eds), *Business Networks: Prospects for Regional Development* (Berlin: Walter de Gruyter, 1996).

Index